ELEMENTARY GUNSMITHING

A sporting Springfield .30 '06 fitted with modern telescopic sight and restocked by the owner to suit his own ideas. A first-class job in every respect, yet there are hundreds of self-taught amateurs who can do equally well at such custom gunsmithing.

ELEMENTARY GUNSMITHING

A Manual of Instruction for Amateurs in the Alteration and Repair of Firearms

by

PERRY D. FRAZER

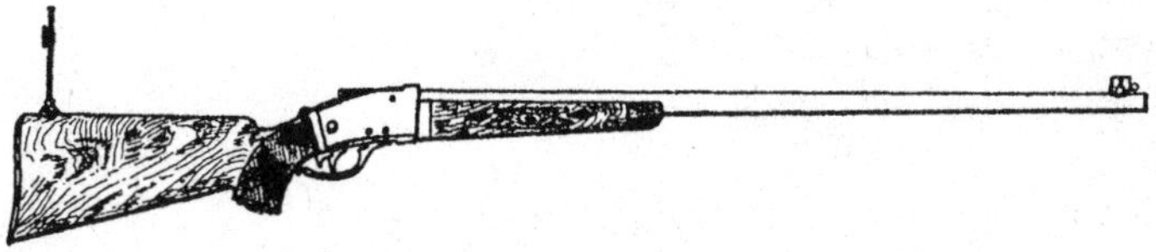

Skyhorse Publishing

First Skyhorse Publishing edition 2015

10 9 8 7 6 5 4 3 2

Library of Congress Cataloging-in-Publication Data is available on file.

Cover design by Richard Rossiter

Print ISBN: 978-1-62914-439-9
Ebook ISBN: 978-1-62914-932-5

Printed in the United States of America

EDITOR'S NOTE

PERRY D. FRAZER'S
ELEMENTARY GUNSMITHING

by Dr. Jim Casada

In the years from 1926 to 1954, Thomas Garvine Samworth's Small-Arms Technical Publishing Company produced a total of forty-three books by thirty-one different authors. The press also published four booklets and two prints. One of the full-length works was a two-volume effort (Townsend Whelen's *Small Arms Design and Ballistics*), and three were reprints (Arthur C. Gould's *Modern American Pistols and Revolvers* and *Modern American Rifles,* along with *The Gunsmith's Manual* by J. P. Stelle and William B. Harrison). This is an impressive record for what was always a one-man operation, with Samworth doing all the editing, arranging for the works to be printed, handling sales and distribution, and keeping track of royalties.

Even more impressive is the fact that Samworth managed — by dint of his character, production of good books, forthright honesty, and exceptional knowledge of the subject matter covered — to cultivate an extraordinary stable of authors. Names such as Townsend Whelen, Elmer Keith, John "Pondoro" Taylor, E. C. Crossman, Henry Edwards Davis, and C. S. Landis remain standards, despite the passage of more than half a century, in their various fields of writing.

Perry D. Frazer was not nearly so well known, at least in literary circles, as the aforementioned authors. Yet from the standpoint of useful knowledge, it would have been difficult to find someone more suitable to write the book being reprinted here, *Elementary Gunsmithing*. Samworth's promotional material for the volume went to the heart of the matter: "Who is better qualified to guide the beginner into the intricacies of guncraftsmanship than a professional gunsmith with more than 50 years' practical experience at the workbench? Yep, we think so too, and Perry D. Frazer turned out a masterful work on this most difficult subject."

It is likely that Samworth envisioned two types of audience for the book. His promotional leaflet mentions it as a "first book buy for youngsters" along with suggesting that the work would appeal to "any person just becoming interested and enthused in firearms. Whether this interest is fired by the individual taking up the love of firearms as a hobby or whether he wishes to go a step farther and make it a part of full-time business, he can get a solid foundation of the fundamentals of gunsmithing in this volume." My personal observations of perhaps a score of copies of this book over the years suggest that "Mr. Sam" was eminently successful in his goal of making this a "working" title. Far more often than not the dust jacket is missing. Similarly, the first printing, with its pebble-grain leatherette, invariably shows cracking and flaking along the spine and hinge. This is less a product of fragility than of long and loving use.

The first printing of the first edition (1938) is readily distinguishable from a Samworth printing that took place in 1946. The binding of the 1946 printing is different, with dark blue buckram being used instead of leatherette, and the location for the Small-Arms Technical Publishing Company has been changed from Onslow County, North Carolina, to Plantersville, South Carolina. In addition to these two Samworth printings, the book was reprinted (as was the case with many Samworth titles) by the Stackpole Company. There were two Stackpole printings, in 1953 and again in 1958. This spread of four printings over the course of a full two decades attests to the book's enduring appeal.

Other than the somewhat sketchy information available in Samworth promotionals, I have not been able to find much biographical data on Frazer. He contributed a single article, "Scope Sight Target," to the February 1940 issue of *The American Rifleman* magazine, but no other evidence of literary endeavor has come to light. In all likelihood Samworth knew or knew of Frazer through his many contacts in the world of guns. Samworth had worked for several years as an editor with the National Rifle Association, and he carried on extensive correspondence with individuals interested in all aspects of guns — hunting, precision shooting, ballistics, gunsmithing, and more. Another possibility is that one of the other gunsmithing writers in the Samworth stable brought Frazer to his attention. More than a dozen books bearing the Small-Arms Technical Publishing Company imprint dealt with some aspect of gunsmithing, and eventually four other volumes — Clyde Baker's *Modern Gunsmithing,* Roy F. Dunlap's *Gunsmithing,* Walter Howe's *Professional Gunsmithing,* and W. F. Vickery's *Advanced Gunsmithing* — would constitute what might at first glance seem to be directly competitive printings.

Such is not the case though. All of these gunsmithing works are more advanced, and at the time *Elementary Gunsmithing* first appeared, only Baker's *Modern Gunsmithing* was available. According to Brian Smith in his important reference work on the Samworth imprints, *Samworth Books: A Descriptive Bibliography,* the book "was commissioned by Samworth to fill the vacancy in his product line for a 'low end' inexpensive book on gunsmithing for the beginner." Published in 1938, just as the worst of the Great Depression was past, it cost only two dollars. The book includes plenty of diagrams and other illustrative material, and the intention of both the author and publisher was to offer a text that would allow someone with nothing more than ordinary hand tools to perform basic gunsmithing work.

In this regard, Brian Smith rates the book quite highly, saying, "One would ordinarily not expect too much of such a work [but] *Elementary Gunsmithing* does have its share of useful tips and information." Similarly, W. F. Vickery thought well of the book. He recommended it as a companion work to his effort, and it seems clear that Samworth envisioned the two as being complementary.

These days *Elementary Gunsmithing* might initially be viewed as a period piece of little contemporary use. Yet its attention to fundamentals, along with the clarity of the prose (probably as much a result of Samworth's editing as of Frazer's skills), gives it an enduring practicality. It also serves as a useful reference guide to the evolution of gunsmithing, and like any Samworth imprint the work is solid from informational and technical perspectives.

Jim Casada

ROCK HILL, SOUTH CAROLINA

CONTENTS

FOREWORD

When we discussed this book for the first time, the publisher gave me free rein to write at some length a book that any young man might use as a guide in making and repairing firearms equipment; work to be done without the help of machine tools—at small expense at first. So far as has seemed practical I have followed this idea, though in places I could not well avoid mentioning processes that must of necessity involve some use of a device to spin round work—not necessarily a lathe or a drill-press, but something a bit more versatile than a hand-drill; for there are drilling, reaming, polishing and other work that cannot well be done in the hands alone. I have tried to justify this divergence by the fact that a small lathe may be picked up for a song, almost or any boy can rig up a foot-treadle and fly-wheel to spin devices held in the chuck of a cheap polishing-head, which, for many small jobs, will do very well in the lack of a good lathe.

In these machine days the growing boy looks forward with pessimism to the possibility of getting into some work through which he may advance. He may get a job in a motorcar or airplane factory, and become an expert in slamming small parts to and from a conveyor belt; but after he has been there awhile, he cannot say he is a finished mechanic, or that his future is assured. He may believe there is no field for one who devotes a lot of time to learning to work on such things as guns and rifles with simple hand tools. He will be wrong, as I will try to show in these pages. There is always work for the man who is an expert with a file—and pages might be written showing the various things it is possible to make with a vise and a file and very few other tools. Of course one who works at a given thing for any length of time will "accumulate tools," which, once acquired, will last a lifetime, if they are good; so this matter of tools will take care of itself in time, and the expense can be distributed over weeks or years, making the cost of each one a very small item.

The firearms turned out by the factories today are almost the last word in elegance of form and perfection of mechanisms; but do not tell me that there is nothing more that may be done to make them still better, since they were made to suit the average over-the-counter buyer, and the expert, who knows very definitely what his gun must be like when it is ready for use, may not be able to make the changes he has in mind, but is willing to pay well to have this done by a good workman in wood and steel.

And so I feel justified in telling the young man who likes working at a bench that he may start with a vise and three files and develop a real honest-to-goodness profession, hang out his shingle, and earn as he learns, as the old saying goes. There is no disgrace in working with the hands. If one makes a living at it, that is about all the average man can do, and it will keep you busy, once you have interested the right clientele and satisfied the sportsmen of your town that you can do good work.

Let me point with pride to the gunsmiths I have watched and wondered at, then tried to emulate: George C. Schoyen and Axel W. Peterson, who came here from far Northwestern Europe, learned our language and showed us what graduate apprentices of old-world gunshops could do at the bench; Harry M. Pope, who started in a very small way and became one of the best barrel-makers in modern times; Otto Niedner, who grew tired of working in machine shops for other people, and is now a famous riflemaker; Frank Nowicki, (deceased) who could do more with a common file than any other man I have ever known; the late Carlos Gove, who made and shot his own muzzle-loading rifles, one of the best weighing forty-nine pounds with its full-length telescope sight; and dozens of other fine workmen whose names are familiar to all of us. They all turned a simple trade into a well-paying profession. Any boy at all handy with tools can at least follow in their footsteps and work into a good honest line of endeavor.

When all is said, there is the sheer fascination of working in wood and metal that every gunsmith thoroughly enjoys. I have made split-cane fly rods, tinkered with cameras, worked on cedar canoes, but gun work "gets one," sooner or later, and I know of nothing more satisfactory than turning out gunstocks for customers who appreciate one's best efforts. There is something about building up a gun or a rifle that warms the cockles of one's heart. Nothing else I can think of equals the satisfaction one feels when he has finished a piece of work that is flawless. And as you grow into the work, you will feel that you are mastering something you will never grow tired of or forget—something no one can take away from you.

THE AUTHOR.

Ridgewood, N. J., April, 1938.

Chapter One

STARTING IN BUSINESSLIKE FASHION.

Assuming that you have a more or less roomy and comfortable place in which to work; that you have a substantial bench, a vise and a few simple but good tools, before you start work sit down and do some thinking. Write down some of your thoughts, and put them under several headings, something like this:

Policy and Declaration of Intentions: I am starting in with what I hope will be my life work. If I am compelled, in order to make wages as I go along, to fix locks and sharpen lawnmowers, until I can afford to devote all my time to altering and repairing firearms, I will do this, but if my first job is to make a key, I will make a good one, being sure that my customer will tell his friends what a nice key I have made for him, and they, too, may bring in something for me to fix. I will not cater to this class of customers right along, and will eventually refuse their work, but as it will be my policy to earn as I learn, I will have to work out of rather than into this sort of thing until I can consider my business as established.

Until I can build up a bank account of my own, I will not buy anything on credit, but will do without, for the time, things I cannot buy for cash. With this reservation: If or when I have enough work to justify it, and I feel that I can work to better advantage with a good lathe or drillpress, I may buy one or both on the time-payment plan tool manufacturers urge prospective customers to take advantage of. With a year or more to pay for a $100.00 article, there may be wisdom in this installment plan, even though I will have to pay a 6% premium on the privilege, knowing that buying for cash saves one the customary 2% cash discount.

This venture of mine is not just a temporary tinkering job, but an institution. In time I will acquire a clientele of the sort of men I wish to attract, and doing good work will be my best advertisement.

As I go along I will determine approximately what my time is worth to me, and will charge for it accordingly, say at so much per hour, but will increase this as I gain skill, until every job will pay me well. My physician does not charge me $3.00 for a visit because he devotes $3.00 worth of his time to it, but because that fee must be credited to the time he has devoted to acquiring the skill and knowledge he has to work with. He, and I, too, must charge for overhead, money and time invested, though it is not my intention to clutter my books with accounts I can never collect, as the doctor does—or as so many of them are compelled to do.

As I progress, I will inevitably come to know customers who will insist on keeping an open account with me, and it may be good business to fall into their ways of doing things, but cash-on-delivery will be the best policy, and I will try to make casual customers respect it.

Borrowing and Loaning Tools: If I have a prospective job that will call for tools I do not at the time possess, I will refuse it, for I will not borrow tools of any sort to work with. Per contra, I will not loan a good tool to any person, be he a member of my family or a neighbor. I will put a memorandum card in my cap, with this legend on it, in heavy black letters, where I can see it, and act accordingly. It will speak for itself, and save me from embarrassing situations:

No Free Repair Work.
No Tools Loaned.

Promising and Producing: I will not take in a job and promise that it will be finished at a given time, unless I am sure I can take it up and finish it on time. I will not follow the practice of so many old-time gunsmiths, of promising a job "right away," when I have other work that must be done first. There is nothing that will drive customers away so surely as to be put off from day to day. Every job should be put on a mental conveyor-belt, to be delivered in the order of its receipt.

I will inevitably have customers of the simon-pure crank variety. I will not poke fun at what I may know to be fool notions, but will humor them, if suggesting something sensible will have no effect. Many of these men have been sneered at by the letter-writers for the big factories, who tell them that the factory can do any inventing that may be needed, and drive them to men like myself—men willing to concede that no man is a fool until he has given concrete proof that he really is one.

I am naturally fond of shooting and experimenting with firearms, and as I can afford the time and expense, I will take part in the activities of shooting organizations in my neighborhood. There I will meet the experts, get their views, learn what they want, and in time they may come to know me better, and turn some of their work over to me.

* * * *

This matter of loaning tools is a thing that must be stopped before it is started—if you will forgive the bull. You will leave your shop unlocked now and then, of course, and your worst enemy may come in as a privileged friend and ask to use your pet carborundum grinder on his axe or hatchet, leaving the tool cockeyed or chipped, to be put in shape again by you at a time when you are busy with other things. Or he may carry away some tool you will need very badly before he is out of sight. If you ask him what you are supposed to do in a case like this, he may laugh and say that that is a problem you can solve yourself when the occasion arises—but he will keep your tool for ten days, or probably return it only when you go for it.

Order. Another thing you should keep in your mental book is Order. Establish a place for every article you use right along, and when a job is finished, put every tool where it belongs, sweep off your bench, and start the next job with plenty of elbow room. There is nothing worse than a bench heaped with tools, metal and wood scraps, and dust. Gun smiths are notoriously careless along these lines, but there is simply no excuse for it. One of these men, who tossed tools aside as he went along, when asked how he could find them again, replied that that did not bother him, but if someone else used a tool and dropped it where used, he, the gunsmith, would probably never find it.

Gunsmiths who are often asked to do some minor repairs for which they have not the heart to make any charge will appreciate the late George Schoyen's favorite joke. When asked, "How much, George?" he would reply, "Oh, $4.00 will be enough for that job; it did not take long." "But, George," the surprised tight-wad would sputter. "Oh, well," George would say, as if a pound of flesh were being asked for, "I'll make it up some other time." Better have a minimum charge, and stick to it.

Chapter Two

MODELS, TEXTBOOKS AND REFERENCE WORKS.

There are books that you will want, as you go along, but these should be purchased as the real need for them arises. It is assumed that you have a fair knowledge of the various types of guns and rifles, and have handled them and examined their mechanisms. This is an important part of your education. Never neglect an opportunity to inspect all the firearms you may see in stores and at tournaments and club shoots. By visiting museums and the homes of collectors of ancient and modern firearms, you will see fine examples of what our daddies used in their target practice and in the wars they took part in, if any.

Do not turn up your nose at flintlocks and Kentuckies, which seem outrageously clumsy and awkward now, accustomed as we are to the handsome guns and rifles the factories and private makers are turning out in all their beauty of blued steel and selected walnut. It is probable that your great grandfather took just as much pride in his long pea-shooter as you do now in your pet Stevens or Winchester. And if the opportunity is offered, ask to shoot some of these old guns—you may be called on to doctor their ailments yourself some day.

Make a collection of cartridge cases, adding to it as opportunities are offered; then, when some particular cartridge is mentioned, you will be able to show a specimen to a customer and explain its merits. Obtain, if possible, one new cartridge from every lot of ammunition you may have access to, at shoots. It will, in a way, serve as a guide and a die very many times in your work. Shotgun cartridges you can inspect by slicing a piece off one side, then paste around one of them a slip of cellophane. This will prevent the contents from spilling, but will give you an inside view of what special or regular loads look like, their wadding, etc.

Start your rifle-cartridge collection with a new .30 '06 government cartridge. It is a sort of standard for comparison, for it is the service cartridge; it will fit the chamber of any service rifle and all factory and special rifles of that calibre. Later on you may be called on to work on rifles of this calibre, and then you can see how your specimen cartridge fits the chamber of each one—for this cartridge is made to fit the smallest chamber as well as the largest one that it may be shot in, hence it is made with sufficient tolerance so that it will not stick in a tight chamber nor wabble about *too* much in a loose one. If you shoot it yourself in a pet rifle, and will try the micrometer caliper on both the new cartridge and the fired one, you will ascertain just how much the case expands in the chamber of that particular rifle, and will decide right there that that case, expanded slightly in your own rifle, will be gas-tight and work beautifully in it when the case is filled with your pet load of powder and a well-fitting bullet. This will give you a lesson in reloading, too—for if you are observant, you will learn that loads carefully prepared by an expert may prove more accurate than other loads that are made up to suit the mill-run of shooters, for either target or hunting, and which may not be the very best thing obtainable for one or the other, and especially those in which the bullets are crimped in the cases.

Send a dime to the Government Printing Office, in Washington, and ask for a copy of *The Handbook of the Rifle.* In it you will find every detail that has been ascertained by the experts in the arsenals and on the target ranges concerning the Service Springfield rifle. Read the book carefully, for it contains exhaustive descriptions of every pin and screw and spring used in fabricating this wonderful piece of wood and metal.

Add to your collection all sorts of bullets of every calibre. They are interesting in themselves, and are also useful in helping a customer to select a suitable rifle for either target practice or hunting. For example, he may ponder long and carefully over a 7 mm or a .270 rifle, but if you can show him the very slight difference, possibly that may aid him. And in the spring, search for bullets behind the butts on rifle ranges. Lead bullets do not break up so readily as the jacketed ones, and now and then you may find almost perfect specimens; that is, those showing the land marks distinctly, and the shape in which the powder charge left the flat base. A bullet that fits a rifle should, if picked up unmarred, show a base almost as free from whiskers as one that has been pushed through the same barrel with a rod.

Send to all the arms and accessories companies for catalogues, and study these carefully. Some firms issue to the trade component-parts catalogues, and these you should ask for every year. In these days of interchangeable parts it does not pay to make by hand a part you can obtain by return mail if sent for, and all parts of every model are illustrated, so one may order by number. This applies to most foreign-made firearms, too, for in the large centers replacement parts are stocked by agents. Mauser receivers, for example, are always in demand, especially the short receivers that are adapted to the making up of rifles with special barrels for smaller cartridges than the German army rifle cartridge. Not that they are better than our Springfield, Remington or Winchester Models 54 or 70, but every man has his favorite, and it is not for the young gunsmith to argue the merits of a certain article when the customer has already made up his mind as to what he wants.

Let your friends call you a catalogue fiend, if that pleases them, but get the catalogues. Some of them are worth preserving. You will notice in the exchange advertisements in magazines like *The American Rifleman* that these old booklets have a real value. As an illustration, a Sharps catalogue, dated 1876, sold recently for $15.00, and you may never get a copy at any price. Old catalogues often help one puzzle out the intricacies of obsolete actions. I still remember the first time I dismounted a Winchester carbine. I had horse sense enough to place the parts in order on a table, but when an old cow-waddy came along and asked me if I ever expected to get half the parts back again, I was stumped for the time being. They were, however, quite simple. The old Winchester single-shot rifle puzzled many an amateur gunsmith until, by long trial and error, he found that the breechblock would only submit to a peculiar partial assemblage before one could replace all the parts. And I saw one of the officials of that company fail to replace those parts until a by-stander took them in hand and manipulated them until they slid back easily. The bolt assembly of some rifles, simple though it may be to one familiar with it, does not readily respond to the efforts of the beginner, who tries to work with his hands only, whereas the assembler had special jiggers for holding springs, etc., and could put the thing together in two shakes in the dark.

Chapter Three

THE SHOP AND ITS EQUIPMENT.

The young gunsmith's shop may be any convenient size that will accommodate a good work bench, that may be heated comfortably in winter and be well ventilated at all times. It should have plenty of light, and this should come preferably from the left hand. One can work in cramped quarters, but he must have good light.

The Work Bench. Of course the bench one is to use is of first importance. There are all sorts of so-called boys' work benches. Forget about that. Build one instead. Have it exactly as you think it should be for your particular needs. Its size will be important, so do not cramp that feature. One likes to have plenty of space to spread out on. Make it twelve feet long, if possible, and three planks wide—say thirty inches. And have the planks good and thick, so it will be solid and strong, and so that, as the surfaces of the planks become worn and rough, they may be turned bottoms up or ends for ends, or the front planks be put at the back—any way to keep the surfaces as smooth as may be.

Build the supports from 2 x 4-inch planks, and secure their backs to the wall, for you will want a bench that will not shake or sway, no matter what sort of work you may be doing; so brace the frame in all directions, using bolts, lag-screws or heavy nails, and fasten the legs securely to the floor. Attach the top planks with long finishing nails, sink these well down, and putty the holes, to prevent the pos-

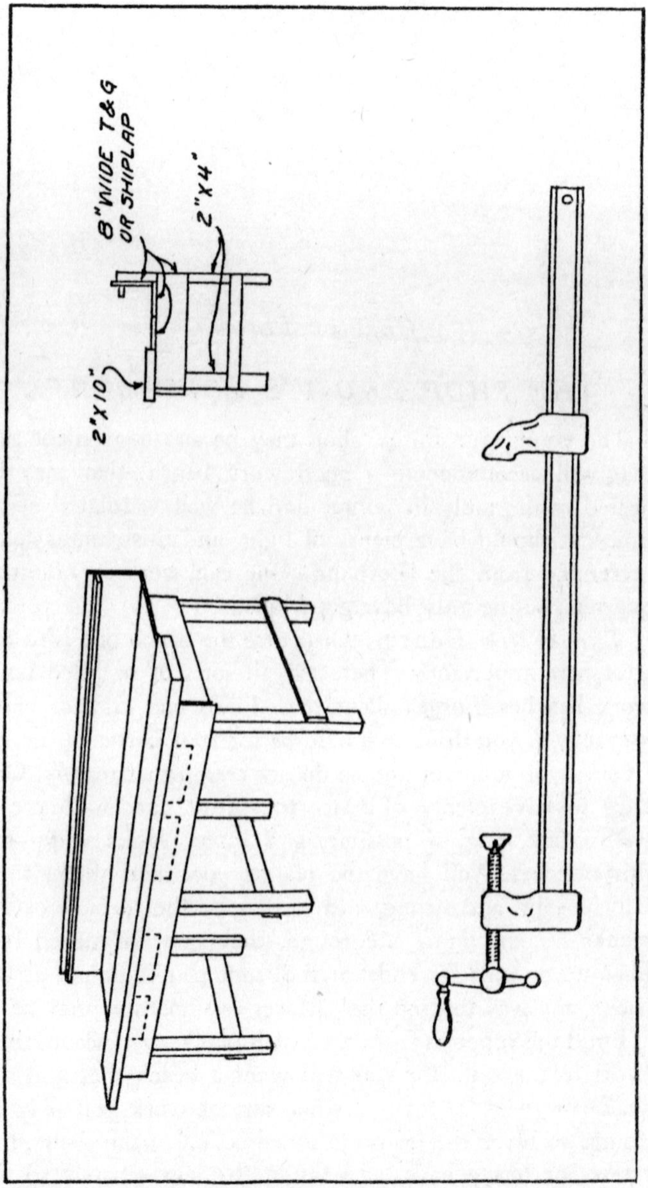

Figure 1. Albert H. Leigh's suggestion for a simple work bench; and a long self-locking clamp used in clamping stocks to actions and tips to forearms.

sibility that a nail may work up above the surface and mar a stock or a barrel that may be laid on the bench.

Albert H. Leigh's design for a bench you may see in Figure 1. The back-board gives space for tool-clips handy to the vise, and the trough, lower at least by the thickness of the front planks, will keep chips and tools away from the working front, and these may be cleared out at the end of the day.

Face the bench with a ten-inch board; then, as you find need for them, saw sections out of this plank and put in small drawers, readily made from odd boxes. The locked-corner cases shotgun cartridges come in are fine for making drawers. Smooth off the ends and put knobs or regular drawerpulls on them. As you progress you will buy a lot of valuable small articles, such as taps and dies, drift-pins, center-punches, gauges, etc., and these should be separated, each sort in a shallow paper box, handy to see and pick out as needed. And they will be right under your hands as you work.

Shelves? Of course. One cannot have too many, for they are great space utilizers, and getting into the habit of putting away one's tools when a job is completed will prevent cluttering the bench with them. Place on the lower shelves those tools that will be used most often, with the higher shelves for materials and parts. Get a number of discarded cigar boxes or small paper boxes, and put in them nails, screws, brads, bolts and nuts, rivets, tacks, washers and such things; small files in one box, larger ones laid flat on a shelf, not touching one another; pliers, wrenches, hammers near at hand, abrasives in other boxes; bottles and jars for various compounds. If there is available wall space, drive some nails there, for saws, braces, hand drills, spokeshaves, large calipers, etc.

The All-important Vise. Now for a good vise. Your bench should be three feet high, to be handy for all sorts of work. The common wood-worker's vise may appeal to you, but not to me, as it is too low for most of the work one will do on guns and rifles. A sturdy iron vise with steel jaws, standing about eight inches high, will bring your work almost breast high as you stand. On long jobs this does not involve bending over very much; that is a thing always to be avoided, for it is neither comfortable nor healthful. The vise must be provided with smooth leather or felt slip-on jaws, anyway, for most of your work on guns; sheet brass and sheet lead jaws will be needed too, for certain kinds of work. Splurge on this one item, as your vise will be your best friend for many years to come, if it is a good one. By all means buy a swivel vise; and, if you can afford the extra cost, select one with swivel jaws, too, so you may adjust it readily to hold any object that is tapered, curved, or odd shaped, as for example, the grip of a gun. If space is too much restricted, mount the vise on one end of a two-foot 2 x 8-inch plank, the other end of the plank bolted to the top of the bench, so the whole thing may be turned entirely around, out of your way when you are working on something that need not be secured in the vise. While this method of fastening a vise is less steady than when it is bolted to the bench, for light work the arm carrying the vise may be turned in various directions, even at right angles to the bench—supported with a length of plank placed underneath.

A still better plan is to mount the vise on a pedestal—a three-foot-high stand made from several pieces of 2 x 4-inch planks, with a base made fast to the floor-beams with lag-screws. Especially when you are shaping up a stock, or checking one, using vise or cradle pivoted on a pedestal, you can walk entirely around your work without shifting it continually. This is quite a feature in getting the best possible light on your work. The ideal arrangement is to have one solid pedestal for the vise and another one for the checking cradle, both within reach of your most-needed tools. Figures 2 and 3 illustrate some handy wrinkles for shop equipment. M and P show thin wood pieces best used

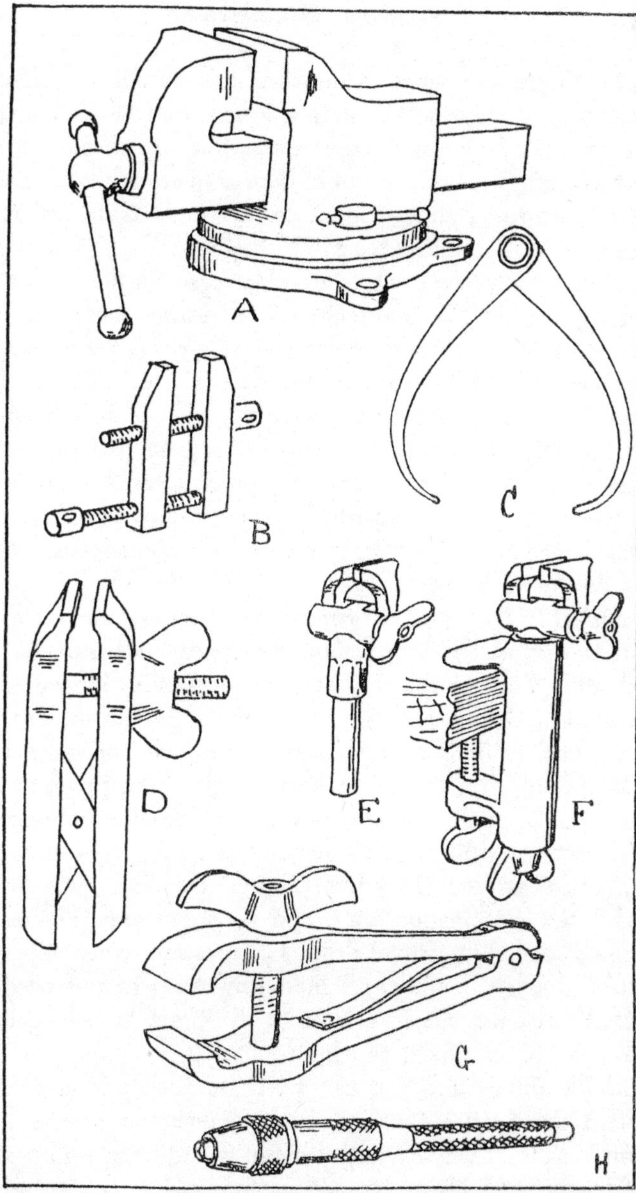

Figure 2. A, Parker swivel-base vise. B, parallel-jaw gunsmith's clamp. C, outside caliper. D, Billings parallel-jaw hand vise. E, Billings hand vise. F, clamp for attaching this vise to a bench. G, old-type gunsmith's hand vise. H, pin vise.

in holding stock blanks in the vise, their cutout lower ends straddling the vise-bar so they will not drop out when the vise is opened. Cut another set of thicker boards, glue thick leather or felt around the tops, then connect the two pieces with a strip of thinner leather or fabricoid, so the set may be lifted out as a unit. (See S, Fig. 3.)

In making a new stock from a blank, using the old stock as a pattern to which you will refer frequently, make a stand like R in Fig. 3 from two pieces of soft wood, the grooved top lined with felt. Place this beside the vise, with the old stock lying in the crotch, any side up, right alongside your work. This saves hunting around for your pattern every time you must refer to it. You may prefer thick felt padding for your slip-in jaws, but this is prone to pick up scraps of metal that will mar a stock set in the vise. Soft leather will not do this so readily.

Small Vises and Clamps. In working on a small part that must be turned about frequently, a hand vise is indicated. There is the old-fashioned gunsmith's hinged vise pictured in G, Fig. 2, I use one of these a lot, but prefer the better one, E. This may be held in the hand, or set in its holder, clamped to the bench, and swiveled. The parallel-jaw vise (D) is equally handy for some work, like holding a long piece of drillrod for threading or filing, or a sear or trigger for stoning. This is a Billings tool. The same firm makes the combination set E and F. A pin vise (H) may be used for holding small drills, scribers, and, when slipped into a wooden handle, will hold tiny reamers and needle files. I often use one in a lathe or drillpress, to hold drills too small for the fixed chuck.

In the dime store you can purchase C-clamps in small sizes. One of these, capacity about an inch, can be used in countless places where a larger clamp would be in your way; but as this type clamp has an insecure swivel on one end, and this end is prone to slip when least expected, it is not so good for holding scope-blocks, for example, while holes

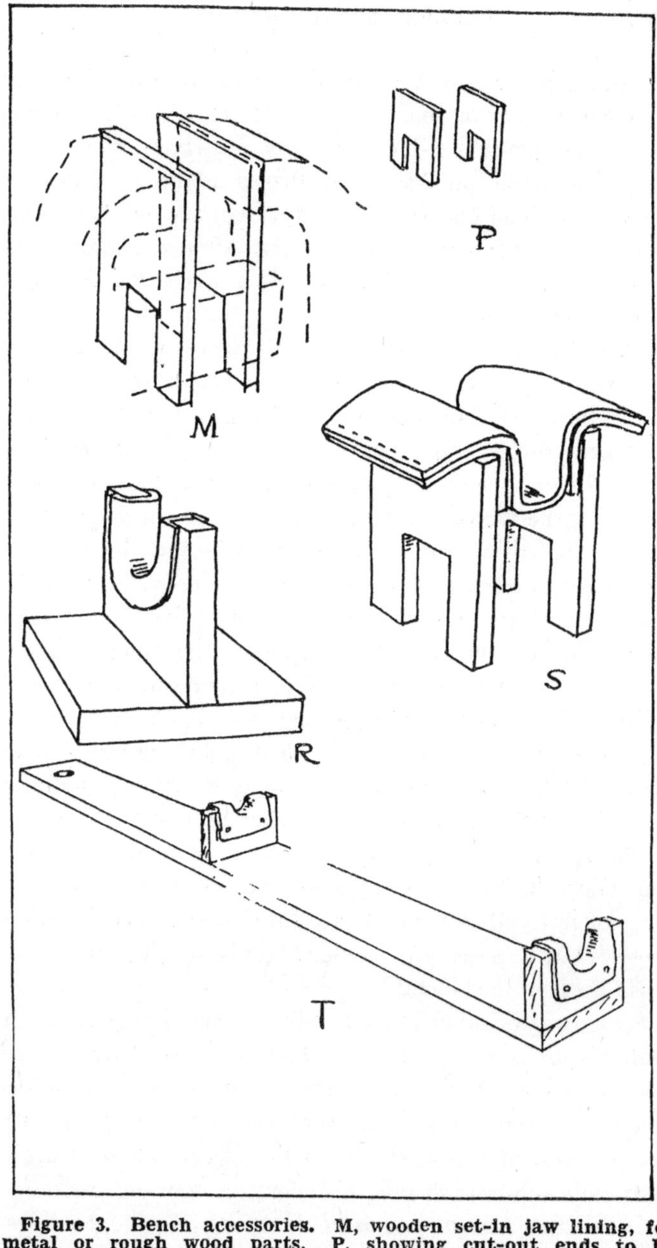

Figure 3. Bench accessories. M, wooden set-in jaw lining, for metal or rough wood parts. P, showing cut-out ends to be set over vise-bar. R, stand for holding old stock while copying it in a blank. S, leather faced slip-in vise pads. T, rifle-cleaning rack, used also for holding metal parts of a gun while one is working on the stock.

are being bored and tapped. For work of this character parallel-jaw clamps like the Starrett set (B, Fig. 2) are almost indispensable. The members are about two inches long. C shows an outside caliper that is used a great deal in stock work. The one I use has arms eight inches long, but these may be opened fourteen inches. After a measurement is taken with it, the caliper is placed on a rule and the exact figures taken from that.

Treadle and Polishing-head. Next in importance to the vise is something with which one may spin round things, polish, buff, drill holes, ream, etc. Before I acquired a lathe I worked with a simple treadle and fly-wheel, connected by a round belt to a cheap polishing-head like the one shown in Fig. 4, the whole shooting match costing much less than $10.00. Something similar is the treadle and flywheel arrangement in a boy's jigsaw stand. If hard pressed one might use the stand from on old-fashioned sewing machine, though the treadle lacks power. The principle of the thing is shown in Fig. 4, but it would be handier to have this treadle and polishing-head unit attached to one end of the work bench.

Do not bother with one of the small polishing-heads, with slender spindle. Get one with a chuck accepting anything up to half-inch. Another even cheaper head may be set up on the bench about a foot to the right, to be used as a makeshift tailstock. Take its spindle out and use instead a smooth piece of rod with a pointed end, fitted with a sleeve with a set-screw in it. This will provide a fairly steady support for anything held in the chuck.

Some time or other every boy buys a small electric motor with his savings. While the cost of firearms has advanced with leaps and bounds in recent years, motor prices have declined. A motor the size of your cap, rated at one-eighth horse-power, may be had for less than $5.00. Hook it up to your polishing-head. It will save many an hour on small jobs.

Heat for Soldering and Brazing. If you have gas handy, a very good heater may be made up by using one

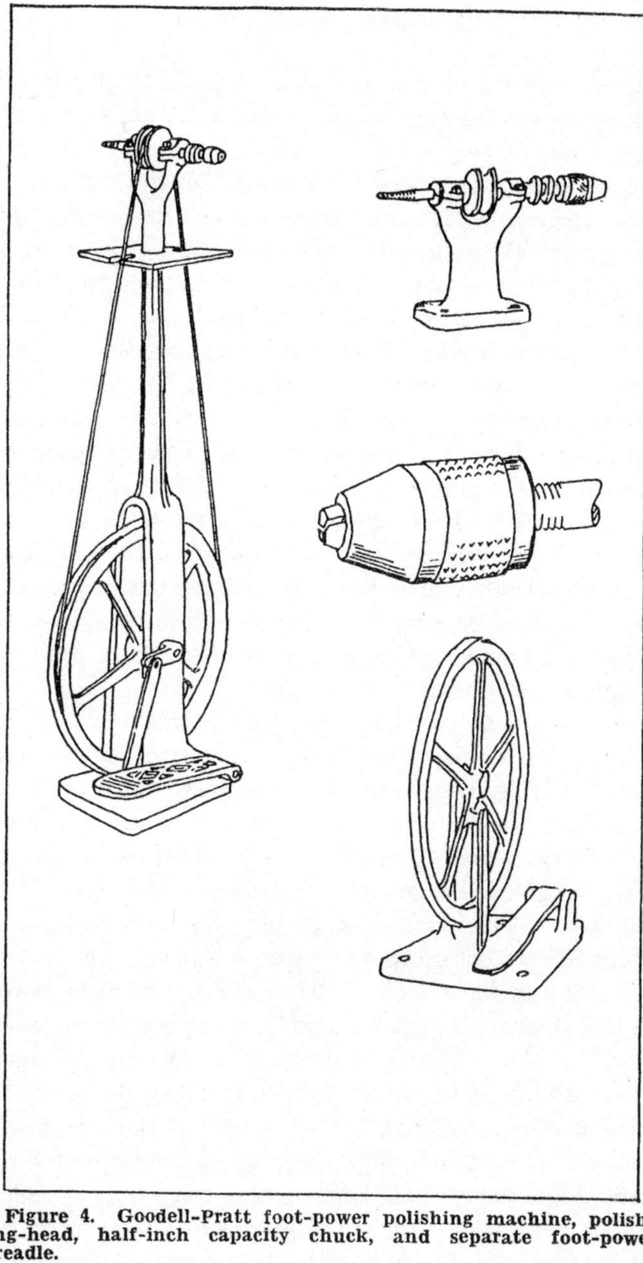

Figure 4. Goodell-Pratt foot-power polishing machine, polishing-head, half-inch capacity chuck, and separate foot-power treadle.

burner from a discarded gas-stove. This will be priceless in casting bullets, heating water, glue, etc. A cheap bunsen-burner will be used even more, and a blow-pipe to go with it, for spot-annealing, heat blueing small articles and marred spots on firearms. Soldering coppers and brazing work may be heated with it and a two-story glue pot is a necessity.

Holder for Parts. While you are working on a stock, something must be done with the metal parts of the gun, to have them handy but protected from accidental injury. Make up a holder like the one shown in Fig. 3, T. Use a narrow board about forty inches long, nail two cleats on top, groove them and protect the grooves with leather cemented on. Cut a hole in the far end of the board, this to be hooked over a brad set in the bench. While the unit may be turned this way and that, the brad will prevent it from skidding while you are cleaning barrels, adjusting sights, etc. While working on a stock, lay the barrel and receiver in the grooves, handy for reference but protected from scratches and dust.

Proper Lighting for Work.

There is one thing about bench work that is seldom mentioned in print, though it is quite important—adequate lighting. When one sets up a bench, in attic, basement or garage, he will try to have one window, at least, behind the bench. Electric light, of course, when available, may be brought to the place where it is needed, by using extension wires or a device like the one shown in Chapter XV, which, by the way, my wife called a rubberneck lamp, the first time she saw it in use. Anyone can copy it readily, using a weighted wood block for a base. The stem consists of several six-inch lengths of flat steel, with small bolts to hold them rigidly in any desired position. An ordinary lamp-socket is clamped to the top section of metal, with an aluminum reflector for the lamp. Mine stands about two feet high when fully extended, but by manipulating the joints the base may be set back, out of the way, and the lamp turned this way or that, to reflect the light where it is most needed. This is a great help when one is checking a stock on a dull day. If the lamp be set well back but low, the shadows thrown by it across the grooves one is cutting will give the contrast one needs to prevent the tool from riding out of the grooves, as may happen when one works toward any light source.

If the vise or cradle may be swiveled, or set on a pedestal, as previously mentioned, one can work all around a gun or a stock, and take full advantage of the best light. In poorly directed light one may easily cut deeper on one side of a stock than on the other, whether shaping or checking. This is similar to aiming, as you believe, at a bullseye when the thing is distorted by mirage; or trying to see the front sight distinctly when strong sunlight comes from one side.

If your light source is not generous, rig up a reflector of some sort. A sheet of white cardboard set opposite the window and not far behind you will serve. Tilt it this way and that while observing just where the reflected light falls as you work, then support it at that angle with thumbtacks on a board or box. Tinfoil, so-called, cemented on a sheet of stiff pressboard, is good material for a reflector. This is much used by camera men in the making of motion pictures. An old mirror will serve, or a window shade may be suspended from the ceiling and pulled down behind you as you work, then snapped up again when not needed.

In cutting a barrel channel at a time when the light is not good, there will be a lack of contrast between the top of the blank and the part where you are working. You start with a block the top of which has been planed flat and straight, and as the edges of the channel must never be bruised or marred, some contrast will help. Blacken the top of the blank with amyl acetate and lampblack, or with prussian blue. A thin coat of the former will dry at once and show you distinctly where your channel edge really is, and all cuts will appear to be lighter. Remove the black with acetone, the blue with turpentine.

A trouble light may often be used in searching for small drills, screws and pins, that one is certain to drop now and then. There is one thing that is dropped oftener, when one is making a stock and fitting the parts to it, than any other one article I can think of. This is the miserable archaic push-button (called release-plunger by the makers) by which the Winchester Model 52 magazine is released. Hundreds of times, in removing the parts from the stock, have I let this plug fall out of its recess in the side of the stock; and every time it rolled under my bench, to be dug out of shavings and other trash that always finds its way under there.

If a flashlight is not handy, use a discarded lamp-cable, with its plug, socket and lamp, to be carried to the seat of trouble. The rubberneck lamp, already mentioned, is useful here, too.

For shop use with a magnifying glass, make up a holder from scraps. Any one of a variety of shapes may suggest itself. One is to attach a length of fairly rigid electrical wire to a base, the wire to be bent in any handy way the nature of the particular job you are working on may suggest. Shape it like a desk lamp holder. A better device may be made from a 12-inch length of stiff wire set in a lead base. To this vertical wire fit a wooden ball or a piece of waste bakelite, set another piece of wire in the ball, too, and attach the reading glass at its end. A set-screw can be put into the ball, so the arm holding the glass may be set at any desired height above your work, then secured at that place. There are numerous small jobs that can be done much better with a low-power reading glass than without, but the glass should be at least two inches in diameter, so one need not squint and strain the eyes in focusing.

Chapter Four

NECESSARY TOOLS—AND OTHERS.

Anvils and Substitutes. A careless workman is quite likely to use one end of his bench vise as an anvil. This is not good practice. Small anvils, weighing ten pounds or so, are not expensive, but if you can find a short piece of railway rail, or something similar, that may be set up on your bench for riveting, forging small articles of metal, and such things, it will serve splendidly. At one time I picked up a short piece of three-inch shafting in a foundry, intending to saw off sections to make grooved pulleys, but it was so handy on the bench that it has been there ever since. Whatever the article is, it should have one level, flat surface and be quite heavy—say around 15 pounds.

File-cards and Brushes. Of course you will obtain and use a file-card. Clean all your files regularly with it. A file the teeth of which are clogged with steel or bits of brass may ruin any work it is used on. Next in importance is a brush, one with real bristles, good and stiff. It may be 3x5 inches, and should have deep, close-set bristles. In checking a stock it will be used every few minutes. Keep it free from oil and grease, and keep an old brush for jobs where grease must be used.

Never let members of your family discard used toothbrushes. Have several of these, some dry, others for oiling and cleaning sights, locks and small parts. Use one with gasoline, as for removing the packing cosmoline from rifle bolts and bolt-channels; another one for turpentine or acetone; a dry one for sweeping out the checking on a stock after an application of linseed oil. With a small round, stiff, paintbrush you can get into crevices that cannot well be reached with any other device. And keep a whisk-broom handy, for cleaning the work bench between jobs.

Screwdrivers. The careful workman cannot have too many screwdrivers. Like his bench vise, a good screwdriver is an institution, to be respected and treasured. There is no such thing as an all-round screwdriver, for the driver *should and must* fit the particular screw-head one is working on. Take an engraved screw-head in a high grade double gun. If it be of foreign make you will notice that all screw-slots are in line with the stock and barrel. On this side of the big pond our workmen are not so meticulous; they are satisfied when the screw is seated as far as it will go. This is a matter of appearances, of course, but in small things appearances count, too. Your drivers should resemble the plain one in Fig. 5. It is short and stubby, has a good grip, and when it is used on a screw whose slot it fits, something is bound to happen when you put strain on the driver.

Not always, it must be admitted. I have had on hand several guns and rifles the screws of which seemed to have been set with a drop-forge, then brazed in. One Springfield receiver screw resisted my best efforts. I called in a neighbor, the ice-man, and finally a husky mechanic, but we could not budge that screw until we had tapped it lightly, then warmed the metal around it with a soldering copper; then, with one man using a wrench and two on the driver itself, the screw finally moved. Make it a rule never to seat a screw until the threads have been coated with grease or oil. Plain bullet lubricant is good, and this can be used to advantage on all wood screws. Soap helps, too, on stock screws, as it prevents the threads from skidding out of their original path. Something of this sort will insure a good grip on the wood without splitting it.

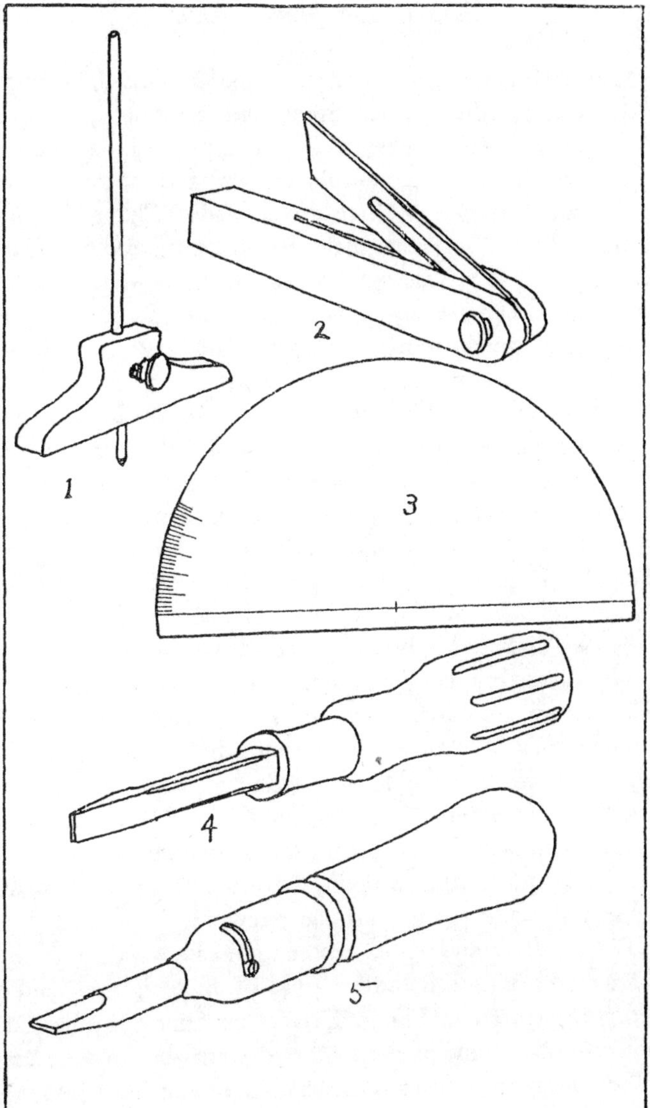

Figure 5. Suggestion for making a depth gauge, 1. Bevel protractor, 2. Pyralin angle protractor, 3. Goodell-Pratt machinist's screwdriver, 4. Yankee ratchet screwdriver, 5.

Now and then one is called on to loosen a too-tight screw in some one's rifle receiver. Some screws cannot be moved with any hand driver, even if a wrench be used, too. This is where a ratchet brace comes into its own; and for every brace there should be two or three driver blades. Clamp the rifle in the padded vise, brace both feet and put steady pressure on the screw. If this does not work, set the brace so you can strike the sweep a sharp, quick blow with the palm of the hand. This usually brings results, but the blade must fit the screw-slot perfectly, else it will ride out and mar the screw. This can be remedied by grinding the head, polishing it, then annealing it. Heat it to a good dark color, then plunge into cold water, so it will be hardened and blued, too. Try to seat all screws so they will be parallel with the barrel rather than pointing every which way. Sometimes it is necessary to grind the point or shoulder until the aim is attained, but with wood screws a quarter turn up or down will do the trick.

Screws that cannot be moved at all with a driver may be loosened, sometimes, by tapping smartly with a hammer, followed by the soldering-copper stunt mentioned above. If a screw must be removed by boring a hole in it, anneal the head as much as possible by holding a blazing hot copper against it for a time, then prick-punch a spot on the head and drill into it about ¼-inch. Grind one end of a broken drill to a square tapered point, drive it into the hole, attach a hand vise and try to start the screw.

For small screws to be seated in hard wood, a ratchet screwdriver is a time saver. One of these is the Yankee No. 12, pictured in Fig. 5. Drivers with long handles lack power—as do some of the ratchet drivers—but may be used to advantage in numerous corners. Do not be taken in by the alleged advantages of combination tool-handles and their mediocre contents. The only combination that is really good is one providing about three driver blades of different widths, all hard and dependable and with a chuck that will hold. The tool companies make some very good ones. One of these is made up with two hollow brass members fashioned somewhat like cartridge cases but with matching flutes and a good steel push-in chuck. These are made, I believe, in Saint Etienne, France, and are sold by sporting goods dealers. Each blade has a flat side that wedges solidly in the chuck, and holds until the cows come home. There are four blades, one quite small. The blades are a bit too hard, but this may be remedied by annealing the points a trifle.

Set a driver in a screw-slot and note how snugly it fits, or doesn't fit. If the blade skids about, use a wider one. On rounded heads a loose driver will ride out of the slot at one side, marring the heads. It is the practice of some makers to bevel the points of the blades. This may be all right for flathead wood screws with deep slots, but for the rounded machine screws found in most guns and rifles, the blade should be shaped like those sketched in Fig. 5—a gradual straight taper with straight sides.

After you get going, make up a few drivers yourself. This works well for very small drivers, to fit special screws like those found in sights and in revolvers. Make them from annealed steel bars, which may be obtained in various shapes from supply houses. The more useful ones are square, $\frac{3}{16}$ by ¼-inch; flat, ⅛ by ⅜-inch, and ½-inch.

Never use a tool-handle that has been battered or split. New ones are cheap. Keep several on hand or make them yourself, from scraps of walnut or red cedar.

It is only a step from drivers to scratch-awls and scribers. Buy a few harnessmakers' awl-blades. These are diamond-shape in cross section, are of good hard steel, and may be ground square, round or oval, or left as they come.

Space limitations forbid going into the subject of tools exhaustively, and any way, every person has definite notions as to what he may need in his work. A good one-pound ball-pien hammer, and a smaller one will be needed; pliers, a hacksaw with eight-inch blades for soft and hard metals; a small fine-tooth back-saw, and rip- and cross-cut saws; a few

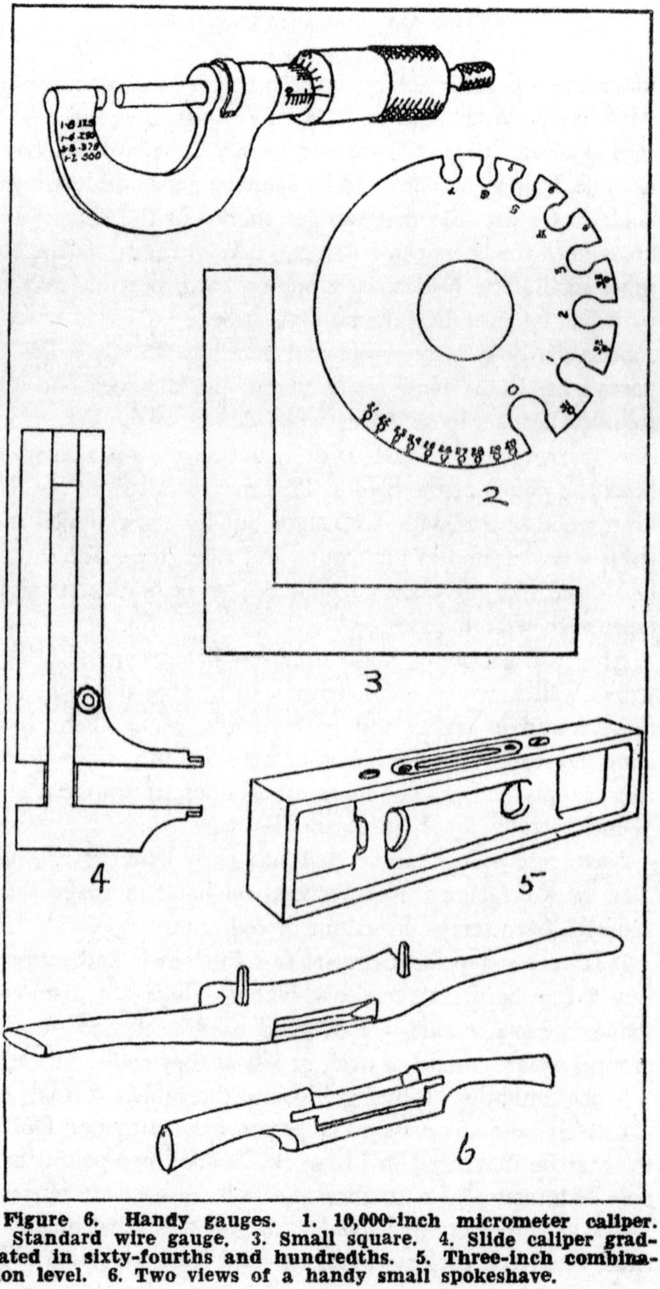

Figure 6. Handy gauges. 1. 10,000-inch micrometer caliper. 2. Standard wire gauge. 3. Small square. 4. Slide caliper graduated in sixty-fourths and hundredths. 5. Three-inch combination level. 6. Two views of a handy small spokeshave.

chisels and gouges; files of various shapes and sizes; a couple of C-clamps and one with a bar about thirty inches long (Fig. 1), for clamping fore-end tips and butt-stocks. A hand-drill will be used a lot, or a brace that will take bits of various shapes—and there is nothing else so effective on stubborn screws as a good brace and a blade that fits its full length in the screw-slot you wish to use it on. Some workmen like the draw-knife but few master its peculiarities fully. A small spokeshave of the pattern sketched in Fig. 6 may be used instead; better still, two of these, one with a very short blade. Planes, particularly the smaller ones, will be needed, say four- and six-inch lengths. To me the metal spokeshaves are a menace—they balance badly, and any way, the lighter wood-handle ones are very efficient. Work with a draw-knife, as some men do, if you like it and can afford to spoil a stock now and then; but if you do buy one, let it be short and compact, then, when it skids it will not spoil so much work as will the mill-run of such tools. It is fine for lopping off corners of a blank. A rasp is better and handier; but with the small spokeshave, with its razor-sharp two-inch blade, you can work all around a stock blank when a rasp is not wanted, and it will not start splinters nor mar thin edges of a stock.

Measures and Gauges. Under this head the most important articles are given. Start with a micrometer caliper, if you can possibly raise the price; if not, a simple slide caliper or gauge similar to 4, Fig. 6. This is a button gauge, very handy, as with it both outside and inside calibrations may be taken. It opens two inches. Select one that has graduations in sixty-fourths on its face, hundredths on the reverse side. I have made numerous split-cane flyrods with only this gauge and a 25-cent center-gauge to measure with. The micrometer caliper, while it costs quite a bit, will more than pay for itself in a moderate time. A typical one is shown in Fig. 6—all the tool-makers supply them. The better ones measure up to one inch, in thousandths and ten-thousandths. The anvil may be locked by turning the milled ring on the anvil, and the small nib on the end has a ratchet that is very sensitive. Never use this tool as a clamp, as I have seen careless workmen do. In most shops doing this is sometimes the equivalent of stopping one's pay.

A steel square, with one- and two-foot arms, of good steel but furnished in the white, may be had for about a dollar. When you get going with your blueing tank, blue it, too. Its longer arm will serve as a straight-edge when you are planing and shaping the sides and top of a stock blank. Another square, each arm about three inches long, like 3 in Fig. 6, is one of the handiest measures I have, for getting into small places in mortising. It is a Browne & Sharpe device, with graduations of sixty-fourths and sixteenths on one side, thirty-seconds and sixty-fourths on the other. A 12-inch flat steel rule may be used as a straight edge, but a handier one is the 6-inch, with graduations on both faces and on one end—also useful in close quarters.

Some workers like a folding rule several feet long, but I find that a seven-foot strip of hard wood is more useful in many ways. Mark it yourself, in feet and half-feet, with inch-marks on the first foot. Fig. 6 shows a standard wire gauge that you will find handy for selecting pin stock, picking drills for holes to be tapped, etc. And there is one of rectangular shape, too.

For very little money you can buy a three-inch level that will help a lot in trueing up sight-slots and scope-blocks. The Starretts make one of this length with bulbs or plumbs for both vertical and horizontal use (Fig. 6).

Elsewhere I have referred to a depth-gauge you may easily make yourself. Fig. 5 shows the idea. It is priceless for measuring screw-holes, the depth of mortises, etc.

A bevel protractor (Fig. 5) may be used in restricted places instead of a mitre-box, as for example in cutting to form the lower edge of a pistol-grip. Cheap, too. The angle protractor (Fig. 5) may be an elaborate steel affair, but you can buy one for a few cents if made of thick pyralin.

A reading glass will be a real help in shop work. It should magnify about four diameters. Provide it with a stand and holder similar to the rubberneck lamp mentioned in Chapter III. For work on tiny parts that may be placed on the bench, with the glass set the proper distance above, you can work with both hands instead of being compelled to use one hand to support the glass. You will appreciate the value of this device when you attempt, for the first time, to replace broken crosshairs in a rifle telescope.

Dividers will save time in your work. Get the so-called firm-joint kind which will stay put wherever they may be set; length six inches. In measuring for mortises in a blank, you start from the forward end of the receiver cut, let us say, then measure from that point to various other points where cuts are to be started or ended. The dividers will give exact limits, and a square will confirm these, so you may go right ahead with full confidence.

Hammers. About hammers again. Try several before you buy one, to determine whether the handle, held normally, is true or crooked. If the latter, you cannot do good work with it. Woodsmen are very finicky about this thing of a straight handle. One whose shape will guide the blade wrongly may cause serious mishaps in the woods. There are jobs where one can do better work with a mallet than with a hammer. When it comes to the finer operations on a stock, one must use the chisel or gouge somewhat like he would a pocket-knife, but the cutter must be razor-sharp. For preliminary cuts the mallet will be an aid. If your left hand is not to be depended on absolutely as a guide, forget about mallets, but if you are ambidextrous, you can use a mallet to advantage, even though you merely tap lightly with it. For cutting off the sprew from a bullet mould, a light mallet shaped like the old-time potato masher is the thing, if the grasp be thin, so one may hold it and the dipper in the right hand. I like locust for mine, length about eight inches—in fact, a miniature baseball bat. Locust or apple wood for a mallet to be used on stocks; length ten inches, diameter of the business end about 2½ inches. A mallet of this size is effective for short swings, close to the hand, and once accustomed to this priest, you seldom go wrong with it. I always think of a mallet as a priest, for the reason that that is what old fly-fishermen call it, and they use the priest to humanely break the necks of trout before dropping them into the creel. The word occurs frequently in all old fishing books. Remembering that good old Irish song, "Father O'Flynn," I have often wondered if one of his fishermen parishoners gave that name to the club used in killing trout. The good father, according to the song, "had a way wid him" in dealing with the lazy and half-witted members of his flock in which his shelalah was used often and vigorously.

Saws. Two common saws will often be needed for wood work. Medium lengths will serve, but both should be good steel—one for cross-cutting, the other for ripping.

The Starrett No. 141 hacksaw, taking eight-inch blades, is versatile in that it may be shifted in a jiffy so a blade will cut to right, left, up or down.

Braces and Hand-drills. As one must set certain standards for his work, it is well to consider drilling devices. As I use a lathe, a drill-press or a polishing-head whenever this is possible, I naturally prefer round-shank bits, as these may be used in a chuck to better advantage than those made for square-jaw chucks. Almost any brace will take round-shank bits and hold them securely until unusual strain is put on it, and the larger breast-drills will take round-shank drills up to half-inch. If a brace be purchased, however, its sweep should not be too great or it will have a tendency to wabble. A small hand-drill, capacity ¼-inch, will be used oftener, as a general thing, than any other drilling device. It is more economical in the long run to purchase twist drills, augur-bits, etc., in sets. For the very small sizes so often used for cutting holes for pins and tiny screws, buy duplicates, as they are so easily broken. Forstner bits cost more than others, but

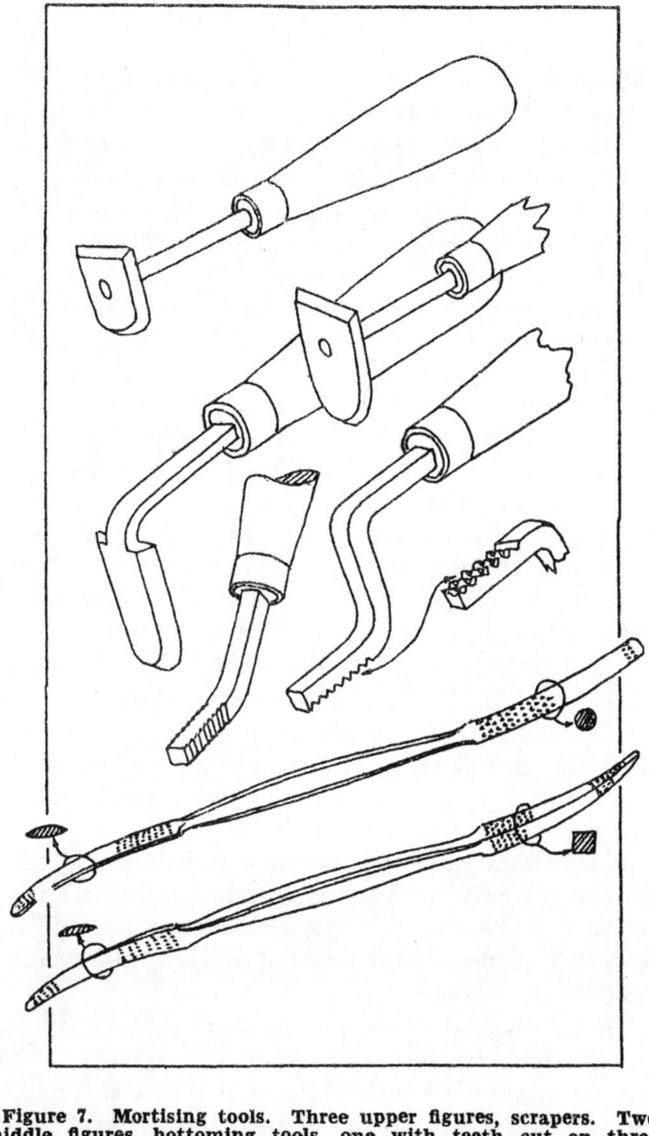

Figure 7. Mortising tools. Three upper figures, scrapers. Two middle figures, bottoming tools, one with teeth cut on three faces. Bottom, woodcarvers' rasps, round, oval, flat, square.

they cut nice clean holes, so it is worth while to have a few, say ¼, ⅜, ½, and ⅝-inch. A center-reamer will often be used on metal and a rose countersink for wood. Buy one flat steel scraper, and collect an assortment of thin glass, to be used in finishing stocks. Visit a professional photographer, who will give you all the discarded glass plates you will want. These are thinner and harder than ordinary window glass, hence they have sharper cutting edges. The convex edge of a tiny piece will remove scratches readily without setting up more of its own.

Files and Rasps. This is a large subject, and my advice to the novice is that he visit a cabinet-maker and ask him to show what sort of files and rasps *he* uses on hardwood; and any good mechanic will help with files for metal. Then buy a couple and experiment with them until you may decide for yourself what lengths, shapes and sizes you fancy. Roughly speaking, the commonest shapes are flat, square, three-square, round; others are flat, the sides parallel, or flat, tapered; flat on one side, rounded on the other; flat on both sides but tapering to an edge like a knife blade, hence the term knife files; needle, with rounded cylindrical shanks, usually made in small sizes and all shapes, including double convex surfaces.

If you are still in doubt, buy these: One 14-inch, fine cut; one 14-inch, coarser, double-cut (that is, grooved in two directions, both at an angle); one 12-inch, half-round, coarse; one round (rattail) and one three-square, eight-inch; and a couple of needle files, one knife, the other three-square. Rasps in 14-inch length, may be coarse and medium, half-round. Fit a handle on each one.

These tools, and a couple of woodcarvers' rasps (Fig. 7) will give you a fair start on either metal or wood work. You will need bottoming tools for work inside stock mortises. For some cuts one of the woodcarvers' rasps may be used, but for other cuts it will pay to make your own cutters as the need for them occurs to you—and any way, every workman makes the tool he fancies will help him most. You can readily design and make up specials by bending or shaping annealed steel bars of small size, cutting teeth in them, then hardening them—not too hard, but so they may be sharpened often with a file, this giving you lessons in shaping cutters at the same time. The sketch shows a few shapes, and also some simple scrapers that are often used for cutting round and angular corners in mortises or smoothing barrel and receiver channels.

There is one file little is heard about in gun books. This is the square double-cut file. One of these, length 12 or 14 inches, largest diameter 1/2-inch, is exceedingly handy in many ways. If you have one of these square files with one of the four faces smooth, it will be still more useful in countless ways.

When a file gets so dull as to be of no use as a file, make something else of it. A ten-inch knife file makes a wonderful knife if re-shaped and ground. Anneal it by heating a low dull red, grind it to shape on an emery or carborundum wheel and hone it to a good edge, then heat and plunge in oil. Small flat files, ground then forged to shape while hot, make excellent chisels. Forge both edges to a long taper, similar to the Addis paring chisels. It is a bit more difficult to shape gouges, but this may be done by clamping one edge of the tool in the vise with a piece of round steel and tapping first one edge then the other until the metal is hollowed sufficiently. Heat and quench, then grind to a good edge. Gouges less than a quarter-inch wide will be used often, and chisels no wider are always useful in corners. Scribers made from needle rat-tail files hold their edge but may snap off if bent. Small screw-drivers made from files, annealed but not hardened afterward, are better than some of the very hard drivers that will chip off when used on case-hardened receiver screws.

Chisels and Gouges. These are very important. Buy Addis chisels, ¼, ⅜, ½ and ⅝-inch wide, straight edges; an equal number of gouges, of the same widths, all deeply curved save one, which should have the merest suggestion of a dished end. Fig. 8 shows a few shapes. These tools are to

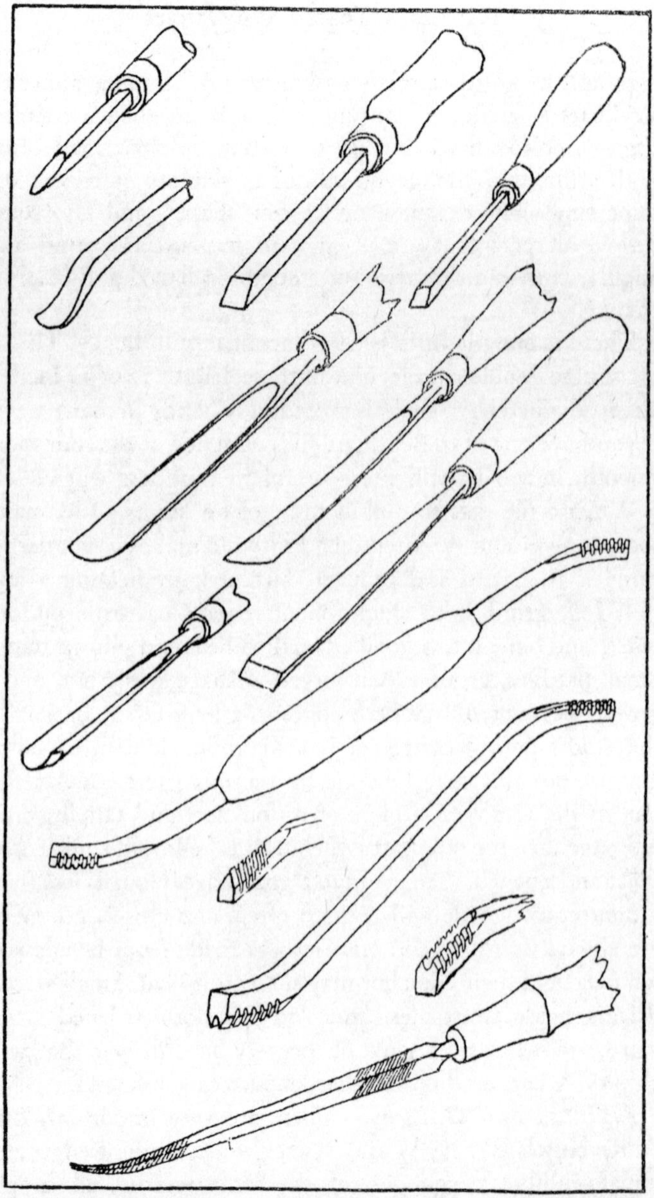

Figure 8. Upper group, chisels and gouges used in mortising and shaping rifle and gun stocks. Lower group, single and double toothed checking cutters, and a bent three-square file.

be honed on both sides, as they are tapered, not beveled. Do not be satisfied until you can shave with every one; and keep them in fine condition. A lot of mortising must be done by cutting across the grain of the wood, the point of the tool being guided by the left hand while with the right you push the tool along very gingerly. For rough cuts a mallet may be used for tapping the tool, but not for close, precise work.

Planes. Only a few planes can be used to advantage in stock-making, but these must be kept very sharp. For dressing the top surface of a stock blank, and the right side—both to guide you in keeping all your cuts square and true—use a 15-inch jackplane. For roughing out a blank, the rasp is handier than any other tool, and really cuts faster without spoiling material, although some lopping off of corners may be done with a short drawknife; but one tiny plane and another one five or six inches long will be used a lot for short cuts on both round and flat surfaces.

The jackplane, and one or two of the iron planes, will be used to cut down to your established lines, and they should be beveled on the under surface of the cutter-bit; but for very fine cuts in hard wood the small planes, with irons beveled on the top, are really scrapers, in that they will not raise slivers, but may be safely used against as well as with the grain. Small iron block-planes, intended for shaping the ends of planks, are excellent tools, but for shaping the butt of a stock, for example, they are not so useful as a coarse file or one of the woodcarver rasps. Cutting across the butt will mar the further edge, any way, so most of this work is done by draw-filing, from heel to toe or the other way. The curved rasps help here, too, if you will always cut from the edges toward the center. With most buttplates the center of the wood must be hollowed a bit, to let the screw-hole bosses down far enough so the edges of the plate will meet the edges of the wood without a suspicion of gaps anywhere.

The checking tools shown in Fig. 8 are referred to in their turn in XIII and other chapters.

Sharpening Stones. One reason our daddies' tools were kept in good condition is that they were generally touched up now and then on large water-moistened grindstones. The boy who turned the thing with a small crank could not possibly generate much speed, so there was no burning—overheating—the edges of tools. We have emery wheels and carborundum wheels handy, and altogether too often these are spun much too rapidly while a tool is being ground, with the result that the edge of the tool is softened more than you would think by heating. It is well, when you are doing this work, to lay out all the edged tools you have that need sharpening. Take these up one at a time, sharpen lightly, lay aside for another tool, and go over all of them several times. In this way one is not tempted to finish up with any one tool too rapidly.

If possible, buy one of these old-time grindstones, set it up on a pair of wood standards, bend a piece of rod crank-shape, and turn it with a makeshift treadle, with a mere trickle of water from a can, to keep it wet while you grind. Finish sharpening tools on an oilstone, then on a very fine-grit Arkansas stone, and finally strop on a length of thick leather glued flesh-side up on a board.

Shotgun locks, sears of all firearms, bolts and their parts, must not be ground at all. For these the exceedingly fine-cut slipstones are all you should use, and this work is honing, always, never grinding. As a general thing all that the parts mentioned need is polishing, and some of them should not be stoned at all, but burnished with a tool shaped like a knife blade but with smooth round edges.

Electric Hand Tools. Amateurs are doing so much work nowadays in the way of dolling-up their stocks, as special ornamental work is called, that some jigger for doing this work in a creditable manner is in demand. Several devices have been put on the market recently, and after the gunsmith has used one of them awhile, he will wonder how he got along without it. One can do a lot of things with a chisel or gouge, but when it comes to setting inlays in walnut, cutting intricate borders around a checked design, engraving monograms in silver or bakelite, and the like, the electric hand tool is in a class by itself. One of these devices is the Hand-ee electric tool, made by the Chicago Wheel & Manufacturing Company. Reproductions of the tool and its container, and some of the bits and cutters that come with it, are shown in Fig. 9. There are several patterns but the least expensive one is very complete, with its equipment of drills, burrs, reamers, brushes and routers. The tool itself fits the hand comfortably, and has a length of cord for plugging into any light socket. There is a sleeve switch, and the speed is said to be 13,000 and upward per minute, according to the model. The tiny drills run so smoothly that one may easily write with one as he would with a pencil, for labeling jars and bottles for shop use, initialing articles in a shooting kit, engraving numbers on bolts, and marking small articles to prove ownership.

I have referred in several places in these pages to some of the things that may be done with the Hand-ee, and others will occur to anyone using the device for awhile. One of these that the gunsmith is often asked to do is to set small gold or silver shields, monograms and such things in gun stocks. This is very tedious work if one has only ordinary hand tools, but with the electric jigger one need only outline the plate to be set in, then rout the wood out and set the plate in with cement. There is a complete set of grinding wheels, and cutters of every imaginary shape, some of which are given in the illustration. I know of nothing so handy for cleaning out mortises after one has completed the rougher part. And the real workman likes to finish the inside work on a stock so it will bear inspection. I have seen some stocks that were beautifully finished outside but with rough, ragged cuts where these would not show normally. Not for me!

Checking Tools. These can be bought singly or in sets from firms specializing in such tools. The American

Swiss File Company's die-sinkers' rifflers, and some of its silversmiths' rifflers serve well in place of bent files, but as every gunsmith has definite ideas as to what checking tools he will use eventually, it would be well for the beginner to make his own checking tools, learn how to use them by working on some old stock, then depend on his own resources afterward.

From annealed tool steel ⅛ by $\frac{3}{16}$-inch the two most-used cutters can be made by anyone handy with small knife and three-square files. Heat a five-inch length of this steel and turn up one end for a distance of ⅝-inch—edgewise. Let cool then heat and turn up the other end in the reverse direction, for a double-end cutter. With a hacksaw make a deep cut in one of the curved ends. Put it in the vise and with a three-square needle file shape the cut to 60 degrees. File the outer edges to the same angle, leaving two sharp cutting edges spaced—to begin with—about twenty to the inch.

With a knife file cut teeth all along the outer edges, spacing them about $\frac{1}{32}$-inch. File these teeth just as you would the teeth of a cross-cut saw blade, then smooth up the inner edges with the three-square file. This will give you a spacer that will cut two grooves.

File the other end of this tool to a 60-degree V, then cut teeth on both sides. Heat the ends dull red and quench in hot water or oil. They should not be too hard, as it will be well to touch them up frequently with a file as you work along. Wind a strip of gummed paper or linen around the middle of the tool, for a handle. This is a handy tool, but if you prefer to have separate ones, use shorter pieces of steel and fit a handle on each one. Several shapes will be seen in Fig. 8.

Heat the tip of a three-square file dull red, bend it the merest trifle in the vise, reheat then quench as before. For some work the three-square needle file is best used as it comes, but bent files are useful in finishing checking patterns.

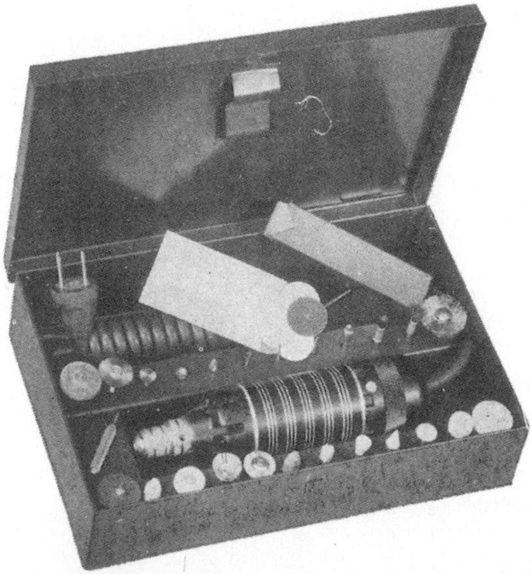

Fig. 9. The Hand-ee tool described on page 37. A most useful gadget to have at hand—doubly necessary to the amateur upon occasions.

Miscellaneous Tools. Tempered steel straight-edges are made by several of the tool-making concerns, in all lengths up to six feet. If you have a square, one arm of which is two feet long, this will often be useful as a straight-edge, but if you have neither, when you purchase annealed bars of steel, get one at least thirty inches long, and use it in trueing up plane surfaces like the top of a stock blank. Grind one edge of the bar to a bevel, and use that side for marking lines, too.

Wood is less dependable than steel, but if you have no choice, try to utilize a long, narrow piece of seasoned birch. Being very hard and dense, it is not easily marred, and is not prone to warp, particularly when it is rubbed with wax over a gas flame until the pores are well filled. I have had in my shop for forty years two five-foot pieces of birch that have never been oiled, but these are as true and straight now as when they were sawed from the plank for me. Sixty-degree grooves were cut in them, one or two on each face, and they were used as shooting-boards for planing the strips of split-cane rods.

In planing or filing to a straight edge in the vise, use a length of tool steel as a guide. Place it parallel with the cut you wish to work down to, but a shade lower than your mark, of course, and when you have cut down almost to the steel, prove up for correctness in your work, then test the surface planed or filed, until perfect.

A pair of tin snips will often save time in cutting thin metal, such as front-sight material, and sight-covers or shades; and brass or aluminum pieces that may be used around the shop. Barrel bands are often cut from strips of soft steel, then blued after they are made up, and can be cut with snips.

The gunsmith is often asked to reload rifle and shotgun cartridges. Even if he does no reloading for customers, he will probably do this for his own shooting—for there are few gunsmiths nowadays who are not shooters, too. Every rifle cartridge case, after having been fired once, must be put in shape for reloading. The first thing to do is ream the inside of the mouth slightly, just a mere bevel, which, when the bullet is seated in it, will not shave the lead. This is sometimes done on a lathe with a rose countersink, but the Hand-ee tool, already mentioned, will do this much more quickly. One of the little burring reamers is used with a very light touch, the tool being held steady on a block of wood.

Primer pockets in cases that are to be reloaded eventually fill up with primer residue. For the best results they should be cleaned out occasionally, and this may be done rapidly with one of the little brushes that come with the set, or by cutting a thin slot in a discarded drillshank, to hold a tiny square of crocus cloth in the tool.

Rifle cases from the Frankford Arsenal have the primers crimped in, and before they can be reloaded this crimp must be reamed out. Do this with one of the burring reamers; or, if much of this work is to be done, make a special reamer for the purpose—one that will remove the crimp and polish the walls of the pocket at one operation. Tools of this sort may be readily made by altering the point of a twist drill, somewhat like the Morse combination drill and reamer. In carbon steel one of the Morse $\frac{13}{64}$-inch drills will fit the Frankford case pocket. One of these costs twenty cents. The reamer is cut at sixty degrees.

Chapter Five

LABOR-SAVING DEVICES AND GADGETS

A Guide for Measuring and Shaping Stocks. The young gunsmith should collect, and keep, tracings in full size of various gun and rifle stocks he has made or had access to. These he can refer to at any time, and they will be a great help to him. On each sheet of paper with the traced outline, set down all data—where the blank came from, what sort of walnut, when made and for whom; length of stock; center of trigger to center of buttplate; trigger to forearm swivel; pitch and breadth of butt; point of comb to rear end of tang; center of trigger to forward edge of grip; width, thickness and smallest circumference of grip; drop at comb and heel; greatest depth and thickness of forearm at center of receiver; length and breadth of cheekpiece, and whether hollowed or rounded.

Next, procure a sheet of tough wrapping paper, at least four feet long. The plan is sketched in Fig. 10, at 1. Draw a heavy straight line A-B, the metallic-sight line; and a shorter base line (B-C) at right angles to the first one, to be used in measuring the pitch of the butt of a gun or rifle, length of trigger-pull, etc.

In measuring the dimensions of a given rifle, remove the bolt and place the rifle flat on the paper, the top of the front sight and the aperture of the rear sight exactly over the long line on the paper guide. Check this by stretching a thread through the rear sight aperture and touching the top of the front sight. With small square prove that thread and mark coincide.

Make a complete tracing of the rifle and stock. An ordinary pencil is too thick for accuracy. Use instead the lead from a pencil set in a piece of copper tubing ⅛-inch in diameter, and hold this upright while tracing. (Later on you will want to trace the stock alone).

Mark all important stations—front and rear receiver screws, location of cut in stock for bolt-handle, magazine cut-off or safety lug; front and rear ends of mortise for receiver, end of tang and front center of trigger.

Now attach the telescope sight that is to be used with the rifle, and after careful measurements, draw the line D-D2, the line of sight through the scope.

Any other gun or rifle may be compared with this one by placing it on the paper guide and noting various details. In making a new stock the guide will be invaluable, particularly when changes are contemplated; and you will refer to it right along as work on another stock progresses.

Move the rifle about on the guide sheet until both the heel and the toe register with the base line (B-C) and center of rear sight is over the line A-B, then measure from the top of the front sight to the line A-B for the pitch of the butt. Some well-known shooters prefer to have the pitch three inches, while a few say it should be five or six inches. The Springfield sporter stock has a pitch of about three inches, the plate has a symmetrical curve, and it seems to fit most men in the prone position. In other positions the plate hooks comfortably over one's shoulder, and helps soften recoil of rifles like the .270 and larger calibers. The plate of the Model 70 Winchester is of practically the same shape, and the pitch is about the same, but to me it is a better fit than the Springfield sporter. Men who, in the prone position, drop the butt below the shoulder, feel the recoil more at the heel—it is not distributed, at is should be, the full length of the plate.

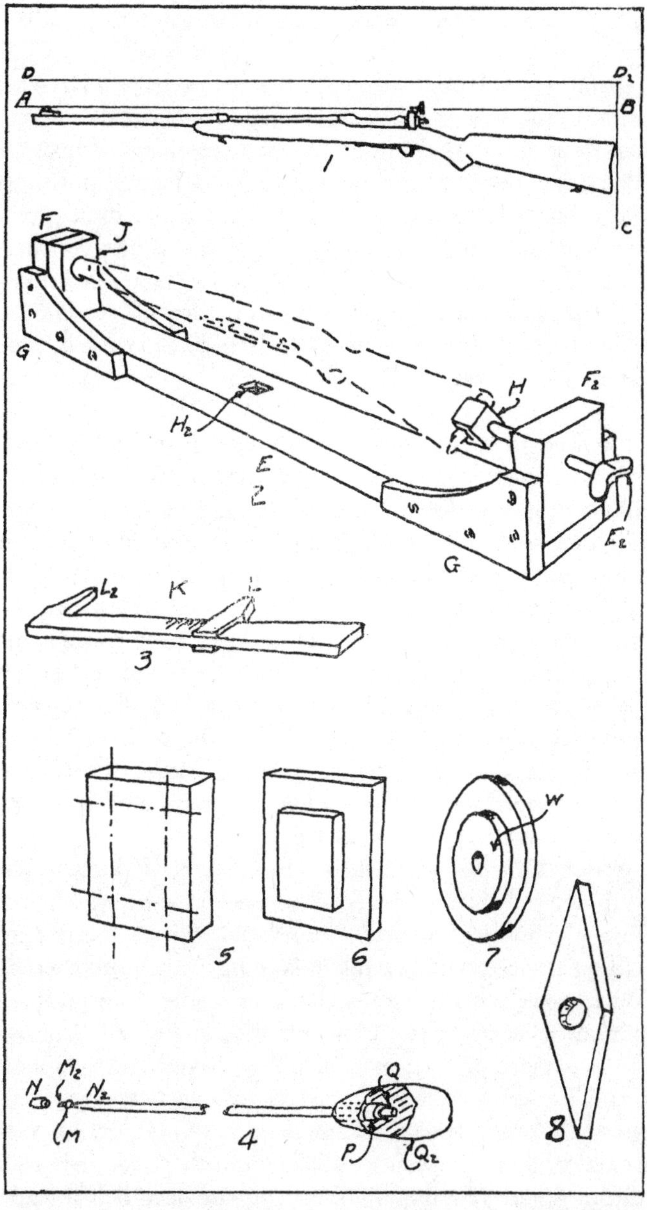

Figure 10. 1. Guide for taking measurements of rifles and stocks. 2. Stock cradle or vise. 3. Trigger-pull length gauge. 4. Building a cleaning rod. 5-8. Method of making grip-caps by hand.

In my work I prefer to leave the butt a trifle long when finishing up, fitting the plate roughly, with smaller screws than those to be used finally, ask the customer to shoot the rifle at the range, then suggest changes in length and shape of cheekpiece or comb, pitch and drop; make these alterations and ask him to try it again. Personally I like the shape of the Model 1897 Winchester shotgun buttplate, mentioned in Chapter XII. It curves nicely, with a sort of mound just below the heel, and it seems to me less pitch, with it, gives the most comfortable fit with high-power rifles, in all positions.

Needless to say, the trials mentioned may best be made after the stock has been worked down and sanded just enough to give it the feel of a real stock. I have even worked with a customer on the rifle range to make slight alterations, using rasp, file or sandpaper. The length and curve of the pistol-grip are often altered slightly at such times. One can start with a pitch of 3½ inches and prove up by reducing this ⅛-inch at a time, if at all, until the buttplate bears its full length on the shoulder. It is not a bad idea to use a temporary sole leather plate, attached to the stock with brads, until the length-pitch question is settled. Pieces of cardboard may be slipped under the leather at toe or heel, tried and shifted until the pitch seems right.

Stock Clamp or Cradle. In Chapter III I mentioned a support for rifles or parts while one is working on them (Fig. 3). Something more substantial will be needed for holding a stock securely while it is being shaped and checked. You can easily make such a clamp or cradle from odds and ends. An efficient device is shown at 2, in Fig. 10. The base (E) is a piece of 2 x 4-inch plank 38 inches long. Supports F and F2 are 2 x 4 x 8-inch pieces securely attached to the base with long screws. Triangular pieces G-G may be metal or wood—their use being explained further along. For the adjusting screw E2 use a half-inch square-head bolt threaded its full length, and with two nuts. Cut pockets in the upright

F2 for the nuts and cement one nut on each side with thick shellac. The swivel (H) is a piece of hardwood notched at one end to fit butt of stock. Bore a half-inch hole in the other end, almost through the block. Ream it out just enough so the end of the bolt will turn freely but not wabble, and coat end of bolt with soap or grease. A large wing-nut may be turned up against the square head of the bolt, then solder sweated into the threads will prevent the nut from moving. H2 may be a bolt of any handy size, for attaching cradle to bench or table. J is a loose block that may be set in the recess formed by the pieces G-F-G. Bore a two-inch hole through it and bevel and round one end of the hole, for a forearm socket.

To center a stock in this cradle, it may be necessary to set in one or two blocks between F and J. Cut a piece of thick soft leather, round, wet and stretch it to fit the hole in the block J, using a ball or old door-knob, and when the leather dries, cement it into the block J. Before the fore-end is rounded it may be held in the hole with a wad of paper; afterward that end of the stock will rest securely in the hole without injury.

Another use for this cradle is to clamp tips to fore-ends—horn, bakelite, etc. The stock may be turned bottom up and blocked underneath, so the tip will be aligned with the stock, cement applied, then the stock left over night with just the right amount of strain to secure a tight joint. After a stock blank has been sawed to rough shape and is ready for inletting, it may be held securely in the cradle and turned about as work progresses through inletting, roughing off, sanding and checking, but for this the device should extend at least one-third its length over the side of the bench and be supported by an upright under the free end. It may be turned end for end and at any desired angle. You will be astonished to find how rigid this cradle is if 2 x 4-inch stuff be used in making it. The stock is supported at its ends, as it should be, yet it may be turned bottom up or on either side merely by giving the adjusting screw a couple of turns. In final polishing alone it will be found exceedingly useful, as one may rub with one hand or both, turning the stock as desired.

The long clamp shown in Fig. 1 is a cheap but efficient device that will often be used by the gunsmith. The bar is 32 inches long, and the sliding member locks by friction wherever placed. It can be used for attaching fore-end tips, holding receivers and buttstocks of double guns or two-piece rifle stocks. Clamps of other shapes may be made from fairly stout iron bars. Still another shape may be made with two pieces of hardwood with inserted bolts with nuts. A clamp may be made from scraps of wood by nailing three or four pieces to a board set fairly close to a shotgun stock, with two wedges behind the butt. Still another method is to thread both ends of a long bar, bend it to long U-shape, fit a piece of iron or wood across the open end, with holes to fit the ends, then turn nuts down as required.

A much more simple checking board can be made in a few minutes from scraps. The base may be a board 20 inches long and 6 inches wide, with a cleat three inches high nailed on each end. Groove one cleat with a 2-inch cut, the other wider. Glue leather on both. In use, place the board on the bench, lay the stock in it, and shift both stock and board so you will get good light from your right hand. When you wish to reverse the stock, lift the board and the stock intact. The stock is held, or turned, with the left hand. The device is especially handy for checking under the grip and all around it; and the forearm, too.

Trigger-pull-length Gauge. One of the important measurements of a firearm is the distance from the forward face of the trigger to center of buttplate. As a quarter-inch too little or too much is sometimes really important, an accurate gauge is a good thing to have. Make up one yourself from a piece of hardwood and a scrap of brass, as shown at 3 in Fig. 10. K is a length of hardwood ½ by ¾-inch, sawed out to leave the arm L2 at one end. L is a piece of metal bent entirely around the bar K and friction tight. On one face of the long member scribe marks 1/8-inch apart from 12 to 16 inches. In use the arm L2 is held against the front center of the trigger and the slide L adjusted to touch the center of the buttplate, then the length of pull read on the scale. Of course the device may be used for other measurements, in which case mark inches or fractions on the long member as may serve best.

Trigger Pulls and Weights. To weigh the trigger-pull of any firearm, fill muslin bags with lead, pebbles or sand, these weighing 1/2, 1, 2, and 3 pounds respectively. Cut a length of hard wire, bend one end at right angles, the other end as a hook. Catch the hook in a string tied around a bag, and holding the firearm upright on a bench, slip the other end of the wire over the trigger and let the bag swing free. If for example the trigger will support three pounds easily, add the half-pound weight, and if it releases the trigger, go back to the three-pound bag but suspend from the wire small articles until the trigger just trips, then weigh bag and all. In smoothing up parts of the mechanism of a firearm or reducing a hard or rough pull, the device may be used at different stages of the work, with no guessing. Lead weights are most reliable, as they will not change with atmospheric variations. Make them by holding the bent end of a length of wire in a small paper box, pour melted lead into the box, holding the wire until the lead cools, then trim the lead until a given weight is found.

Testing Rifles for Accuracy. No doubt you will often be asked to test rifles and cartridges for accuracy, and this calls for a solid rest of some sort. Where it is possible to set up such a unit, an elaborate bench made from concrete is the best bet, but wood will serve, and even a portable rest will be steady enough if well braced and its legs set in the ground.

If its weight does not matter, build it from 2 x 4-inch stuff, put together with screws or heavy nails. It may be any convenient height, but 30 inches will serve, as this height will enable you to sit alongside the rest on a box or stool, or to kneel while firing, though this will grow very tiresome after awhile. Five feet is about right for length, two planks wide—say 22 inches. Spread the legs quite a bit, like a carpenter's saw-horse, and nail a brace across each pair. At the forward left side add another plank three feet long, bracing it underneath, to support your left elbow as you sit in the recess formed by the added short plank.

At the front end fit a 2 x 4 across the top of the bench, nailed securely. Cut at least three more pieces of plank of equal length, and keep them handy, so they may be used to increase the height of the muzzle-supporting front end, as needed. Support them with cleats nailed to the lowest piece. This is one of the simplest forms for adjusting the height of the barrel support. Another one has a slotted upright in the middle of the front, with a piece nailed on top, for a rest for the barrel. Half-inch machine-screws and wingnuts furnish means for adjusting the height.

On the left side fasten to the bench a short plank with a lagscrew, so it may be turned. Top it with a piece of plank grooved on top, to hold a spotting scope, swivel that piece, and you will have the glass close to your eye as you shoot but movable in two directions.

To complete the unit, nail a two-inch cleat on a piece of thin board, and shift this about on the bench for a support for the butt of the rifle. The incline of the board should be toward the rear, so the butt will slide downward and backward with the recoil. The other way about will influence group centering unfavorably. Finally, use a small muslin bag filled with dry sand on the muzzle support. Some shooters prefer instead a short block clamped on the barrel, as shown in the small sketch, Fig. 11, on page 53. One of this sort may be made with a hardwood block grooved to fit the barrel, a bent aluminum piece, two small bolts with nuts, and two pieces of soft leather, so the device may be clamped tightly around the barrel without marring its finish. In this shape the clamp will hold the rifle rigidly upright on the support, and in aiming there will be no excuse for canting the rifle.

This device is a makeshift imitation of the solid bar the old-time rest shooter used years ago at the Walnut Hill (Mass.) rifle range. That was a three-inch bar of iron fitted to a dovetail slot in the under-side of the barrel near the muzzle. The bench top was leveled, the bar plumb, so in aiming it was only necessary to hold the front sight under or on the bullseye, or, with a scope, to quarter the black. A refinement of this plan is to fit two metal cleats on the top of the muzzle support, cut two grooves in the wood block, and have this slide on its "ways" when the rifle recoils. The bench-rests used at Walnut Hill and elsewhere had screw adjustment for the muzzle support.

Rifles with heavy barrels shoot better with solid muzzle supports than do light-barrel rifles. Some of these will perform better when a sandbag is used and the barrel supported just forward of the forearm end. Remodeled Sporter Springfields and the Winchester Models 54 and 70 are in this class, and some light barrels are tricky if shot in the sun on a hot day.

Lacking anything better, the old-time crotched stick is not bad. Rest the toe of the rifle in the palm of the left hand, and use a sling-strap. Very close grouping is possible.

Bullet Catcher. When one purchases a new rifle, the first thing to do is ascertain what sort of ammunition will work best in it. If a .22-calibre, this may be done by shooting several groups on a rest with ammunition of different makes, then using right along that brand which will group best with that particular rifle. If a center-fire rifle, try another stunt. Seat a bullet in an empty case, put the dummy in the rifle chamber and close the bolt. Take the dummy out and examine the bullet with a glass, to see just how far the bullet may be loaded ahead of the case. The lands in the barrel will mark the ogive or shoulder of the bullet 1/16-inch or so, and this is what you want, as it will prove to you that the bullet lies true in the throat or lead at the forward end of the chamber, so that, when the powder charge is fired, the bullet will move along in perfect alignment with the bore, with no jumping or wabbling to twist it out of shape.

Measure the over-all length of the dummy and make a gauge from a scrap of metal, loading all cartridges to that standard length; provided, of course, you get close groups on the target with that length; if not, seat the bullet further out or further in until its grouping improves. Uniform length of cartridge makes for close grouping. And if the powder charge be less than a shell full, be sure to tap the cartridge slightly, to settle the powder down against the primer just before firing. In the excitement of shooting, however, one may forget this detail. Forestall the possibility by using a loading-block. It should be added just here, however, that the dummy must also be tried in the magazine, since some magazines will accept a cartridge of standard length only. Anything longer will not feed through into the chamber. In a well-known model, the first four cartridges will go into the magazine nicely but the fifth one will jam in the top of the follower and must be pried out with the fingers or a screwdriver—a pretty situation to be in if a bear is on his way to visit you!

Bore fifty (or any convenient number) of holes in a hardwood block, but stop the drill within $\frac{1}{16}$-inch of the bottom, so the block may be carried about with its contents intact. Have the holes just a bit larger than the head of the case. Fit the block into a paper box with a snug cover. Stand each case in a hole in the block after filling the case with powder —so it cannot tip over—then, after the bullets have been seated and the finished cartridge wiped off, return them to the block, bullets up, and carry it thus to the firing-point. Make it a rule to tap the box slightly every time you line up to shoot. In this way the depth of powder will be the same in every cartridge, and this spells greater uniformity

You may know the bore and land diameter of your barrel, and can swage your bullets to fit the bore snugly, but if you shoot plain lead or gas-check cupped bullets, it is well to know just what a bullet looks like after it has travelled a hundred yards or so. Specimens may be found at times behind the butts in soft soil or in snow, but finding a specimen that will clearly show the imprints of the lands on a bullet is another story. A better plan is to settle this matter in the shop. Take a gun-shipping-case at least four feet long, fill it with fine sawdust, saturate the dust with any old waste oil, and nail the cover back lightly after removing one end and covering that end with a sheet of pressboard.

Set the box in a place where no harm will be done should the bullet pass entirely through the box—a remote possibility—aim at the center of the paper end, and fire two or three cartridges, then remove the cover and dig the bullets out. They will penetrate the oiled sawdust anywhere from one to three feet, depending on power, and the bullets will come out almost perfect, so you may examine them with a glass or caliper them and know just what your particular bullet does after it passes through the bore. An example: A .270 rifle shot 136-grain gas-check bullets very accurately, but 110-grain plain base bullets went wild. A test in the shop developed the cause. The rifling had been cut with four lands about $\frac{1}{32}$-inch wide, and these were very clean and sharp on the heavy bullets recovered from the sawdust, but the land marks on the lighter bullet were more than a sixteenth wide, and were not clean cut—showing that without any doubt the lighter bullet had turned part way 'round on its axis in the bore—partial stripping, that is. Usually a fault of this character may be remedied by making the bullet from harder alloy or reducing the powder charge.

Indications of Head Spacing. With the fit of bullets we turn naturally to the subject of head space. In black powder days the term head spacing was called bushing up; that is, when a gunsmith fitted a barrel to a receiver he used a certain cartridge or case as a gauge for chamber form and length; and the distance between the rear end of the chamber and the face of the breechblock was carefully gauged so the case used would fit with only a minimum of play. He had in mind the fact that other cases would be used in that chamber, some of them shorter, thinner, or with smaller heads than his gauge-case; and larger cases would be tried, too. So he finished the job with sufficient tolerance to admit the use of cartridges of different makes, and called his work "breeching up."

Conditions today require more care. With high pressure ammunition a cartridge that is too large for a rifle it is tried in is not used at all, so no harm accrues. But if one is used that is short from head to shoulder, with an ill-fitting head that does not closely fill the space between chamber end and bolt face, it is a potential menace to the one who fires it. The excess space along the neck and the taper to the shoulder and part way back of the shoulder may permit gas to escape; the excess space around the head will allow the case to set back. Anything may happen, the least dangerous thing being a jet of gas or powder residue projected far enough to injure the shooter's face or eyes. If the primer be loosened or punctured at the same time, the consequences may be more serious.

Head space as applied to rimmed cases like the Hornet and the Krag is the space between the rear end of the chamber and the face of the bolt when locked, ready to fire. It follows that gas may find its way back along the case if it be shorter or slimmer than normal, but as the head covers the chamber end, this gas may not so readily reach the recess between chamber and bolt. A rimless case head has nothing behind it but the bolt, so head space as applied to it means the fit of the case from its seat in the chamber, against the bolt, along its main body to the shoulder.

Risk may be avoided usually by using new cases. The first time a new cartridge is fired the case will be expanded to a close fit in that chamber. The neck and the taper to the shoulder may be blacked more or less. Polish this stain off, and after firing again, examine it. As it was neck-sized before it was reloaded, the neck may be stained a bit, but the taper and shoulder will be bright, so there is nothing there to worry about.

Head-space gauges are expensive. They are used in the factories, so it is safe to assume that a new rifle has been measured for cartridge fit.

Figure 11. Bench rest with adjustable muzzle support, wider top at forward end, swiveled holder for spotting scope, and inclined board for toe rest. A Winchester Model 70 rifle being tested, with a 6X Malcolm scope.

Chapter Six

MATERIALS AND SUPPLIES.

You must not get the impression, as you read these pages, that all of the things I have mentioned are necessary in order to do some work. You can go without a lot of them or pick up here and there articles I have not mentioned. I have merely tried to cover the ground in a general way, and to suggest things that old hands believe they must have. One buys a tool here, another there, some from the dime store even, and plugs along with what is available—which is really half the fun, since one learns to appreciate the few things he can work with.

Abrasive Rolls and Discs. Consider abrasives. You will need several kinds as you go along. Sandpaper, as it is called, is the commonest one. The British call it glass paper, although ours is often flint-coated. Garnet paper is very good, harsh and durable. I have seen it produced, and have actually waded through great heaps of beautiful garnets, obtained by crushing boulders quarried from the mountain sides in the Adirondacks (and elsewhere). The garnets are separated from the worthless parts of the stones, washed, pulverized, sifted, graded, and spread on tough paper about 9x11 inches, also on smaller paper that is put up in handy packs. Use will be found for all grades in stockmaking, particularly the very finest, which is best for the final sanding at the end of the wetting stage.

Emery cloth will save labor on metal work. Select coarse,

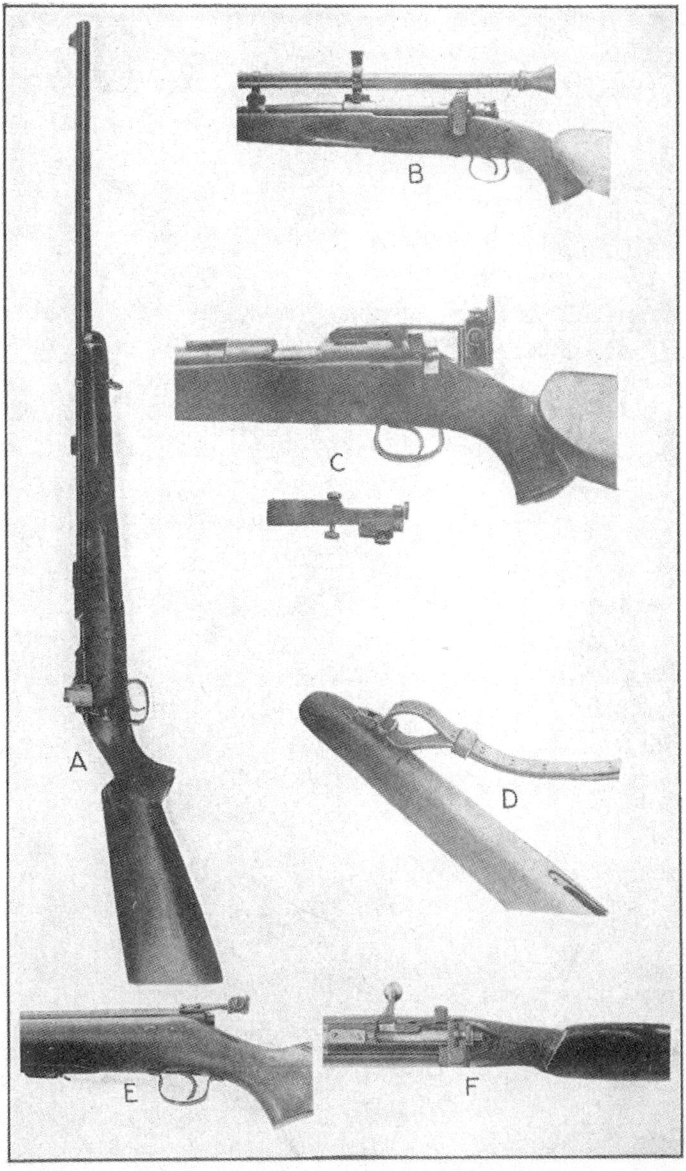

Fig. 13. A, restocked Model 52 rifle, with snobble fore-end and self-spring magazine catch. B, Model 54 rifle, high scope mounts and raised comb. C, two types of extension sights. D, four-inch swivel-plate on the Model 416 Stevens rifle. E, Model 55 sight and extension on the Stevens 56C rifle. F, Monte Carlo cheek-piece on restocked Stevens Model 416 rifle.

medium and fine; crocus and carborundum cloth as well, for the final stages of metal polishing; and coarse and fine steel wool.

There are numerous places on a stock where something more effective than a rasp will be needed. For this work a few sandpaper rolls should be made up. Take round pieces of wood, like chair-rungs or rake-handles, saw them to convenient lengths, say eight or ten inches, and glue sand or garnet paper on them. All sizes from half-inch to two inches will come in handy. Cover some with coarse, others with medium and fine paper. Emery and crocus cloth, made up in this shape, will be good for smoothing steel surfaces. Cut the paper so the edges will just meet around the stick, coat stick with glue, then roll each one in a sheet of paper and put aside until dry.

Sandpaper blocks may be purchased in stores, provided with wire clamps to hold the paper rigidly. Pieces of suberit (cork chips and glue, compressed) or belt leather make good holders. These should be about five inches long and two inches wide. Rounding all corners saves paper from cutting at folds, and one may more readily work into curves. Pieces of porpoise hide, which are often an inch thick but flexible, are good. A disc of this hide, fitted to an arbor, will often be used in the polishing-head for buffing metal. The periphery becomes soft with use, so it may be oiled and sprinkled with rottenstone, pumice, emery or tripoli, according to the work in hand. The side of one of these discs is fine for polishing some surfaces.

Rolls of varying lengths and diameters, each equipped with a mandrel of its own, are often used in the chuck for polishing. I use a number of these, the diameters from one to seven inches, but unless these are used in a lathe having a tailstock spindle, they should be quite short, to turn smoothly. For a mandrel use a piece of round steel two inches long, carefully centered and driven into one end of the roll.

Discs are even handier than rolls. Make them any size the

polishing-head will accommodate, though five to eight inches will be best. They may be cut out with a compass saw from pieces of half-inch pine board. Glue abrasive paper on both sides and provide each one with a headless bolt, two washers and two nuts, as described further on for making pistol-grip caps. The best ones will be surfaced with coarse grades of sandpaper, but others covered with medium and fine sandpaper and both emery and crocus, will be used more frequently than you may think.

After a stock has been inletted and you are working on the outside, if the stock be held on its side in the vise, protect the edges of the barrel channel by using a round piece of wood in the channel. One of the sandpaper rolls will be ideal if it fits the channel, as it will not drop out every time you shift the stock, as a smooth stick will do.

Now and then you can use a long strip of sandpaper in smoothing a stock that is nearly finished. Work with it as a bootblack does with his cloth. Another thing to be used in this way is a strip of coarse duck, folded two or three times and coated with pumice or some other abrasive. Use it wet for final rubbing, or with crude oil. This will save much hand rubbing after a stock has been oiled.

Always keep on hand two or three buffsticks, for polishing metal surfaces. Make them from pine an inch or more wide and a foot long. Glue duck on one, saddle or strap leather on others, and use each one with a different abrasive. In a pinch you can strop cutting edges of tools on one of them. Use the stick as you would a long file, with both hands.

Soak a long strip of flannel with any thin oil, and keep it in a drawer, away from grit, when not in use. Rub soiled stocks with it now and then, and all metal parts, following with a dry wool strip. Soaking a gun with oil, to keep moisture away, is a messy thing, but a clean oily cloth is worth preserving. And it is bad practice to let lubricating oils soak into barrel and receiver channels, to rot the wood where it cannot be seen.

Coarse and fine steelwool pads are always handy. The finer grade is good for polishing, but for very particular jobs it is best to use it with crude oil or oil and pumice or rottenstone. On stocks it must be used across the grain, as otherwise particles of metal may be rubbed into the pores and cause trouble later on. In oiling a stock, after the wood has had several coats and the oil starts to gum, cut it down to a smooth surface with wool, pumice and oil. When spar varnish is added to linseed oil, to really waterproof a stock, the last coat will leave a gloss almost like white shellac or lacquer. This most owners object to because of its varnish-like appearance. Remedy this by rubbing with fine steel wool and pumice. This may be done at any time. You may smear a heavy coat of spar varnish on an old stock, and when that is dry, cut down all gloss, leaving a matte surface almost as dull and smooth as the famous London finish, but this requires practice in rubbing very thoroughly with just the right pressure on the pad. Wool alone will leave fewer scratches than fine sandpaper, but wool, oil and pumice or rottenstone will give a smooth dull surface on any finished stock, old or new.

When a stock has been used all season, and shows scratches, finger and perspiration marks, treat it with boiled linseed oil and turpentine, half and half, with a few drops of clear Japan dryer, on a bit of coarse flannel; then, when dry, cut the surface down as described above. The result should be satisfactory. Crude oil is a real aid in polishing wood. In my canoeing days our club members rubbed their cedar canoe hulls in the winter with sandpaper, gave them two coats of boiled linseed, rubbed these down, then two coats of spar varnish, this treatment giving a beautiful finish and protection against bruises and wear all season. Pumice and water were used first in rubbing, then pumice and crude oil, followed with dry cloths, then warmed varnish on a fine day, in the sun.

The Viscol Company, mentioned elsewhere, sends out with

its leather dressing a small package of acuin, intended for dressing razor strops. This is a very fine abrasive you may use to advantage on a strop for chisels and gouges, but do not push the edge of the tool away from you, as you would with an oilstone; pull toward you.

Keep powdered abrasives in pint jars on a shelf, where each one can be selected at a glance. Instead of using stickers that are always falling off, etch the legends with the Hand-ee electric tool referred to elsewhere. One of the tiny grinding discs is the thing to use, and at the high speed of the tool you can trace a name on a jar in a jiffy. The matte white lettering can be seen at a distance more clearly than if it be written in ink. Brown jars and bottles lend themselves to this scheme, as the contrast makes the letters stand out clearly. You will need a small supply of each, emery powder, flour pumice, whiting, tripoli, flake orange shellac, lampblack, graphite, and a brick of rouge, good for buffing metal.

Shellacs and Lacquers. Buy orange shellac in flake form, shake a little of this into a fat jam jar, and pour just enough wood alcohol in to make the mixture thick and gummy. Leave a short brush in the jar, where the spirit will keep it soft. Use this thick stuff on hurry-up jobs where heated glue is not needed. A finished grip-cap, put on a slightly hollowed grip-end with this stuff, then the screw turned down, will stay put; then, when you finish it up, along with the wood, there will be no gaps between wood and cap. It will look as though it had grown there. If thinner shellac be needed, pour a bit into the jar lid and thin as needed. The ferrules of fishing rods never loosen when set with thick shellac; and while you are aligning a set of scope-blocks on a rifle barrel, if a trace of shellac is put under them, they will stay put until you can spot the screw holes. If the comb of a gun is too low, put on a temporary pad of cotton and chamois secured with shellac. You can remove both at any time with alcohol on a cloth.

White shellac, if you use it, is best in solution, as it does not keep well if exposed to the air. Thin as needed with alcohol.

DuPont clear lacquer is useful in many ways. A stock may be finished with it and nothing else, if you do not object to the high almost transparent glass-like surface. It may be had in tints, too.

Celluloid lacquer may be made up as needed, and if lampblack be mixed with it, it is sometimes useful on wood, and may even be used as hurry-up blacking on small parts, say a sight-cover or that part of a service Springfield barrel that is left unblued at the arsenal. To make it, put a little acetone in a screw-top bottle. Drop into it small scraps of pyralin or celluloid. These will dissolve in a day or two; add a little amyl acetate (banana oil), lampblack if desired, and stir frequently. Old photographic films will serve after the emulsion has been cleaned off with hot water, but the present-day acetate safety films will not dissolve readily. Apply with a soft brush, polish with a wool cloth, add banana oil to thin. Clean the brush with acetone, and keep all these away from a flame.

Hard maple gunstocks may be darkened with various substances, among them potassium permanganate and Indian red (oil-soluble red, as it is known by color makers). Minwax furniture stain, sold in department stores, is another one. The stain penetrates hardwood nicely, and after this has been rubbed down, Minwax is warmed and rubbed in over a flame, leaving a velvet smooth but not glossy surface. The wax is made from tung-nut or chinawood oil. This oil dries in a short time without the gumming that is inherent in linseed oil. The prepared wax may also contain furfurol, a comparatively new liquid that is extracted from wheat hulls in the breakfast-food plants. Combined with benzol, this has a pleasant odor. In this it is unlike chinawood oil, which alone has a very disagreeable odor. Chinawood oil is extracted from the seeds of the tung "apple," in China, and recently from trees grown in our Southern states. The raw oil dries nicely in a few hours, and does not sweat afterward and become gummy, as linseed oil does. Shortly after the World War linseed oil became scarce, and the raw product was combined with cottonseed and menhaden oils. Manufacturers of varnishes, paints, lacquers, linoleum, etc., turned to chinawood oil, which is not much affected by grease or hot water, and this is commonly used in many ways now. Soy bean oil, so highly praised as a food, a drink, and the body for various varnishes, may become the successor of linseed—who knows?

Miscellaneous Items. Bow and arrow makers use this formula for making waterproof glue, a necessity for bows and arrows that are often exposed to the weather: "To liquid glue add a slight amount of potassium bichromate. Expose to the sun, after which the glue will become insoluble in water."

DuPont household cement is a reliable adhesive for small jobs, filling wormholes in wood when combined with wood filings, etc. It is not affected by moisture. Thin with amyl acetate.

Emery powder is used on metals, rottenstone and pumice on wood. Tripoli or rouge is better for steel polishing, as neither one leaves scratches. Coarse pumice powder is preferred to fine for preliminary rubbing.

Prussian blue was used a lot by old-time gunsmiths; it still is. Its color contrasts sharply with metal surfaces, or metal and wood, and is never mistaken for grease marks, as with lampblack. Lampblack is cheaper and very satisfactory for inletting work. Put a little of the powder in a shallow tin, mix with crude oil or any substance that does not gum, and apply it to metal parts with a stick covered with a piece of flannel. For inletting, smear all the metal parts liberally, set these in your mortise, and reduce the spots that are blacked. It can be removed with turpentine.

Glue. Assuming that you have an ordinary water-jacketed glue pot, what will you use in it? Years ago I made a good many split-cane fly-rods, and the glue then popular was Coignet No. 1, a French product which, when combined with a small part of Russian isinglass, would join the glassy hard strips of Tonkin cane so firmly that no silk windings were necessary to hold the glued-up joints of cane against parting when wet. That glue works best when fresh and loses strength after being warmed over a few times. Italian glue works well even when quite old, though with it, or any glue, a small quantity of acetic acid should be added before setting the pot aside after use, particularly in summer time, when any animal derivative is likely to go bad from heat and moisture. This glue hardens over night and makes a perfect joint, wood to wood, though it is not so effective as other adhesives, perhaps, for joining bakelite to wood. Bakelite, or any smooth substance, should be scored before attaching to the smooth end grain of a stock.

Common white flake glue is used by many woodworkers, and some amateur makers of split-cane rods claim that cold-water glue will do the job better than some hot glues. I have not tried this, so I *dinna ken.*

Here is another old formula for waterproof glue: White flake glue, one pound; milk, one quart. Soak over night, then heat, adding milk to thin.

Every gunsmith uses paste in some form. Try white dextrin. In a pipkin put a pint of water and a thermometer. When the temperature reaches 160 degrees F, hold it there if possible while you stir the dextrin powder in, then mix with it 5 minims (about one-half thimbleful) each, extracts of wintergreen and cloves, pour into small bottles and let them stand for a week. Makes a good white paste, clean and strong.

A very old formula for making adhesive for bottle labels follows: Cold water, 400 parts; cologne glue, 25 parts; strong wine vinegar, 100 parts; wheat starch, 50 parts; venice turpentine, 20 parts. Soak the glue over night in the vinegar. Stir the wheat starch in the water, then add the mixture to the glue and boil for a few minutes until the consistency suits.

Add the turpentine. This adhesive may be used cold or warmed slightly, but if hot will soak into the label. Keeps well.

Stains. On a hurry-up finishing job, or for darkening places that may have been rubbed—as in raising a dent in a stock by steaming—it is possible to use common iodine as a stain for walnut. Dilute it until the desired color is attained. It may also be used on sight screws which you may want to use as dummies, to fill unwanted holes in a barrel. Sights may be partially rusted in their seats with it, and scope-blocks will seldom work loose if set with a drop of strong iodine. Some rear sights shoot loose on high-power rifles, notably on the Springfield, the receiver walls of which are very thin at the point where most rear sights are put on. I would prefer to enlarge the holes, re-tap them, then put in heavier screws.

Permanganate of potassium, mentioned above, is another stain for walnut. If used, start with a very small quantity of water and a few of the small purple crystals of this antiseptic, stir vigorously, then test the solution on a scrap of walnut, adding crystals until a good brown is attained. While this stain penetrates wood nicely, it fades slightly if long exposed to sunlight. French walnut sometimes develops dry-rot areas where you least expect them, always in the very place where they will prove most objectionable. It is places of this sort that may be doctored with permanganate, or with a paste made from shellac or DuPont cement and end-grain walnut filings. Plastic wood adheres well, but when dry is too light in color to match walnut.

Make up a small quantity of dust for use in filling holes in walnut. Brush a fine-cut file, so there will be no metal scraps in its teeth, then file the end of a scrap of walnut, catching the dust on a sheet of paper, then put it in a bottle. To use, spread a few drops of shellac on a sheet of glass, sprinkle the dust over it, then work it into a paste with the point of a knife. When it is about like thick honey, work it into the hole to be filled, pressing all around with the knife point. Add more after an hour, leave until next day, then rub the patch down smooth with fine sandpaper.

Anyone working with tools is likely to suffer from bruises and cuts now and then, hence it is good insurance to keep antiseptics handy. The old standby is iodine, but if you keep a bottle of it for any length of time, dilute it with grain alcohol, else it will get too strong through evaporation and will actually paralyze nerves in a mild but uncomfortable way. Permanganate of potassium is another good antiseptic. Dissolve a few of the tiny purple crystals in water and bathe a cut or bruise with the pink solution but avoid the grains, which are too strong for direct application.

In an emergency use clear shellac as a disinfectant. While planing bamboo strips on one occasion, three of my fingers were cut to the bone by one of the saw-edged strips. Lacking something better at the moment, I plunged the fingers into a bottle of shellac, then, seeing some clean sawdust, put the fingers into a handfull of that, bound all with a cloth, and next day there was only a little soreness in the seriously gouged fingers.

Keep bottles containing poisonous solutions in a place where no one but yourself may find them. While I was out of the shop one evening, my daughter tried to find a bottle of acetone with which to remove orangetinted stain from her fingernails. She used gun blueing liberally, then hunted me up to say "that stuff" had no effect. No harm was done, but different results might have been attained in case of a cut.

Chapter Seven

ROUTINE JOBS.

Removing Obstructions from Barrels. One of your first jobs may be the common one of removing obstructions from a rifle barrel. Possibly the owner tried to clean the bore with a tight patch. Ask him what is really in the barrel, so you may act intelligently. One job that I recall was removing a section of brass rod, a length of pine, a rag, then another section of brass. At best that was a case of blind reckoning, so light oil was put in the rifle and left until next day, when the barrel was warmed until uncomfortable to touch, then a steel rod almost the full size of the bore was inserted, tapped lightly with a mallet, and finally the bore was freed. It is best to start with a short piece of rod—less springy than a long one—then remove it and insert a longer piece. Drilling cannot well be done without injuring the lands.

If nothing else will function—and at best this drilling is a makeshift job—build up a tool. Take a short piece of steel tubing that will just slip into the barrel. Fit into it a length of drillrod and secure it by threading or brazing. Into its other end set a drill a trifle smaller than the drillrod, and make the drill fast by threading or brazing. Put the barrel in your padded vise and the drillrod in a hand drillstock, and work very carefully, preferably from the breech end, on the theory that the base of the bullet, if it has not been damaged, and is either flat or hollowed, will help center the drill. Work slowly with plenty of oil, taking the barrel out of the vise frequently to tap out any lead that may stick to the drill, as it surely will.

Before a drill of this sort is used, be very sure that it is perfectly straight and will not weave about, cutting more on one side than the other. For some jobs the drillrod can be shaped up to a point, then hardened, but in any event the point should be smaller than the body of the rod.

After a stuck bullet or a section of cleaning-rod has been removed from the barrel, polish the bore with a very tight cloth, oil and tripoli or rouge.

The combination of a rusted barrel and a stuck patch is not pleasant to contemplate. So far as the rust itself goes, kerosene may partially loosen it, if left in the barrel a day or two; and liquid soap may then be introduced, to make the patch slimy. Soda is another thing that may help.

If possible, work down from the muzzle of a rifle barrel, on the theory that there may be a slight taper in the bore, hence it should be easier to push the obstruction toward the breech than toward the muzzle. If or when the barrel is cleared out, polish it diligently with rouge or tripoli on a fairly tight greased rag, followed by oiling. RIG is an excellent grease to use in a case like this, for it will coat the bore thoroughly, and it will not crawl, leaving bare spots to rust again.

Dents. Shotgun barrels are often dented in a fall. Usually a dent may be raised by shaping a short piece of hardwood or steel, tapered at one end, and pushing this plug down almost to the dent; then, while some one taps the rod, you can tap the outside of the barrel lightly with a mallet or brass hammer until the plug will move further down and finally pass the dent. If the dent is very deep, a bit of experience plus suitable tools for this work are indicated. If the surface of the barrel be marred, as one generally is when one falls in a rocky place, smooth it as best you can with crocus cloth, heat the spot with a dry soldering copper and rub until cool with linseed oil, crude oil, and sperm, mixed.

Sometimes cleaning patches of old material cause real trouble, and this should teach one never to use any cleaning patches except those cut from new flannel—a snug but not tight fit. If the barrel is rough, trying to force a patch through will probably wedge it tighter. Pour thin oil in the barrel, let it stand awhile, pour oil into the other end, let it stand, then warm the barrel slightly where the obstruction lies, and try with a full-sized smooth-end rod. If this fails, fit a worm in the end of a rod and pick the patch out bit by bit. The muzzle-loaders had a worm as part of the equipment, but a brass screw set in the end of a rod will do as well if carefully handled.

Common blue (mercurial) ointment will loosen lead fouling from any barrel; in fact, it is one of the best of all cleaners for either rifles or shotguns. You can leave it in the barrel all the time, if desired, without harm. For years I have carried some of it in my rifle kits.

If a case is ruptured in firing, leaving the small end in the chamber, one of the common broken-shell extractors may be used to advantage. In a pinch use a piece of threaded brass rod with a slot cut in one end. Spread this end until it will pass through the bore but stop when it reaches the mouth of the broken case. Usually tapping with a light mallet will start the case, and it may then be pushed out at the breech.

Shortening Barrels. Guns that have been neglected may rust near the muzzle or the chamber, where air gets into them readily. You can cut off a rifle barrel without injuring its accuracy, provided you do not cut it shorter than about 18 inches, but a shotgun barrel is a horse of another color. These tubes are usually made with the right barrel cylindrical or only slightly constricted (choked) at the muzzle, the left barrel choked quite a bit, so the owner may take his choice, be the shot a short or a long one. If he insists on having shorter barrels, on the theory that such a gun will be handier in brush shooting, tell him that while this is a simple matter, if an inch or so be cut off, he will have two cylinder barrels.

If the barrels be pitted badly near the chamber, polish them as best you may with crocus cloth on a tight-fitting rod, or even emery powder and oil. Ream out the muzzles with a rose countersink or a steel ball attached to a piece of drill-rod and worked with oil and emery until no burrs can be felt, then polish the ends with crocus. Pitting will not affect the accuracy of a gun, provided it be cleaned frequently. A pitted rifle barrel cannot be cured at all. It may be lapped with a lead slug, emery and oil, so it will still shoot with fair accuracy, but jobs of this sort are best turned over to the factory, to have the rusted barrel rebored to a larger calibre, replaced, or relined.

Relining has come to be quite common, and there are several good workmen who are equipped to do this at reasonable prices. In brief, the barrel is bored out to ⅜-inch, a rifled tube of this diameter is inserted, soldered in place, then the muzzle is cut off and the breech chambered. One of these processes is called Parkerifling, the tubes coming from a firm of that name in Birmingham, England. It is hardly a job for a novice to tackle, though in time he may try it. There is, however, no reason why our young gunsmith should not consider making a specialty of relining .22-calibre barrels. The tubes and the few tools needed to reline barrels may be purchased from the agents here, and it should not be difficult to find rusted-out rifles to practice on.

Cutting off the muzzle end of a rifle barrel presents no great difficulties. Cut the barrel off with a hacksaw, using a square to guide you. Smooth the muzzle with a fine-cut file, then with emery cloth, ream very carefully with a rose countersink, then with one of the larger bullet-shaped stones in the Hand-ee set, then with finer buffing points in that tool, and finally with a flannel patch dipped in oil and tripoli. The ends of the lands must be smooth as silk, else the accuracy will be impaired instead of improved.

Slugging Barrels. While we are about it, let us look into this subject of what makes a rifle click. At the factory a bar of steel is bored out, the hole reamed smooth then polished lengthwise, and the barrel straightened—in fact, it is straightened many times before it is ready to shoot. A cutter is inserted and pushed from end to end while the tube is revolved just enough to give the cutter a spiral path of one complete turn in a predetermined number of inches. In the popular .22 long-rifle barrels the twist is one turn in 16 inches. In other calibres the twist may be as short or quick as one turn in eight inches.

The first cut is a mere scratch. The next one, with the cutter set a shade wider, is slightly deeper. Several changes are made before this first groove is deep enough. The cutter is then set over and a second groove cut, and so on until four or six grooves are completed. At every shift the barrel is straightened—a complicated scientific treatment that can only be mastered by skilled men after long experience in this one line of work.

A good barrel is one that has really been tuned up to a certain pitch. Grind a flat along one side and it will shoot wild, even though you may not have actually bent the barrel at all. Thinning the walls of the barrel at one place will cause it to spring when it is shot, just as surely as it would if given a hard blow. And this is one good reason for declining to turn a barrel down in your lathe, if you have one. It is true that our Springfield service barrels are turned down slightly, to smooth the unfinished portion just forward of the receiver, when the service sight is removed and the piece restocked as a sporter; but this dressing is usually done by striking, as this is called (draw-filing) instead of with a fixed lathe cutter, often while the barrel is held in a vise. And mere scratching of the heavy end of the barrel does not set up unusual stresses. Blueing that part, or all of the barrel, follows.

At the government arsenals all barrels are measured internally with a special instrument. Starting at the chamber, the exact calibre is taken every inch to the muzzle, and these data are set down on a card which is sent out with that rifle. Here is a copy of the record of one of these rifles, calibre .30 '06: Diameter at breech, .3081; at muzzle, .3081-inch, with no variations between those two points. That was called a star-gauged barrel.

You can slug a barrel and get measurements almost as accurate as this. Select a bullet, preferably lead, oil it and the bore, take a brass rod a foot long and nearly bore diameter, and with the rifle held in the vise, push the bullet into and along the rifling; then, with a longer rod, push it entirely through the barrel, making mental notes as you go along as to the tight or loose fit encountered at different stations. If there are loose places (pockets), less pressure will be needed to force the bullet along; and be sure the bullet fits as closely at the extreme muzzle end as it did on starting. At first a mallet will probably be needed, to get the slug moving, but if so, tap very gently, so the slug will not be crushed out of shape. Measure the bullet with micrometer calipers reading to ten-thousandths-inch. This will give you the groove diameter, and that is all you need to know, although you can turn the bullet down in a lathe to get the land diameter, then measure it again. Several barrels that I slugged at one time varied only three-ten-thousandths, which is fine enough to suit almost anyone, or so it seemed to me. Any way, all those rifles shoot about as close as any factory barrel, which is far better than you and I can hold.

Lapping Barrels. If there is only one pocket in a barrel, and that one is at the muzzle, I for one would not care especially to own that rifle; but if there is a pocket midway of the barrel, it is possible the accuracy may be improved, in this fashion: Take a piece of brass rod as long as the barrel and the receiver but smaller than a rod you would use for cleaning that barrel. File two or three notches at one end, wind a bit of cotton around the rod about four inches down, merely tight enough for a snug fit, warm the barrel slightly, then pour melted lead into the muzzle until it is filled. Push the slug out of the barrel just enough so you can trim it smooth at the end, coat the slug with oil and emery powder, then pull it down to the chamber—never further until this particular job is completed. Push the slug up the barrel as far as the pocket, then work it back and forth, adding more emery and oil as the first coating dries. Always permit the slug to follow the grooves easily.

Work at this lapping until you are positive that you have increased the diameter slightly from the chamber to the pocket to match the diameter at the pocket, then work slightly beyond the pocket, and remove the slug at the breech end. Oil the barrel, clean it thoroughly with a bristle brush, then a dry patch and an oiled one. Try another bullet for fit, and if it goes through without slipping, getting tighter toward the muzzle, throw the old slug away and forget your troubles, for the grouping should show improvement. If you are not satisfied, cast another slug and try again, but do not attempt to put the old slug back into the barrel.

This work will be of real value to you when you are asked to do something to improve the accuracy of a barrel that is not satisfactory to its owner. And while you are about it, insert a dummy cartridge in the chamber, bullet seated out of the case further than it is seated normally, close the bolt slowly, then withdraw the dummy and examine the bullet with a glass, to see how far into the lands the bullet will go without forcing it. That gives you the maximum length to which a cartridge for that rifle may be loaded, if case and bullet are to be kept intact. Of course you can seat the bullet in the lands just ahead of the chamber, if more air-space is sought, and put a thin wad in the case neck, to prevent the powder from spilling out. In that event make a bullet-seater from a case with the head bored out just enough to permit using a plunger in it. The bullet is put in the case, the case inserted in the chamber, then the bullet is pushed through into the lands, always a uniform distance. This is the old schuetzen plan of loading for extreme accuracy, but it is not so much in vogue now. The maximum length of cartridge that will function in the rifle is found by trying five cartridges in the magazine. If one is too long, it will not go down smoothly, and when the bolt is operated the top cartridge will jam in the follower—at least in some of the most modern actions. Make a length gauge from a piece of flat metal, and set the loading tool to that length, as previously mentioned.

In passing, it may be interesting to some of the rifle shooters of today to know that when the .22 long-rifle cartridge was being tested by Dr. Walter G. Hudson, Harry M. Pope, William Tewes, and others, back in the 1890's, components were purchased at the factories and the filled cases and bullets seated separately in the rifle after the method described above. Some of the tools used then are still in the hands of collectors. One of these old bullet-seaters is pictured in Fig. 12.

Etching Steel Surfaces. Some curious and rather pleasing effects may be obtained by treating polished steel surfaces with fruit juices, and this reminds me of something that was brought to my attention by a friend who had invented a sheath-knife the haft of which was cast aluminum into which a blade of most excellent steel was set just far enough to leave the top end of the device hollow. Into this was fitted a cap, in the under-side of which a tiny compass was set. The cap was threaded, and in the recess a dozen common matches could be carried. I used my knife a lot until the loss of those caps in the woods prompted me to cement the cap fast; after which my bill for caps became, as Mark Twain once said of razor-strops, a mere bagatelle. The knife was used mostly to cut oranges and apples after lunch on the trail, and in time the blade took on the most beautiful case-hardened effect. This attracted Chet's attention, and he asked how the mottling was attained. Jokingly, I told him that was a deep secret, but I would sell the formula very reasonably! Every country-bred boy, I expect, has experimented at one time or another with citric acid and soap as a medium for etching initials on knife-blades. Soap is smeared on the blade, the lettering traced with an awl, then the acid is poured on and left awhile to eat into the exposed steel.

Something like this may be done in a jiffy by etching steel surfaces with one of the tiny grinding wheels of the Hand-ee set, mentioned elsewhere. The speed of this jigger is so great that one may really write words or figures on any metal surface almost as easily as with a pen. The surface need not be touched deeply, but the result is permanent. It is a good thing with which to mark rifle-bolts or any part that might be mislaid. In a match, at cleaning time some one is likely to mistake another's bolt for his own, but this marking is proof of ownership.

Pistol-grip Caps. Making a pistol-grip cap by hand may be simplified in this way: Saw a 1½ by 2-inch piece of black bakelite. Scratch straight lines a quarter-inch from and parallel with all edges, as shown at 5, Fig. 10. Saw halfway through the piece on these lines, then saw down to these cuts on all edges; the block will then be like 6. Bore a hole in the exact center for the screw. Find a little stove-bolt $\frac{11}{64}$-inch in diameter, the size of the screw-hole, turn a nut down to the end of the threads, put on a washer, then the block, another washer and a second nut. Set both nuts up tight, cut off the head of the bolt, and you have a mandrel to hold your work in the vise or your polishing-head. File to shape, using at first a washer or some circular article to guide you in rounding the ends. Work the ends egg-shape rather than round, measuring from center frequently to insure symmetry and coincidence of curves in crown and block. The crown (7, w) may be reduced to ⅞ by 1⅜-inches. The crown should be high enough to insure a neat shape, while the base of cap need not be more than $\frac{3}{32}$-inch thick. A ¼-inch rattail file is used to cut these curves. Smooth with emery cloth, polish with crocus, then with water and pumice or rottenstone. Rub now and then with thin oil. Bakelite makes a nice cap. It will not chip easily, provided no strain is put on the edges—for sheet bakelite has grain running lengthwise, somewhat like pressboard. If buffed it will take a high gloss, and its color is so much like that of blued steel that it is in harmony with it. In mounting a cap, cut deeply with a rose reamer, and use a flat-head screw with the edges rounded, blued.

If preferred, make the crown of the cap diamond-shape, but in that case the diamond may be the full length of the cap. Easy to make, this shape is quite neat with curved edges.

If something fancy is asked for, grip-caps and fore-end tips may be made from ivory or even from the plastic stuff now available in tubes, rods, sheets, and in all imaginable colors. It is very dense, can be worked with any tool, and some of the wild colors can be expected to attract attention, if not admiration. I have seen very nice stocks that were made from Southern juniper, the heart wood, of course, and Oregon myrtle is also used occasionally. Both varieties of wood are very contrasty, so perhaps pink or vivid green ornaments might be worked in for stocks of this sort!

While jazzy fittings do not appeal to most riflemen, copper may be used in combination with bakelite for bases of grip-caps and swivel-stud bases (8, Fig. 10). Aluminum or copper bases should be about $\frac{1}{16}$-inch thick, cemented to the bakelite while being shaped, then buffed to a high gloss. A bakelite diamond can be set on a sheet of very thin copper or aluminum, cemented, then the edges turned up so there will be no wrinkles, then both smoothed up to leave all edges square. The diamonds may be made from ¼-inch bakelite, cut down to lie flush with the wood, or about ⅛-inch thick when finished.

A bakelite sight-blank can be made in a few minutes like O in Fig. 12; or an old barrel-sight may be cut off, as indicated at T-T, and shaped up so both ends will be alike.

All sorts of grip caps may be made up to customers' orders, if you are handy in making up and executing designs in bakelite, copper, silver, and steel. With the Hand-ee tool you can etch or engrave a design in a piece of dense wood, and have casts made from it in any desired metal; or cut these designs in a block shaped to fit the grip. One of my friends, an amateur but very expert metal-worker, has a rifle that is trimmed with African ivory. The grip-cap is rounded, the fore-end tip is of conventional design, there is a diamond-shaped inlay on each side of the receiver, and the comb is tipped with a piece of ivory cut in an intricate series of angles. All joining is perfect. The contrast is not pleasing—that is to my eye. Two varieties of wood might be better—we have already heard of laminated-wood stocks. I have made fore-end tips from juniper, but if woods as contrasty as this be used, there should be a grip-cap of the same material. I like better the idea of setting copper pieces under caps and inlays, and some day I mean to line a buttplate with thin copper. It would go nicely with a Belding & Mull trap buttplate, I think.

Cleaning Rods. Make it a rule never to insert a cleaning rod in a rifle barrel until the rod has been wiped clean. Why attempt to "clean" a barrel with a rod coated with grit? One is often told that a steel rod is the only sort suited to barrel cleaning, but it should be hard steel. Nearly all the better supply houses carry drillrod in three-foot lengths, which is just right for almost any rifle barrel. If no lathe is handy, it is not difficult to fashion a good rod with a file. Other forms may suit your fancy better than the one shown at 4, Fig. 10, but that one is practical. The simplest way is to so file one end that a knob will be left, its length ¼-inch, diameter the full size of the rod, which for the .22-calibre may be .190″, and for the .30-calibre .219″. The throat is carried back an inch, leaving it strong but only half the rod diameter. The design shown in M2 is for a swivel at this end of the rod. With a swivel handle this is not really necessary, though the method may be followed in making a brass instead of a steel knob. I find a brass knob securely fastened less likely than a steel knob to injure the lands. For the swivel knob a thin collar is left at M. A bit of tubing is then fitted over M2, not quite a tight fit. The end of the rod is spread or upset just enough to prevent the sleeve from pulling off. This may be done with a nail set and a light hammer while the rod is held securely in the vise.

The handle end of the rod need not be reduced in size. It may be cemented into a suitable wooden handle, but if that end of the rod is to be made to swivel, as it should be by preference, a two-inch length of brass tubing (P) can be fitted over that end and anchored with a pin (Q); but the length of this pin must be less than the diameter of the tubing, or it will jam. A hole is bored in the handle (Q2) into which the tube is to be pushed, a coating of thick shellac helping it along while fresh but cementing it firmly when dry. A drop of oil now and then will keep the swivel working. Before using, rub the rod with something like rough duck, then with several pieces of clean cloth, to be sure no filing chips are left on the rod. Polish with tripoli on a cloth. These commercial drillrods are almost smooth enough as they come, but polishing will make them still better. Being very hard, the rod will not pick up dents and scratches, and if a patch of new cloth is used in cleaning, there are very few chances that any barrel will be damaged by the cleaning rod.

Hard brass rods are good, provided they are rubbed down frequently; but the material is soft and easily scratched, and grit may get into these places. To be strong, a brass rod should be only a trifle smaller than the bore of the rifle.

Shotguns are usually carried in leg o' mutton cases. Sometimes there is a jointed cleaning rod in a pocket. A better item is a tubular rod, made in this way: Procure a piece of tubing the length of your barrels and ⅜-inch outside diameter. Cut a thread in each end. For a handle insert a piece of brass rod, threaded to fit the tube, in a tool handle. For the other end provide another short rod, threaded to fit the tube and with a cylindrical wooden knob the right size to carry a generous cleaning patch. In traveling the tube will go in the case alongside the barrels, the ends in the spare pocket. Various shapes of cleaning ends may be made to interchange, among them a brass scratch-brush.

When a new rifle comes from the factory, it will function perfectly, but that does not mean that you cannot improve it by hand work. One likes to tinker with these men's toys, anyway. Polish the bolt for hours, if you wish, using valve-grinding compound and thin oil. Never use sharp abrasives or cut down any corners, else you may change the headspace. Stone all flat surfaces lightly with a fine-cut slipstone and oil, smooth all bearing surfaces of sears, triggers, hammers, but do not actually cut any of these parts down enough to cause misfits and trouble.

Chapter Eight

SIGHTS AND SCOPE BLOCKS.

Making Front Sights. It is good fun to make sights. For a front sight use a block of steel ⅜-inch thick, shape it like a slot-blank, then cut through the center with a hack-saw (A, Fig. 12) half the depth of the block, widen the slot with a knife file and set a flat piece of steel (B) in the slot, for a blade. For target shooting .070″ to .090″ will serve for width. Cut the top square, polish all surfaces, then drill a small hole through block and blade and put in a pin or braze the blade in place, using borax and soft silver solder to sweat the blade in (C).

For a hunting sight lay a small piece of round electricians' wire atop the blade (D) and braze it on, heat in a flame until dull red, then wipe until cool with mixed linseed, crude and sperm oils.

Hooded sights may be cut from an old rifle barrel and sawed and filed to shape. The length may be ¾-inch. Bore a half-inch hole lengthwise, cut a slot across the tube from the top and fit in this a disc aperture or post sight. Ream the tube a bit with a taper reamer, then fit a short piece of tubing, also tapered, so it will be friction tight, to hold the disc in place. Cut two slots in the outer end of the inner tube and you can remove it with a coin spanner.

A handier plan is to make the tube, cut the disc-slot in it, then attach on the top a self-spring catch like the old Sharps spirit-level-wind-gauge front sight (E). One end of this spring is to be riveted to the hood, so it may be turned aside to release the disc. The other—rear—end has a tiny round lug. When the spring is closed this lug snaps into a shallow dent made with a prick-punch in the hood.

Every enthusiast tries crosswires some time or other. Make a disc for the wires from a thin washer and solder the wires on it. Try various thicknesses until you find the right one. This sight will show quite distinctly against almost any background.

In ordering sights for hunting rifles—except Krags, Springfields, the original Winchester Model 54 rifle, and some foreign rifles—specify what arm the sight is to be put on. Formerly each manufacturer cut his barrel slots a little narrower or wider than other firms; there is more uniformity now, but in any event be sure. In mounting a sight, set the barrel in your padded vise and drive the old sight out of its slot from left to right. For this use a piece of hardwood or copper, as steel or brass may mar the blueing or turn up an edge of the sight-base. Tap very lightly in backing the sight out, then try the new sight, the base of which is tapered, so it must go into the slot small end first. Drive the new sight part way in, then back it out and examine it closely, to be sure it will not bind too much when driven entirely home in the slot. If too tight, file the base of the sight but never touch the dovetail slot in the barrel, as this would widen it and make the seating of the new sight or one of another type a botch job. Line up the sight with the bore, as mentioned elsewhere.

Rear sights, placed on the tang, must be leveled perfectly, else the group center will vary every time the rifle is canted the least bit or the sight is elevated. Level the rifle in the vise and set the sight to coincide. If it cants toward the right, set a shim of cardboard or aluminum under that side and level again before setting the screws down; if to the left, shim the left side of the base. The tangs of most hunting rifles are bored and tapped for folding rear sights, and the holes filled with dummy screws. Some Savage rifles, the Model 03 and 63 Winchesters, etc., may be fitted with folding rear sights secured with short wood screws.

So many ramp front sights are made by various firms that it does not pay the gunsmith to make them. Usually there is a short tube carrying the ramp and the sight, and by reaming this tube slightly or by tapping it with a hammer—to stretch the tube—it may be fitted and sweated in place very neatly without marring the barrel. Line up a sight of this sort by bore-sighting.

For Springfield and Krag rifles, procure a front-sight assembly from the Director of Civilian Marksmanship, in Washington, and fit it to the barrel in a similar way to that just described. The sight-blade fits in a longitudinal slot and is secured with a pin, so that sights of different shapes or widths may be put in at will. To determine the correct height for a new sight, put a piece of brass or steel in the slot, bore sight the rifle, then file the top of the piece of metal until the sights are aligned, or better still, fire a few shots at target. In ordering a new sight, send this bit of metal to the factory, for correct height and width for a new sight. This Springfield removable sight-base may be replaced with a factory target sight, made regularly to interchange in this way, and secured in the fixed base with a screw set in at the muzzle end.

Ramp sights are more popular than they formerly were, and they are neatly matted, so in aligning the sights on target or game, one's eye naturally finds the high front sight, as it is in a way led up to the sight itself without physical effort. The matting offsets glare, and some ramps are quite low, as, for example, the hunting ramp sights made by Dean King.

These ramp sights made by Dean King of San Francisco are splendid ones for the hunting rifle. This ramp can be any desired height—high for the Springfield and Enfield, low for rifles like the Model 70—and it is matted, to kill reflections.

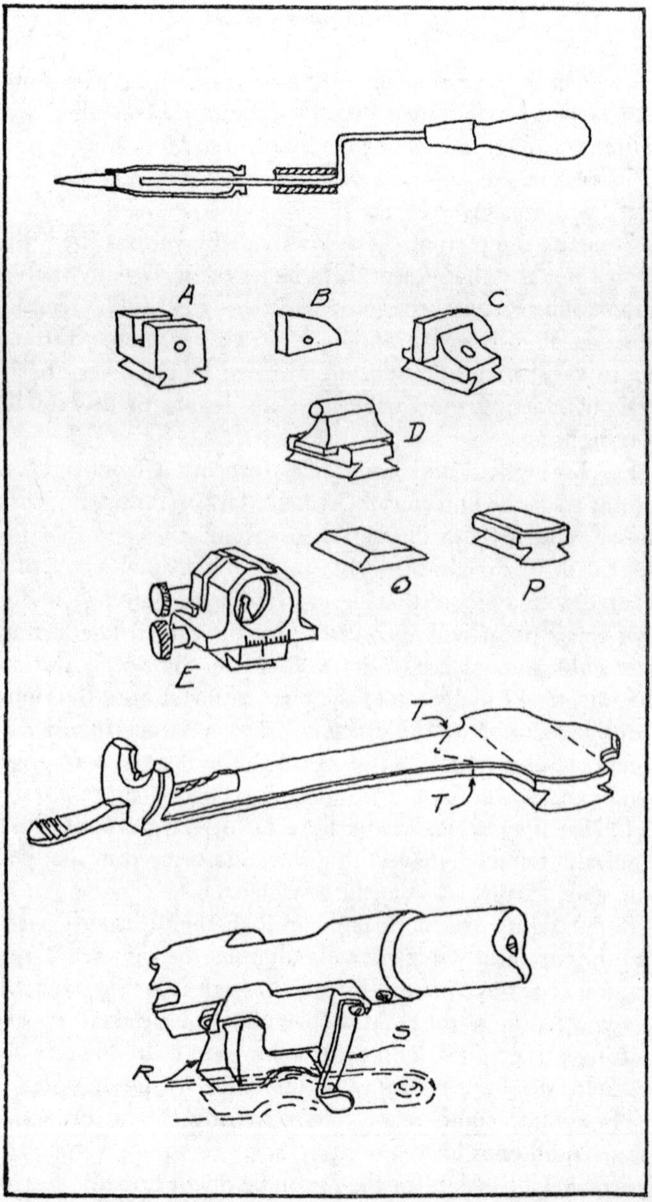

Figure 12. Top, tool for seating bullets ahead of a case in the chamber of a rifle. A. Sight-block. B. Blade. C. Blade riveted to block. D. Copper-bead hunting sight. E. Old Sharps sight. O and P. Barrel-slot blanks. N. Buckhorn sight converted to a slot-blank. Lower figure, self-spring magazine catch for Model 52 rifle.

Any sort of bead will be supplied—ivory, gold, red. A tiny mirror set below the level of the ramp-top, and protected from hard knocks, reflects light toward the bead, rendering it distinct whether you are aiming toward or away from the light. And there are groves alongside the ramp, for a slip-on shade.

Some very handy ramp sights are supplied with low-cost rifles. These need no tube, but are mounted in the same way as a plain hunting sight. The base is beveled, to be driven into the usual barrel slot, and the ramp effect is given the jigger by a separate stamped piece which fits over the body of the sight. When centered the ramp is a close fit on the barrel, and the whole thing is neat and efficient, though the cost is low. Dean King makes some of his rifle sights for mounting in this way, and his hunting sight with dull red head and reflector shows up nicely against dark or light backgrounds. Dean King, by the way, is one of the old-time long range riflemen of the '90's, when Sharps, Ballard and Remington Creedmoor rifles were shot at target. We both shot on the Golden range of the Denver Rifle Club, in company with Carlos Gove, George C. Schoyen, Axel Peterson, Capts. George and Joseph Lower and their father, Pioneer John P. Lower; Henry Simmons, Guy Chamberlain, Harry Willis, John Dean (who, when he did not make a good score, always said he was "unrestless.")

Cable Tubular Front Sights. When everybody was shooting .30 '06 Springfield rifles and service ammunition, after the World War, I shot a great deal at 200 yards with Captain Robert Cable, one of the best metallic-sight marksmen I ever knew. He worked out a front sight that we both experimented with for a long time. It is a good sight, and may easily be made by any one. Cut off the top of a common post front sight and fit a half-inch length of quarter-inch tubing to it by cutting a groove in one side of the tubing so it will fit the post. Braze it on. Ream the tubing and fit in it another tube, tapered to a slide fit. Bore the little tube from each end, to leave a very thin diaphragm with a hole of proper size for aiming—say .090″ or larger, up to 1/10″. Make a set of tubes with apertures of different sizes, and change tubes to suit light conditions. We used a large aperture for indoor and one as small as .070″ for 200 yards.

Marine Corps Front Sights. Eugene Patridge of the Walnut Hill (Mass.) group of shooters in the 1890's proved that the former favorite—the Paine thin bead front sight—was not the best one for accurate target work with revolvers and pistols. Today the wide Patridge sight is standard, used, as it is, with a very wide square notch in the rear sight. The so-called Marine Corps front sight for rifles is merely an offshoot of the Patridge principle, adapted to rifles for target work. Cable and I experimented a lot with this sight, too, but instead of making the post 1/10″ wide, we used sights of .100″, .090″, and as narrow as .070″ for indoor work. Take a post .100″ wide. At 200 yards it looks ridiculous at first to one accustomed to the .050″ service sight, for it covers about two feet (apparently) of the target. Notice, however, that the top of this post looks clean and sharp, so there is no doubt about its exact location in holding below the bullseye; and with it one can hold off for wind very accurately. It helps any shooter who, because of astigmatism, finds it difficult to see the front sight distinctly.

Mounting a Front Sight. If for any reason you are asked to cut off the muzzle end of a barrel, determine before you do this the location for the new slot you will have to provide for the front sight. On the receivers of bolt-action rifles and on the top or side of single-shot and repeating rifles you will find a place to level the rifle in your padded vise. This is where a small level like 5, Fig. 6, will function. Determine the location of the slot, saw several cuts close together, to help reduce metal, then cut down gradually with a three-square file to the full depth, widening the dovetail carefully and keeping it plumb with the level until the sight will go part way into the slot. Most sights are to be driven in from the right, and they should fit flush with the bottom of the cut and be tight enough so they cannot be moved.

Some of the hooded sights that have a hollow plug screwed in to hold the discs are mounted upside down, according to most riflemen; that is, one must place the rifle on a bench and work from the rear, whereas the normal method is to lean the rifle against a bench and work above the muzzle. But the base of the sight is usually wide enough so you can reverse it by filing the beveled edges slightly, then drive it in with the screw-plug up.

If the long barrel of the Krag be cut down to about 22 inches, a Springfield front sight assembly can easily be fitted to it.

The Springfield rear sight fixed base may be removed by driving out a pin from the under side of the front end, then driving the sight-tube off. This leaves an unfinished area at the breech, which may be treated as already described. Usually a Redfield or Lyman receiver sight is put on the rifle when it is converted to sporter type by restocking.

If a complete set of sights is being mounted on a rifle, it is well to mount the rear sight and fix the indicator on zero before any attempt is made to line up the front sight with it. Then drive the front sight into its slot (with the rifle in a padded vise), align the bore on some object, then drive the front sight home so that the set will line up perfectly with the bore. Very often this means driving the front sight quite an appreciable distance to the left of the apparent center line of the barrel. This does not matter except in looks; then, when the rifle is fired, make further corrections, if necessary, by moving the front sight bodily until it coincides with the rear sight, set at zero. This sounds worse than it is in fact, for the front sight will not be out of plumb. Then, if the rear sight has a scale for windage, loosen the screws in the little plate carrying the scale and set the plate over until the rifle will shoot on center without changes of sights. Then, if the rear sight be shifted for windage at any time, it can be put back on zero at the end of the day, and will be approximately correct for the next shooting day.

Adjusting Sights to Individual Eyes. The gunsmith must, in a way, be an optician. The average rifle shooter takes a lot for granted—he does not stop to think that sights are made to suit the crowd. Demonstrate for him the fallacy of this notion. Select a strip of black iron like the stuff put in filmpacks—thin iron enameled dead black. Bore a series of holes in a row in this sheet, starting with one .035-inch in diameter, then .040, and so on to about .120-inch. Remove the disc from the customer's rear sight, and with the rifle steady on a bench, hold the strip behind the rear sight while he sights through the largest hole in your sheet of metal. If he says the front sight does not show sharp and clear when aimed at a mark on a sheet of white paper say 25 yards distant, try a smaller hole, and so on clear across the strip and back, until a certain hole gives clear definition. Ream out the hole in his sight disc to correspond; or, if the hole is too large, put in a bushing and bore it to the correct size. Always ream the hole with a rose countersink on the side facing forward, leaving a clean sharp edge nearest the eye.

This is no cure-all, however. An aperture of a given size will work nicely in a certain light but not so well at other times. The best ironsight disc is the Parker-Hale (and others that are similar), with six apertures cut in a tiny disc set into one side of the sight disc. This is revolved until an aperture to suit the prevailing light comes into coincidence with the fixed aperture. When the light changes, the disc is turned until the most comfortable hole appears.

The Merit Gunsight Co., Berkeley, Calif., makes a rear-sight disc containing an adjustable shutter patterned after the iris diaphragm put in camera lens-barrels. The opening may be set instantly to suit the light. The Wittek Mfg. Co., 4308 West Twenty-fourth Place, Chicago, Ill., makes both rear and front sights with adjustable apertures; and extension rear sights.

One of the most radical changes in sighting equipment has

appeared recently in the shape of sight combinations intended to be raised quite a distance above the line of the bore, so that a rifle built purposely for telescope-sight shooting will fit just as well when iron sights are used instead. The sight makers are supplying sights or adapters made for this purpose, and the change is one that has come to stay—that is, for target rifles only.

Some of the rear sights of this class are set in dovetail or other bases and bound with a set-screw, to enable the owner to set or remove them readily. The device most used at present for securing the removable front sight is the homely base-block for telescope sights; but it is efficient, since a sight may be taken off and replaced at will without disturbing adjustment. This system is found on the comparatively new Winchester Model 52, and the Remington heavy target rifle. No doubt sights made to take care of this feature are obtainable from the sight makers now, so that any gunsmith may put them on a customer's rifle quite easily. This system is not intended for hunting sights, though it can be so used by providing a bead sight to fit the muzzle-block. For purely target shooting it does away with the old objection to stocks that are made purposely for one shooting position but which are not quite the right shape for other positions.

A Vaver device may be used for the front sight instead of the scope-block mentioned above. It is a barrel band with a dovetail slot at the top. Merely set it on the barrel, line it up, and turn the set-screw down.

One of King's hunting sights which is useful to have around is the one which has three beads, any one of which may be turned up to suit the background or the prevailing light.

Barrel-slot Blanks. If a customer wants an open sight removed from a barrel and the slot filled, there are three simple ways to do this: Cut off the old sight as indicated at T-T, Fig. 12; use a factory steel blank (P); or shape up a piece of bakelite (O), tap it into the slot, and look wise. This makes a neat blank, as its color matches steel nicely.

Scope-Blocks That are Too High. On some rifles mounting scope-blocks higher than normal will leave the sight line obscured. This would be especially true of rifles like the Winchester Model 70—with its rear mount on the receiver-ring and the high front mount in the barrel-lug slot—were it not for the fact that scope-blocks intended for such rifles are made with a deep channel along the top. Shorter screws must be used with this type mount. Flat-top mounts may be grooved with a rattail file if you have no round-edge carborundum stone to use for this purpose in the chuck of your polishing head. One of the small stones in the Hand-ee set is ideal for this purpose. If the blocks are casehardened, heat them dull red, let cool, cut the channels, heat again, then quench in oil, to reharden them.

Mounting Scope-Blocks. Fitting scope-blocks to a rifle is a bit tricky. If it is a bolt-action and the blocks are to be mounted on the barrel, take off the stock, set the receiver in your padded vise and level perfectly with the aid of the square under side, by looking through the bore and the sights and aligning the high front sight with your eye and the level. Put the blocks in their mounts and try them on the barrel to determine how far the scope may be shifted forward and backward for different shooting positions. Usually the eyepiece is about flush with the rear end of the bolt for most positions. If the rear mount is put on the receiver-ring—as on the Models 54 and 70 Winchester rifles—it will be so high that the front mount will resemble a skyscraper, so set the rear mount on the barrel just ahead of the receiver-ring and the front mount either 6 or 7.2-inches ahead of it, measuring from center to center of blocks. Run a white thread through the rear-sight aperture, with the other end touching the top center of the front sight. Stretch the thread tight. Set the rear block on the barrel directly under the thread and cement it temporarily with tacky shellac, as otherwise it may slip. Set the level atop the block and sight along the thread and the bore, first from the breech

Fig. 14. K, extra wide, curved cheekpiece. L, Model 416 Stevens in partly finished blank. M, reshaped 416 factory stock. O, the same rifle with stock finished and checked, with barrel-band, swivel plate and trigger stop. N, Model 54 California walnut stock. P, exaggerated comb on French walnut stock. Q, Springfield-Niedner heavy-barrel target rifle. R, speedlock mortise in Model 52 stock. S, Model 54 with California walnut stock, fore-end snobble and trap buttplate.

then from the muzzle until you are sure the rear block is centered and level, then with a scriber mark around the screw hole in the block. Test the front mount in the same way, then remove the barrel from the vise and set it on the bench, provided its surface be level. Test this carefully, then stand a square on each side of the barrel and with a short rule measure from one to the other to prove the hole in the base is exactly halfway between the two and the base is level. Clamp the rear block at one end, select a drill the full size of the screw hole in the block, then with a small hand-drill bore just deep enough to make a distinct mark on the barrel. With the drill to be used for this hole bore a hole in a scrap of metal, tap the hole and try one of the screws, just to be sure you are going right. Now start the screw hole, using the square and your eye to keep the drill plumb. If you start boring with the drill leaning in one direction, then correct it and drill from another angle, you will have a tapered hole.

Set the depth gauge, put a screw in a block and compare both. The gauge must be set for a depth just a shade greater than the distance the screw protrudes through the block. Use plenty of oil on the drill. When the depth is right, oil the taper tap and try it in the hole. It should go in about a sixteenth before it starts cutting. *Turn the tap slowly.* If it springs the least bit, back it up two turns and start over, keeping in mind the fact that a splintered tap is a very nasty thing to remove from a screw hole. These taps are so hard that they will snap like glass if pushed too hard, so keep turning and backing until the tap binds, then remove it and insert the plug tap, but before you do this, square the bottom of the hole with a drill ground to a very blunt point, to ream out the tapered bottom in the hole.

Turn the plug tap very gingerly, and when bottom is reached, remove the tap, oil a screw and turn it down through the block. Drill the second hole for that block, tap, and set the screw. Make all the tests over again, then mount the front block. If you are lucky enough, the first time you try this thing, to get one or both blocks true, you will be doing well; if not, and the blocks are slightly cockeyed, the play in the mounts may be sufficient to correct this. Better luck next time!

With black shellac mark a sheet of glass with a plus (+) mark. Set the glass in a window as far from your vise as possible, center this mark in the bore of the rifle, line up the crosswires of the scope to coincide, and that rifle should shoot very close to center the first three or four shots fired.

Mounting scopes on the Models 54 and 70 Winchester rifles is child's play, provided you are satisfied to set the front mount in the dovetail slot cut for a barrel sight. The distance will be less than six inches—not that that matters so very much on a hunting rifle, however. The receiver-ring is bored and tapped for the rear block, and these holes are filled at the factory with dummy screws. At best the front mount will be quite high, but I for one dislike to cut into the thin barrel to set mounts further forward, where they should be. For these rifles grooved blocks must be used, else one cannot see through the metallic sights.

Some of the light-weight bolt-action rifles may be fitted with scope-blocks very easily by mounting the rear block just six inches rearward of the open barrel sight and utilizing the rear-sight slot and part of the sight for a base for the front mount. Of course a special block to fit in this dovetail may be purchased—such a block is often used on the Models 54 and 70 Winchester rifles—but the old sight may be used instead, by cutting off the rear end, annealing it, then boring and tapping holes in it for the front-sight mount for the scope. Care must be used in threading, as this sight is so hard that a tap may easily be broken in it.

The popular low-priced Weaver rifle scopes are attached to the left side of hunting rifles. There are only two 10/32 holes to tap, after boring, and the generous-sized screws have coin-slots, for tightening. These glasses should be tried first by bore-sighting before the holes are bored in barrel or receiver. The adjustments are all made, afterward, by means of two thumbscrews on the outside of the tube, but in fitting one of them the bracket or the clamps around the tube, or both, may be shimmed until bore-sight and crosswires coincide.

Scope Mounts for Hunting Rifles. There are dozens of styles of mounts for hunting rifles. The Germans display a lot of ingenuity in the making of mounts that may be put on or removed quickly. Some of them are clumsy, heavy affairs which, with the equally heavy short scopes that come with them, would call for a pack-mule to carry them; but those makers probably never saw a real mountain, and cannot realize why our hunters go to the lengths they do in "going light"; so they use plenty of metal and stick on gadgets that are seldom used—such as solid blocks, clamps and turn-screws much better adapted to field guns than light hunting rifles. Some of the big scopes of low power have goose-neck hangers that permit the alternative use of either metallic or scope sights. With two- and three-power scopes these gadgets are a plain nuisance, as one will admit after trying first the iron, then the scope sights, only to rely on the latter for all shots. The field of these large scopes is so wide that one can, with them, pick up an object almost as readily as with the iron sights.

The left-hand side of the receiver is usually employed as anchorage for the excess metal, and in some types the mounts are rather neat, but altogether too many of them merely burden the hunter with useless weight, making a hunting rifle as heavy as one of the old plains rifles. However, there are indications of better designs coming on the market now, and these are produced by our own workmen.

One Use for Offset Adapters. For target shooting the telescope sight is always mounted directly above and in line with the bore. For a hunting rifle many of the low-power moderate-price glasses are mounted slightly toward the left side, in which position, if the mount is rather high, one may use the factory or the scope sight, at his option. Some men, because of some defect in the right eye, seek to have the rifle sights shifted so the left eye may be used for aiming, while the rifle is held against the right shoulder. This you can do by putting offset adapters on the scope, to throw the scope slightly to the left, and by thinning the comb of the stock on that side. The other alternative, which means disfiguring the stock, is to cut a portion of the comb down; and, if the rifle is being restocked, to set the buttplate as far as possible to the right—cast-off, it is called. Theoretically, setting the scope to one side spells inaccuracy, mainly through canting the rifle to left or right. Actually one who holds a rifle in the same position right along, will not be badly handicapped if he uses offset mounts. The better plan is to learn to shoot from the left shoulder, but this some men never do; and a bolt-action rifle is awkward to manipulate from that side.

The Difficult Springfield Receiver. Fitting a rear sight to a war-time Springfield is "something else again." The walls of this receiver are very thin, both sides are hardened by a special process, and boring a hole through them is a thing to be taken seriously. It is possible to locate the position of the sight screw-holes by means of a center-punch, but no drill will take hold until the metal has been treated. Some workmen use a blowtorch, but with it the heat affects quite an area, leaving the place discolored. Better spot anneal the metal where the holes must be bored. This may be done on the outside with a hot soldering copper, but getting next to the wall inside the receiver is not practicable. Anneal the spot to be bored into, bore the hole with great caution, and use the tap as though it were the only one in existence. Be especially cautious when the tap approaches the inner wall, as that is where so many taps are snapped, on the hard skin. If the tap will not go clean through, use a discarded piece from a small rattail file, ground to a blunt four-square point.

Worry this through the hole as best you may, then try the tap again. No hurry-up job, this one.

Cutting holes in most of our rifle barrels is easy, and the average receiver is by no means drill-proof.

Another way to get under the skin of file-proof steel is to prick-punch the location for screw-holes, coat the area with carnauba wax, which melts at much higher temperature than beeswax, remove the wax from the hole with an awl, then fill the hole with nitric acid. This will eat into the steel where the wax does not cover it, but will not affect the wax.

Extension Sights. When bolt-action rifles first came in, the rear sight was moved from the tang, where it should be, to the receiver bridge—even further forward on military rifles. But the bridge sight is too far away from the eye for target rifles, and nothing much can be done about it, for if you set your sight too close to the eye, the safety or the bolt may strike it. Some men like to have a sight mounted on the bolt head, and this is fine for hunting rifles, but target shooters "crawl" up on their sights, and often suffer minor injuries from the recoil. With .22-calibre rifles we are going back to the tang-sight distance just now, with the sight proper mounted on an extension bar by means of which the sight may be set from two to three inches nearer the eye, this increasing sight radius by that much, and certainly giving a much clearer view through metallic sights. A simple device to attain this end may be seen at E, Fig. 13, showing one of the handy little Stevens Model 56C rifles fitted with a Lyman Model 55 adjustable sight mounted on a short bar by means of two sight screws set in the receiver, while at C a Lyman Model 56 micrometer sight is mounted on the factory base of the old Model 52 rifle by means of an extension bar of somewhat different form.

This old Model 52 rifle has a sight of the carbine type, and no one loves it. Any gunsmith may readily improve it, and have a practical extension sight at little expense. To

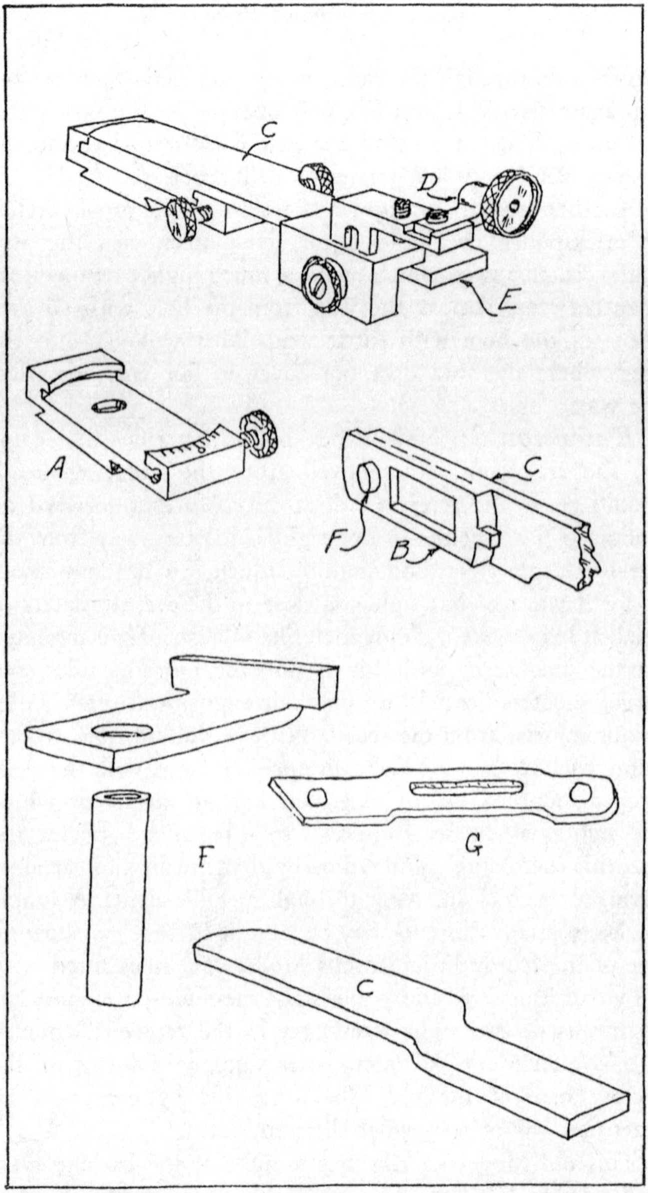

Figure 15. Extension sight adapted to factory base of Model 52 Winchester rifle. A. Original base. B. Leaf base with bar. C. Attached. D. Model 55 hunting sight fitted to bar C. F. Abutment plate set in barrel and receiver mortise of the Model 52 stock. G. Trigger plate for Model 416 Stevens rifle.

do this take out the windage screws and the click springs. Throw the springs away. Shorten the screws. Turn the sight out of its base (A, Fig. 15), cut off the leaf-hinge ears and file the top of the part B flush. Procure a piece of good steel ⅛-inch thick, 4 inches long and an inch wide. Saw and file it to shape (C) then braze or rivet it to the old part B. The sight proper may be any one of several hunting or target sights. The one at D was made for a round barrel, but the under part was filed to fit flush against the new bar (C), then riveted in place on the bar, with the rear end of bar extending slightly behind the sight to protect it. Fig. 14 shows a more elaborate arrangement. This sight was placed as close as possible to the bolt shoulder, and must be turned part way out of base when the bolt is removed. Other patterns of hunting sights, mounted in this way, do not interfere with the bolt at all, and may be left on the rifle when a scope sight is employed, though on some rifles the sight-cup must be removed. The old windage screws are used merely to hold the sight securely in its base (though one or both may be used in adjusting the sight when it is first put on).

The old leaf-sight base (A) need not be moved at all. To attach the new parts, merely turn them at right angles to the barrel, insert the lug (F) in its hole in the base, push the sight into its seat, then insert one screw, and the jigger is complete.

Since the preceding paragraphs were written the improved Model 52 rifle has been put on the market. An illustration of the standard model is given in Fig. 27, together with a sectional view of the trigger and sear mechanism. In this it will be noted that an improved trigger-adjusting screw is placed so it may be operated with a small screwdriver by removing the bolt, as in the older model; and there is also an adjusting screw in the upper part of the trigger, but which can only be reached by removing the stock.

Improving sight discs. Several firms make target front sights and supply with one of these several inserts to interchange. These discs are stamped from sheet metal or cut to shape then filed. There is usually one pinhead, several posts and aperture discs. In the old days of offhand shooting much slimmer pinhead inserts were used—so small, in fact, that the tiny ball on the top of the stem was held in rather than under the bullseye in aiming. This required keen vision, but it was done. Clamp one of these coarse pinheads in a pin vise, and with a small needle file trim it down to decent shape. Improvement in grouping shots will follow inevitably.

Trim a couple of the apertures down, too, in the same way, leaving a mere wire edge. Leave the aperture as it is, unless reaming will give you better definition; and if reamed, do this with a rose reamer on one side only—always facing away from the eye.

Along about 1890 Capt. Joe Lower and I started experimenting with crystal discs for the Sharps Creedmoor rifles. We had a jeweler cut these from optical glass, with an aperture in the center to suit the individual eye and the size of the bullseye. Several years ago I made up similar discs from tinted pyralin and gave them to shooting friends. Some men used them as made; others preferred purple, yellow or blue tints. Still others inserted a fairly wide post behind the transparent disc. This is a good idea if one's vision is not so good, as the post acts as a corrector if the bullseye is not exactly centered in the hole.

Apparently certain manufacturers liked the notion. At any rate they stole the thing bodily, and even boasted that their "engineers" had developed the device.

Chapter Nine

HUNTING TELESCOPES AND MOUNTS

Bridge-type Mounts. The young gunsmith is often asked to furnish or at least mount telescope sights on target and hunting rifles, hence it will be to his advantage to learn everything he may about these useful attachments to all sorts of rifles. Formerly a scope sight cost as much if not more than the rifle it was intended for, but since a number of firms have been marketing low-priced scopes, anyone with four dollars is likely to show up with an outfit for you to line up. You'd be surprised how good these cheap rigs are, too, for shooting at nearby objects. Even schoolboys are buying them, though they do not really need scope sights except for target practice.

It will be worth your while to read Col. Whelen's book on "Telescopic Rifle Sights"; it is certainly not my intention to go into this subject here, for he has covered the subject very thoroughly and interestingly. However, while our manufacturers have long been quite "lame" on real good mountings for rifle scopes, I am glad to say there is improvement in these things now, and one of the neatest of these new mounts is the set made by the Redfield Company, in Denver. These are not target mounts—those things belong on the barrel, immediately over the bore, to be regulated very accurately with micrometer adjustments handy to the shooter's fingers as he aims; but they are good solid attachments for hunting rifles, where a set of mounts must be sturdy enough to withstand hard knocks one encounters in woods and hill hunting, for carrying in saddle-boots, in boats and on pack trips, where one has enough things to worry about without being afraid his rifle and scope will be put out of commission far from repair shops.

These Redfield mounts are affixed on the receivers of bolt-action rifles. The front mount is put on the receiver-ring and is quite low and strong. Its companion member is locked on the tube of the scope, can be moved for adjustment when first put on, but after that it is fixed, as a hunting scope should be. The scope is locked by setting it at right angles to the barrel, then turning it back, where it stays put. The rear mount is set on the receiver bridge, with two set-screws to provide lateral adjustment, then lock it, too. Normally a low-power short-tube scope does not extend very far behind the bolthead of the rifle, for the relief in these glasses is two inches or more, so the eyepiece does not endanger one's glasses or eyes, as a target scope, with its short relief, might do.

The mounts are very simple to attach. They are affixed with sturdy screws, and lining up a scope, in the usual way and by bore sighting, is not difficult.

One sees all sorts of gadgets intended to so place a hunting scope sight out of the metallic-sight line that in aiming the hunter may use the scope or the iron sights, according to light conditions. In two weeks after having my rifle rigged up in this fashion, I was completely cured of any notion like this. I was going on a canoe trip into the squirrel woods of one of the rivers in the Ozark Mountains, and as I knew the light would be dim in the deep woods there, I had the Malcolm Company make a 3X short scope which I fitted on a light hunting rifle. That rifle had metallic sights which I expected to use most of the time in the dark woods, and the offset mounts of the scope placed the glass so that I could look through the glass, then, if the object was not distinct, I could try the iron sights. I *did* try the scope; in fact, I used it for 95% of the shots I made on that and subsequent trips, and finally folded the iron sights down and did not use them at all.

I would not advise anyone to leave iron sights off a hunting rifle, instead, it should be equipped with mounts that can be set up quickly. Carry the rifle and the scope separately in traveling, especially if one is riding a horse; then, if a shot be taken hurriedly, use the iron sights, but if there is time, mount the scope.

In the open one can always get better definition with a low-power scope than with iron sights, and even in deep woods or at twilight, if an object cannot be defined with the glass, be sure you will not be able to locate it at all with metallic sights.

Renewing Broken Crosshairs. If a customer complains that the crosshairs in his rifle scope are too coarse, make a new set for him, in this way: Cut a two-inch hole in a bit of thick paper board (G, Fig. 16), paste a piece of white paper under it, then rule lines across card and paper—one vertical, one horizontal. Place the reticule (G) on the paper, exactly centered. Put a drop of DuPont cement on each line on the card, and stretch pieces of silk thread across the card, holding the ends down with a finger until the cement sets. The silk must be very tight. Now put tiny bits of cement on the reticule at four places, shift the reticule until the silk pieces center it, then lay over all, inside the card, a large washer (J), to press the silk down on the reticule. Leave until next day, then clip ends of silk.

To obtain strands of silk sufficiently fine, unbraid a small piece of bait-casting line or OOO machine twist, wet the pieces and separate two or more—there will be nine or more in each strand—then use the perfect ones. Before selecting pieces to use, compare a strand with the old hairs in the scope, for it is difficult to find silk thin enough for this purpose. The color does not matter at all, since white will look black when mounted in the tube.

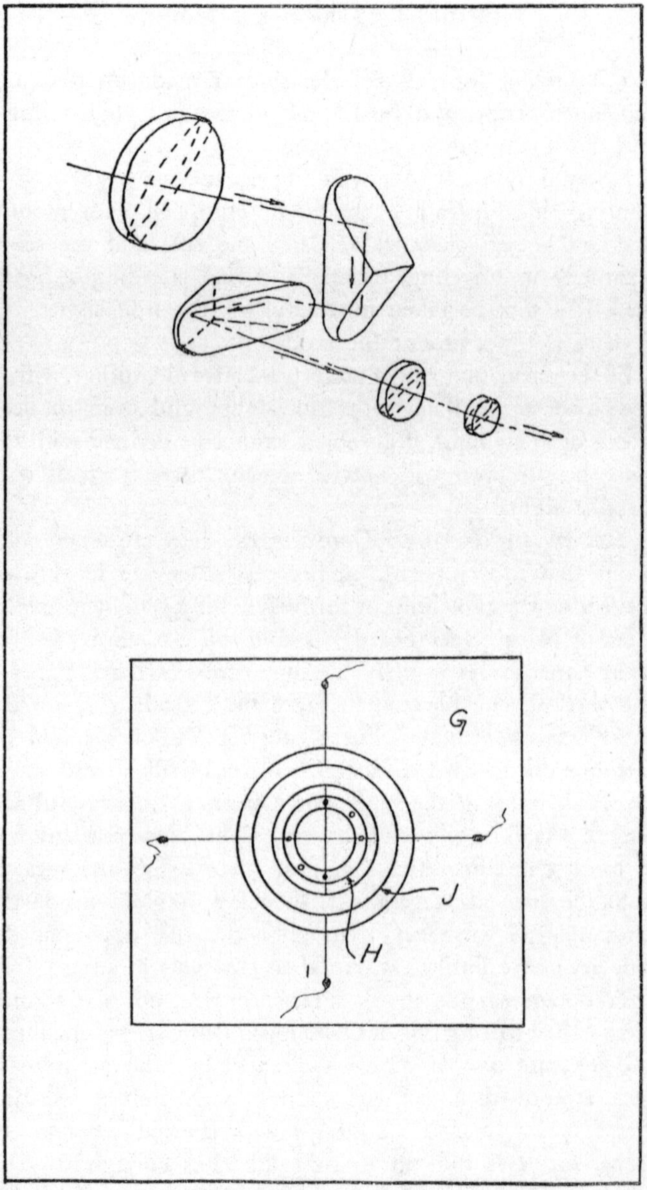

Figure 16. Upper sketch (courtesy Carl Zeiss, Inc., New York City), path of rays of light through a prism spotting scope. Lower figure, method of replacing broken crosshairs in a telescope sight reticule.

When a reticule is removed from the telescope tube, be sure to mark it carefully, so it may be put back right-side up. A tiny scratch on both the reticule and the tube holding it will serve. And read the manufacturer's directions before removing the reticule, as with some reticules, it makes quite a difference which side faces rearward when replaced. With post reticules, one may replace the reticule upside down, and have the work to do over again.

Spotting Telescopes. There is not much the young gunsmith will be asked to do with spotting scopes, unless it be to clean the lenses; but he should have a general knowledge of the workings of these popular glasses. The old-time long-tube scopes are not so popular now as are the shorter ones. Prominent among these are the Bausch & Lomb draw-tube scopes of 20 diameters, and the Wollensack and Mossberg scopes. These have no prisms, but are made on the old Gallilean principle. Carl Zeiss and Bausch & Lomb make prism scopes, the popular ones being around 20 diameters, with tubes not more than a foot in length. And as not everyone understands the principle of these compact glasses, I have asked Carl Zeiss to explain the matter for our readers, and this is given here in a simple drawing showing how the rays of light enter the object lens and are reflected by means of prisms to the ocular lens and the rifleman's eye (Fig. 16).

Chapter Ten

BLUEING BARRELS AND PARTS.

Before you go deep enough into the subject of blueing to become completely fogged mentally, read R. H. Angier's book, "Firearm Blueing and Browning," then select one of the many formulas he mentions and stick to that one, at least long enough to gain experience in the routine of blueing. Mr. Angier is a chemist, and his conclusions, based on his tests of all the best-known formulas, are very valuable to every person who wishes to blue or brown rifle barrels and parts.

Equipment Needed. Very little in the way of equipment is needed. Procure a sheet of plain iron at least three feet long. With square and pencil lay off lines providing for a depth of five inches and width an inch less, but allow about 1½ inches for rolling both edges of the top, for stiffening. You can roll the edges with a piece of rod or tube and a hammer, turning both outward. Bend the sheet over a 2x4 plank, leaving the corners rounded rather than square. Cut pieces for the ends and solder them in—solder outside—and reinforce the ends with wire soldered around them. That is about all.

For a solution you want a simple one at first. Try Hervey Lovell's (the Indianapolis gunsmith) formula, a simple but excellent one. Try it out, any way, before switching to something else. The druggist will make up the solution for you for less than a dollar or at least he should. Here it is:

Bichloride of mercury—1 ounce
Potassium chlorate—1 ounce
Potassium nitrate—1 ounce
Spirits nitre—1½ ounces
Distilled water—1 pint

Simple, isn't it? Start with an old barrel nobody wants. File, scrape, emery, crocus it until not a scratch may be seen. Rub thoroughly with steel wool, wash with alcohol or gasoline, give it a bath of hot soda water—anything to remove all grease and finger marks. After that *do not touch it with the hands,* but fit soft wood plugs in the ends of the barrel, to be used as handles, and use two bent wires as lifters. Put enough rainwater in the tank to more than cover the parts to be treated, then heat the water until it *boils* merrily, using gas by preference. At the same time heat a small portion of the acid solution in a jam-pot suspended by a wire in one end of the tank. For a swab use a piece of stick with cotton bound around it.

Lower the barrel into the tank and leave it for five minutes at least, when it should be piping *hot.* Swab the solution on, going from end to end several times. This will dry in a jiffy, so scrub vigorously with clean steel wool as rust begins to appear, then return the barrel to the tank for another five minutes, take it out, swab with the solution, and so on. Repeat this as often as you like, but five or six treatments should give a rich dark blue.

While the barrel is cooling slightly from its final bath, examine it closely and rub off any rust that remains, then apply boiled linseed oil on a piece of flannel and continue wiping the oil on until the metal cools. If you do not get a good rich dark blue, without spots or blemishes, start all over another time and persevere until the results please you. Remember, it is experience you are trying for, not a rush job. Leave the old barrel as it is for a day, then rub lightly with petroleum on a cloth to remove excess linseed.

The Lovell blueing solution has plenty of latitude. For example, if, in swabbing the hot metal with acid, rust runs in streaks, instead of rubbing with steel wool, rub with a wet cloth until the metal is so cool that no more rust is set up, then return to the boiling water. If the part turns dark in spots but the color will not take in other parts, put a little hot water in the shallow cover of a tin can, add a few drops of nitric acid, and swab the streaked part with this. It will turn the metal white all over. Wash acid off and heat again. Patience is required, since some steel will take the color readily while other grades will darken very slowly.

If your first trial is unsatisfactory under the linseed oil finish, wash completely with gasoline, then with nitric acid, and start all over.

In blueing a Springfield or any similar rifle, strip all parts from the receiver, wipe excess oil from the inside and have the plug for the chamber a close fit. Otherwise the receiver need not be protected, as little rust will lodge in it, and that little may be wiped out afterward.

Some receivers come into the shop to be used in making up complete rifles that have been used so long that they show no color at all. Those originally casehardened have this appearance. You can gauge their hardness with a file, and if convinced of casehardening—which will not take blueing readily—heat the entire piece until almost dull red, plunge in hot water, then blue. Shotgun barrels of the old-time twist variety call for special treatment. For this read Mr. Angier's remarks on this subject.

Small parts you can blue in a pipkin of boiling water, in which the solution pot may also be set while in use. Handle each part with a separate wire.

Store a supply of rainwater in clean cider demijohns, corked, or use melted snow. Rainwater kept in open vessels is likely to be filled with wrigglers in warm weather.

Blueing Small Parts. Another formula that is less poisonous, but works nicely for small parts, is sugar of lead

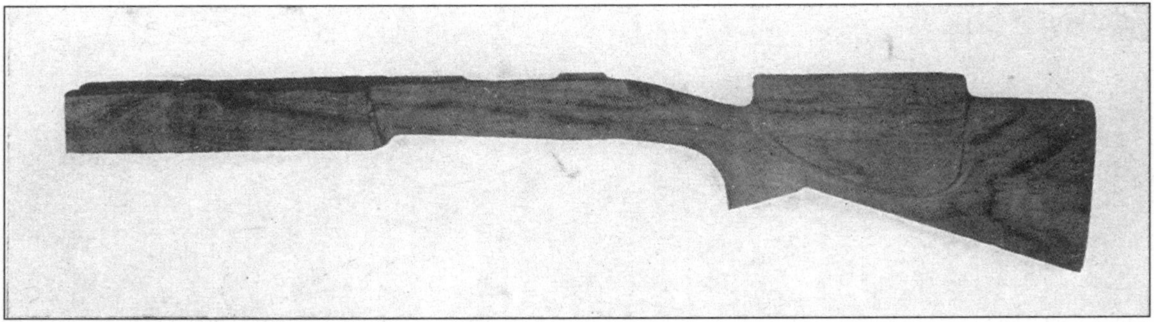

A machine-inletted stock blank such as can be furnished by the National Target and Supply Company, suitable for the making of a custom stock with full, well curved pistol grip, Monte Carlo comb and beaver-tail forearm. A splendidly figured piece of wood for such a low-priced blank. It is a simple job to finish out this blank into a first-grade sporting rifle stock.

and hyposulphite of soda, both obtainable at any drugstore. In a quarter-pint of rainwater dissolve 227 grains of hypo, then in another container dissolve 69 grains of lead acetate, both piping hot but not boiling, then mix. Dip the parts and move them about in the solution heated to about 150 degrees F. This is the Buchner formula.

Another simple formula is made up of a 10 per cent solution of nitric acid in hot water. Dip the parts for several minutes, then put them for three successive periods, five minutes each, in fresh boiling water, to remove all traces of acid. Place on wire gauze over a flame until quite hot, then quench in oil.

Small parts like screws and pins, and even sights, may be heated until dull red in a flame, then, as the color darkens, rub with the linseed-sperm oil crude oil dope, previously mentioned. Cut down the proportion of linseed if a nice blue is wanted, otherwise a reddish-blue will result. Although it is more or less waterproof, the color is not desirable.

With this simple heat blueing watch the metal closely for color. At first this will be deep purplish-blue, then this fades to a gray-blue, to red, at which time it should be taken out and held until the color darkens, then wiped steadily with the oil-soaked cloth. This is very satisfactory for screws and pins, not for large parts. Lacking a screw to match a metal part nicely, take a common wood screw, set it in the chuck and with a file round the head evenly, smooth off the sharp edge, then blue by heat. This makes a nice job when nothing better is at hand. It works well with grip-caps and such things.

Blueing is not all pure joy. Much depends on the sort of steel being worked on, atmospheric influences, kind of water, etc. Read Mr. Angier's comments of various solutions. Very often a barrel and its receiver will react differently, one taking color nicely, the other coming out anything but satisfactory. Some old receivers are so rusted or scratched, through long use, that the amateur cannot tell, until he has tried repeatedly, how the metal was last treated. A carbon steel barrel will not be difficult to blue, but a stainless barrel may not take the color worth a hoot. Water varies. If distilled water could be made available, some common troubles might be avoided, but the best most of us can do is to use rainwater or melted snow, and trust to luck. In theory, at least, that should be pure, unless the water or snow is contaminated on its way to the containers we use in collecting it. It must be remembered that blueing is a chemical process and much depends on the exact composition of the water one uses. A formula that will work nicely in my shop may not be at all good in the State of Washington.

Blueing is so simple, and so satisfactory when well done, that every young smith should practice it thoroughly. Once understood, you can blue a barrel or receiver while a customer waits, if need be; and the cost will be very reasonable. Usually a customer is greatly surprised when he sees his old gun completely refinished, in a few hours. This reminds me of a young man who brought in a wreck of a double gun that had originally cost close to $100.00. The bores were in good condition but the surface was rusted, the stock battered. After a long time the barrels were polished bright, then blued, the wood scraped, sanded and waxed—as it was a rush job—and when the owner saw it he was tickled pink. You could not buy that gun today.

Chapter Eleven

SOLDERING AND BRAZING METAL PARTS.

Old-time gunsmiths did a lot of welding of parts, but this is something the youngster should duck, at least for a time, as there are firms better equipped than he can possibly be that will do jobs in a hurry much better than persons who do this sort of thing only occasionally.

While some repairs should by all means be welded rather than brazed or soldered, it must be admitted that soldering today is not the make-shift thing it was years ago; for aluminum solders are available now that enable one to make a repair of great strength. Not only will this solder join aluminum to aluminum—a thing that was not done until recently—but it will join other metals too. This is obtainable from most supply houses in neat kits containing wire scrapers, bars of solder, and a bottle of the paste that is applied to the parts to be joined. An ordinary soldering copper is used with it. Its chief advantage over brazing is the fact that the parts need not be heated much, hence it may be applied to blued surfaces without marring them, though it may also be used for sweating parts to a joint, as in brazing.

Brazing is best done in the flame of a bunsen burner, as then one has better control than in a coal or charcoal fire, and scaling of the surfaces may be avoided. The materials needed are soft or hard silver solder and a bit of borax. The parts are first scraped bright, then the borax is mixed with water to a thin paste, this is applied to the parts to be joined and left for a short time, then heated slowly until the borax turns liquid, when the heat is raised to bright red. At this stage the solder should melt and start to flow. Its action can be helped by working it with a sharp-pointed piece of metal until it enters the joint. When cool the heavy scale laid down by the borax must be scraped clean and the metal polished, after which it is heated dull red and wiped with an oily rag until the color is satisfactory, without any danger of starting the solder. As the heat that is applied to the solder must be intense, a blowpipe directed on these parts will help matters a great deal.

Pure silver may be used in this work, though the common soft silver solder, obtainable in thin sheets, is handier. Cut off tiny slivers of this, lay them against the work, apply the moist borax, then heat as described above.

If you do take up welding—and it will be very useful to know about it,—first read those chapters devoted to it in Clyde Baker's book, "Modern Gunsmithing." And in the library you may find a copy of the out-of-print book by Charles H. Haswell, "Mechanics' and Engineers' Pocketbook of Tables, Rules and Formulas Pertaining to Mechanics, Mathematics and Physics." Packed into its thousand pages is about everything one can think of that may come up in any sort of shop.

To blacken brass, he says, use 8 ounces shellac, 2 ounces sandarac, 2 ounces annatto, ¼ ounce dragonsblood in one gallon of alcohol. And to stain wood mahogany color, use brazil, madder and logwood, dissolved in water and applied while hot. To preserve leather (as for sling-straps), use beef tallow one part and castor oil two parts, apply while warm.

The melting-points of various metals the gunsmith will be interested in are given in International Critical Tables, as follows: Lead, 621.5 degrees Fahrenheit; tin, 449.2; zinc, 787; aluminum, 1220; silver, 1760.9; copper, 1981.4; gold, 1945.4; antimony, 1166.9.

I would not advise any beginner to take up case-hardening work involving the use of cyanide of potassium—it is too poisonous. Anyway, he would not have at hand a forge in which to heat parts to be treated. Before attempting work of this sort, the young gunsmith should take a few lessons from a veteran, then, if he does work with cyanide, he should keep in mind constantly the danger in merely inhaling a whiff of the stuff. There are several acids that fume when a bottle is opened, and with them this should never be done indoors. For example, the dark-room in which I do photographic developing is about 5x8x8 feet in dimensions. When a four-ounce bottle of hydrochloric acid is opened in it, the fumes are strong enough to fill the room and make breathing difficult—and dangerous as well. Cyanide is stronger still. These acids should be handled outdoors, and one must keep on the windward side of the work.

In making up muriatic acid solutions for brazing and soldering, put a half-pint of water in an open pan and pour a couple of ounces of hydrochloric acid and a half teaspoonful of sal ammoniac into it, then bottle. Never attempt to pour water into a bottle of this—or any other fuming acid. Serious burns may be the result. Cut up small strips of zinc and drop them into the solution, one at a time. The solution will "boil," so do this outdoors. Add zinc until there are no more bubbles, then cork. Apply the acid to the work with a sliver of pine.

According to Baker, small articles may be case-hardened with kerosene. Polish, then coat with soap, heat cherry red and plunge into kerosene.

The same authority mentions cold blueing with nitric acid. The metal part is coated with the acid, wiped clean, rubbed with linseed oil, then burnished with a wire wheel.

In remodeling rifles some men insist on changing the form or pitch of the bolt handle. A bolt handle may be bent down without danger of annealing the bolt itself, but thinning a bolt handle is a foolish thing to attempt. It may seem clumsy and thicker than needed, but you will change your mind on this point if you ever extract a stuck cartridge by hammering the bolt handle with a club, as is often done. The handle may be bent by winding wet cloths around the bolt while the elbow only is heated bright red in the narrow flame of a bunsen burner, then held in the end of a vise while the bend is made with a pair of heavy pliers. Some handles may be left soft, but it is best to re-heat the handle then quench. Before this is done the inner surface of the knob can be checked with a needle knife file, to render it easier to manipulate with cold fingers.

In Chapter III brief reference was made to blow pipes. Perhaps a word or two more will be worth while here. In some cases one must heat a small area on a metal surface without affecting other parts. Reference is had specifically to annealing a small place on a part that has been casehardened. This may be done with a blow-torch or a bunsen burner, but if a flame is directed to the spot to be annealed, in time the color not only of that place but of the surrounding metal will be annealed and stained. Use a blow pipe, a tapered brass tube with a business end having a hole no larger than the point of a needle. The large end is held between the lips while one blows steadily through it, the jet of air streaming out vigorously a distance of a couple of inches. The bunsen burner flame is held close to but not touching the metal to be annealed, the fine point of the blow pipe is held in one side of the flame, and the jet of air forces that flame or rather a tiny portion of it on to the spot one wishes to anneal. This gives intense heat at one point only. You can with this pipe heat a spot no larger than a pea, and this simple device is very effective in heating silver solder, in brazing two pieces of metal which otherwise would have to be heated white hot and possibly ruined by scale. A brazed job may be blued by heat afterward without affecting the places joined, then quenched to harden it. And a blow pipe costs only a few cents.

Chapter Twelve

RIFLE-STOCK JEWELRY.

Barrel-bands and Swivels. It is the custom of some workmen to connect barrel-bands and swivels so they will constitute one fixture, as in 1, 2, 3, 4, and 6, Fig. 17. It is, in my opinion, better in some instances to separate these units; that is, to set in a swivel and its stem and nut without regard to the band. If the swivel is seated about three inches back of the forearm tip, as in A and B, Fig. 21, then a barrel-band may be placed an inch further forward or back of the swivel, as preferred, and the strain on the sling-strap will be absorbed by the stock, with less pull on the barrel. In that case the band would be attached to a plain machine-screw set in an escutcheon instead of the stud usually employed with snap swivels. The band would then act merely as a support for the stock in an accidental fall when hunting, and it could be quite loose over the barrel, if desired.

In Fig. 17 the numeral 1 shows a snap-swivel attached to a common barrel-band the lug of which must be filed square to permit the arms of the swivel to turn. No. 2 shows a band made from ¼-inch flat steel, with the lower ends bent over enough to hold a separate nut. This is brazed, about the strongest method of all those shown. Even solder will hold the nut. The lower part of the band is bent to permit it to be passed over a front-sight lug. This is a much simpler method than filing a band from solid stock, as is sometimes done. No. 3 shows a band with two pins through its base.

This and No. 4 are fitted to the barrel, then the pin is burred while on the barrel—an easier method than one would think. No. 6 has an open-top band cut from solid stock, hardened. It can be passed by a sight-lug and is a strong device for a hunting rifle. Nos. 5 and 7 make a good pair of plain swivels for a strap that is left on the rifle continuously, but a handier arrangement is to use a snap-swivel on one end of a carrying strap and a swivel snap-hook like No. 10 on the other end. For that an eye like 8 is used.

Swivel-studs like 2, 3, 4, and 6, must be made, as they are not supplied with quick-detachable swivels in this handy shape. Hexagon-head machine screws make good material. File the heads round and turn the stems down to 7/32-inch and thread with a 12/24 die. Bore the head for the 9/64-inch pin in the snap-swivel. Otherwise half-inch round stock may be turned to fit, leaving the stem ⅞-inch long, so it may be cut down.

Swivel bows are easily made by bending a length of wire around a flattened tube (12), then sawing through all of them, as indicated by the broken line.

No. 11 shows a piece of steel or brass around which a piece of wire may be bent and fitted to the swivel head in the vise. The wire may be bent to shape, then file the ends round, so they will turn easily in the head. They must fit close enough to impinge on the groove in the head, so the hook will not slip out of its seat.

Target shooters sit up nights planning gadgets they can put on their rifles to increase accuracy and promote their own comfort. One of these has to do with adjusting the distance between the left hand and the forearm swivel. How the gunsmith may do this for customers is shown at D, Fig. 13. From a ¾x4x⅛-inch piece of steel make a plate. Round the ends so the device will be more or less ornamental. Bed in the wood and attach with two short wood screws, one at each end. Bore two or three holes in the plate and thread them to take the stem of the stud of a snap-swivel. Shift the

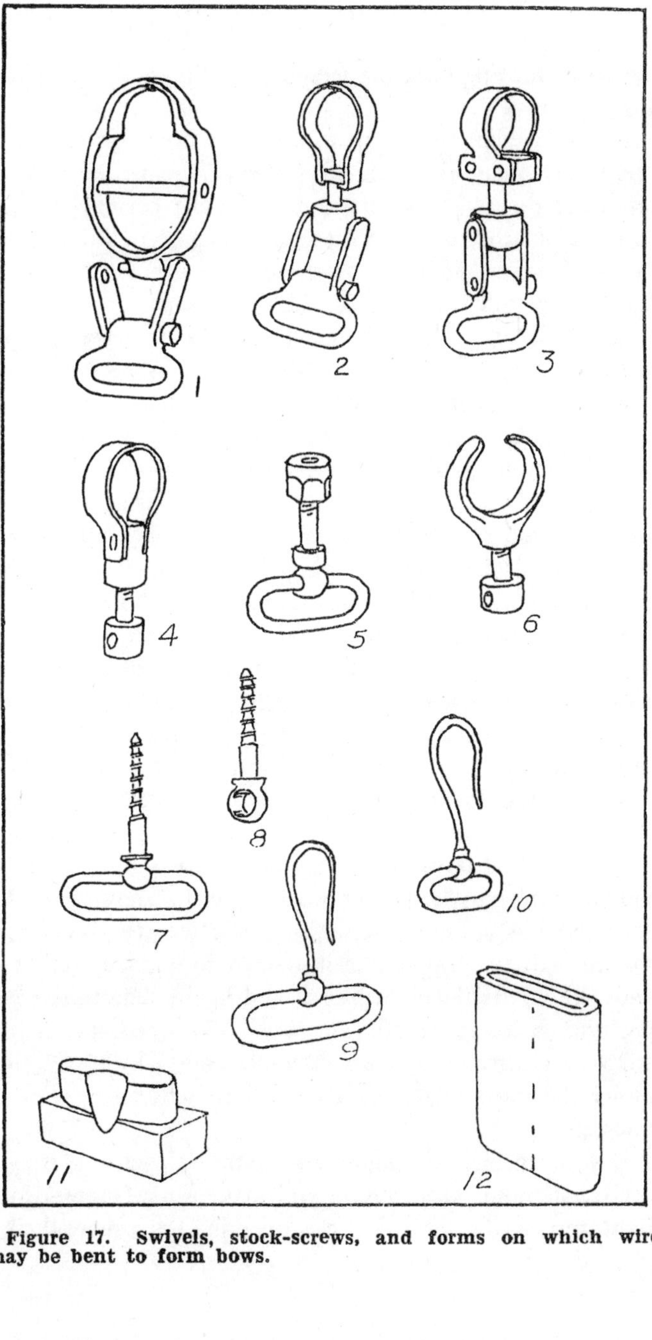

Figure 17. Swivels, stock-screws, and forms on which wire may be bent to form bows.

swivel by turning back the screw, seat it in another hole and turn it down.

There is more to this plate than has been mentioned so far. Carry out with it the idea already mentioned, that of attaching the swivel at one point and the barrel-band and its lug at another point. With a rigid long plate like this one there should be no strain worth mentioning on the barrel-band when pull is exerted on the sling-strap.

Buttplates. The old model 1897 Winchester shotgun buttplate is used so much by gunsmiths and others who make new stocks, that it is almost standard for that purpose. It is long, has good width, and its checking is harsh enough for it to hold well against one's shoulder. A variant is shown in Fig. 18. This plate was cut out and a trap fitted to it. The second sketch clearly shows the method. A lug was brazed on to provide holes for the hinged cover pin, and a piano-wire spring was bent around the plate screw-hole and made fast with a short screw threaded into the plate. A trap plate is handy for carrying small articles such as cleaning materials, oil, a screwdriver, and even a few cartridges. These reserve cartridges often prove handy when one is hunting and game is seen when ammunition may not be at hand.

The adjustable buttplate shown at 4, Fig. 18, is the design of Joseph and John Minarick. It is made from cast aluminum for heavy-barrel target rifles. It is at its best with a palm-rest similar to the one shown in the same sketch. The stem of this palm-rest has a 12/24 thread, and is often used in a hole cut through the trigger-guard ⅝-inch forward of the bow, with the standard-weight barrel, and in the magazine opening with a heavy barrel. The small machine-screw in the adjustable buttplate has a rectangular nut which will slide under the fixed plate, but cannot turn when the screw is lowered.

If you can pick up one of the old-time skeleton buttplates put on shotguns years ago, it will make a nice fitment for a light gun or rifle. This device is thin; in fact, a mere shell to

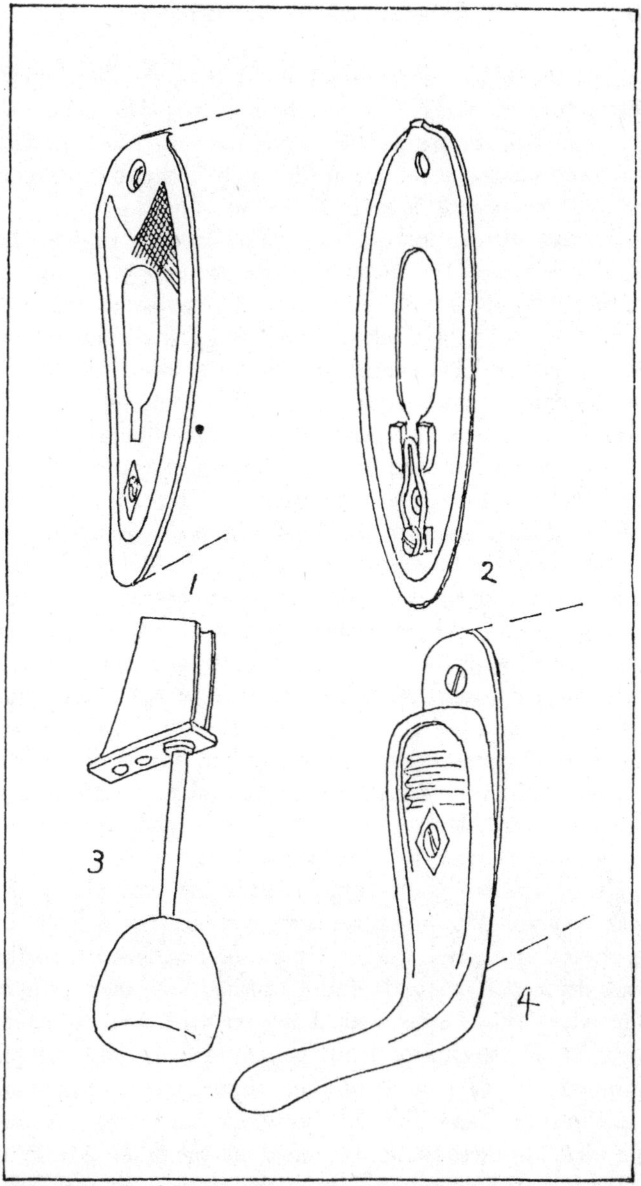

Figure 18. 1. Model 1897 Winchester shotgun buttplate, with hinged trap fitted. 2. Trap-cover and spring. 3. Cedar-ball palm-rest with screw-stem and dummy to fit magazine-well of Model 52 rifle. 4. An adjustable aluminum target buttplate, Minarick pattern.

protect the edges of the wood at the butt, for the center of the plate is cut away. Fit it on the butt so a sixteenth-inch of the wood will protrude, then work steel and wood down to a smooth finish, oil the wood thoroughly, blue the plate, and rub the whole butt now and then with oil.

A great many shotguns are stocked with a rubber plate, to absorb recoil, but some of these plates are so soft that getting the gun to the shoulder quickly is difficult, when one is wearing a lot of thick clothing. Suggest a thinner plate, with a base of hard rubber and only a half-inch of soft rubber. Very little is needed to soften recoil. Some riflemen claim that checked steel buttplates slip on the shoulder, and all sorts of things are tried to make the things rougher. Better use a rubber plate instead, as rubber seldom slips if not too soft. And there are plenty of men who really dread shooting high-power rifles because of the punishment they receive from recoil—some never get over this thing. Humor them with suggestions for rubber plates. You will find them doing better work with their pet rifles. Usually this is a mattter of how the rifle is held. Most men never feel recoil on the shoulder—cheek and jaw absorbing most of it—and some of them shoot by preference, in warm weather, in running shirts. Anyone can learn to give with the shoulder, so the recoil is softened. Even elephant guns are fired offhand by men who know how to meet the recoil correctly.

Steel Pistol-grip Caps. There are several ways to make a pistol-grip cap of thin steel without special tools. One of these is to gouge out of a piece of hardwood a shallow oval depression about half the finished size of a grip-cap. The edges must be clean cut. Lay over the hole a rather thin piece of soft steel, and with the round head of a ball-pien hammer tap the plate gently all-round until it is gradually sunk into the depression. Do not strike hard enough to dent the metal, as these marks will show on the other side. When there is a nice raised oval, trim the plate to fit the end of grip, bore for a screw, polish and buff cap, then blue it.

A cap of this type may be engraved before it is blued. Try your hand with the Hand-ee electric tool; it is easier to cut out a design than you would at first think. Monograms, initials, dates, or a simple scroll may be cut into the metal with one of the tiny grinding wheels. Or an engraver will do the work at small cost.

Templets. Get into the habit of making templets or patterns of things you will use right along. Start with a stock that fits you; use it as a standard for comparisons when you are planning other stocks. When I made my first full-length stock I used several rifle stocks for patterns, and after deciding which shape suited me best, I worked my blank down to the pattern, then, as the blank was thicker than necessary, ripped a thin piece from the left side, smoothed it up, bored a hole in one end, and hung it up for future guidance. I still have it, and as I view it today, I am rather pleased with it, for it shows that I started with a bit more than a vague idea of what I was about to undertake.

I also made stiff paper patterns of all the stocks made during several years; putting on each one the name of the person it was made for, who supplied the blank and what sort of wood it was; all measurements, etc. Referring to those patterns has been a help right along. You can make these patterns quite accurately if you will use a thin pencil to trace the outlines. Use a piece of brass tubing $\frac{3}{16}$-inch thick, fit into it the lead from a carpenter's pencil, and trace very carefully, holding the pencil vertical all the time. Cut out carefully and preserve these templets between sheets of packing board.

Three barrel-channel templets will be useful. One is shown in Fig. 19. Cut templets from sheet brass or aluminum. To make one, coat the edges of a stock mortise with lampblack, lay a piece of stiff paper over the mortise, then press down with the fingers all along the cut, trim along the edges of the marks with scissors, lay the paper on a sheet of metal, then cut it out, try in the mortise until the fit is perfect, and

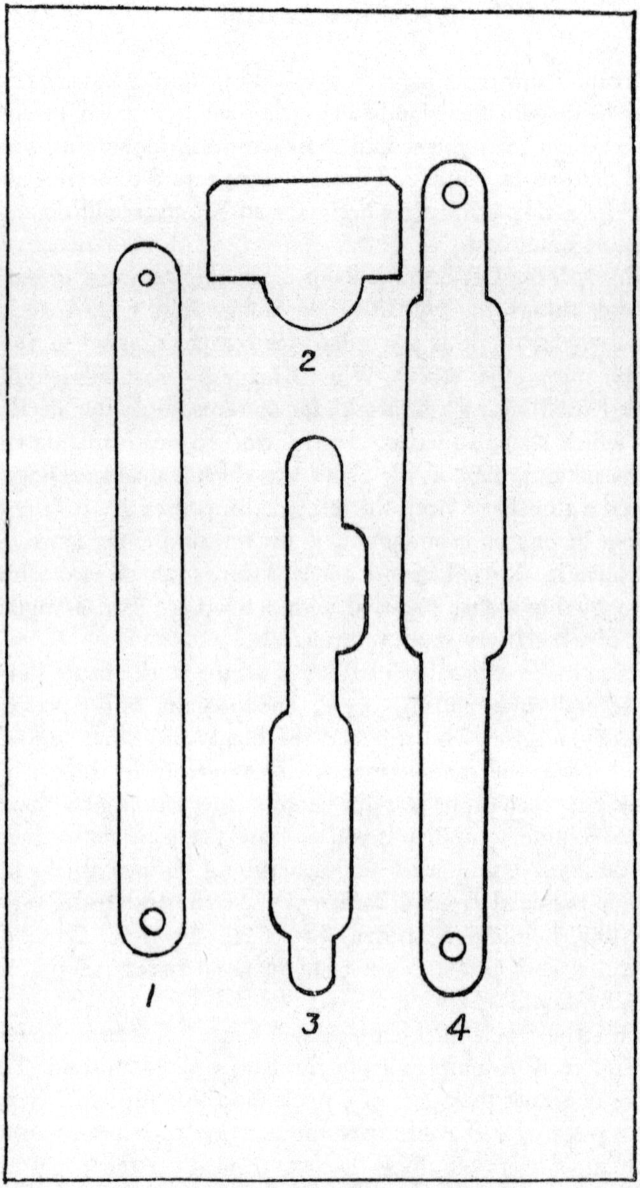

Figure 19. Templets for stock mortises.

use this templet right along in inletting. Memory is fickle; patterns do not change.

After the center lines have been drawn on a blank, and the starting point for mortising determined on—say the receiver-ring screw hole, a templet comes in handy. The one sketched in 4, Fig. 19, is for the floor-plate mortise of a Springfield blank. No. 1 gives the shape of the 1935 Model 52 trigger-guard. No. 3 is the exact shape of the cut in the Model 52 receiver mortise, when allowances are being made for the offset for the magazine, and the increased width toward the after end, to accept the built-in parts of the speed-lock mechanism. No. 2 is a barrel-channel gauge. Two of these will be needed—one for depth at the muzzle end, the other for depth just forward of the receiver-ring.

Two grip-cap templets will come in handy—one the full size, the other for outlining the "lozenge" or crown. Use hard brass. First scratch a mark straight across the piece the long way, one across the brass at a right angle, bore a hole for the screw in the center, then shape the device so it will be two inches long and 1⅝-inches wide. With a hacksaw cut out a piece of quarter-inch bakelite and sand or file it to shape (using a piece of copper or aluminum under it, for contrast, if desired). Cut a second templet ⅞-inch by 1¼-inch, for the crown. Mark fore and aft edges of the bakelite with a knife file—to insure aligning the plate with the stock.

Shaping the plate has already been mentioned. Still another pattern may be made by beveling the cap to the crown templet with a flat wood-carver rasp, then emery cloth. This makes a nice design for either an oval or a diamond-shaped crown. Make the bevel straight or curve it with a rattail file.

Some men have queer ideas about the color of grip-caps and fore-end tips. I had in the shop a handsome curly black cherry buttstock on a single-shot Winchester receiver, but the grip-cap was made from some lavender-hued hard-rubber-like stuff. But the face of the cap was shaped just like the caps the Sharps Company put on its Creedmoor rifles. At the forward end the cap was left full thickness, then a filet was shaped, the curve running out to the flat part of the cap. I have put on guns, as grip-caps, bronze medals won in the National matches. They look well except that they are round.

Grip-caps may be handled nicely by setting one on the end of a bit of wood, secured with a screw, then hold the jigger in the vise while shaping it, or hold it in one hand and grind with an emery disc in the polishing-head.

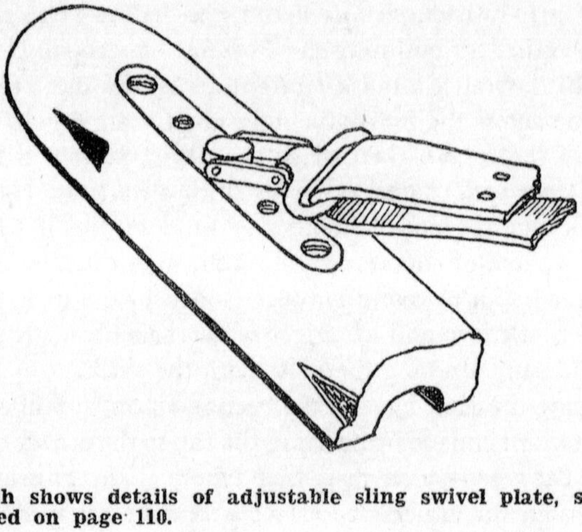

Sketch shows details of adjustable sling swivel plate, such as described on page 110.

Chapter Thirteen

RESTOCKING PROBLEMS.

In recent years great improvements have been made in machines that turn out rough-finished inletted walnut stocks automatically. So many amateurs have demanded these stocks, and so many otherwise idle mechanics have gone into restocking as a business that a number of factories have given this matter attention and have made it possible for amateurs to procure partially-finished stocks at prices never dreamed of ten years ago; in fact, if one is satisfied with ordinary domestic walnut, he can buy a rough-finished stock for about the same price he would formerly have had to pay for a plain blank.

Machine-inletted Stocks. "Would it pay me," the young gunsmith may ask, "to go into this thing myself—and just what are these partially-finished stocks like?" I am no prophet, but in my humble opinion the surface of this thing has not been scratched very hard, as yet, so there would be wages, at least, in buying these stocks for customers and finishing them completely, as is possible, within a fortnight. Rough-inletted stocks that I have worked on are better in many ways than one would expect. You will be astonished, at first, to see how closely they come to fitting the component parts of a rifle of standard make. And if your customer is willing to pay a little more for one, you can order selected imported or domestic walnut, and "doll up" his stock just as he would do himself if he had the necessary time and skill.

Firms that furnish these blanks or stocks may tell you that "about one day's work" is required to completely finish one of them. That depends on the speed with which the average amateur works, so it would be well to be liberal in this matter of time. All cuts are purposely made under size, so the young gunsmith may start in on one of these stocks by blacking the metal parts, trying them, shaving a bit here, rasping a little there, trying the parts, and so on until the barrel and receiver are bedded and the guard and magazine fitted in and locked. Trimming the outside of a stock does not take long, but checking cannot be hurried, and if our gunsmith finishes that one piece of work in five or six hours he will have to keep moving. Surfacing takes much longer, of course, for oils do not dry to order; so, in taking an order for a thing like this, it will be well to ask for a fortnight at least before delivery.

Modern Trends in Stocks. To my way of thinking, we have never had a rifle handsomer than the Sharps-Borchardt target rifle. It was slim and graceful—streamlined, it would be called now. There are only two rifles now that can begin to compare with it—the Models 52 and 70 sporters. The others intended purely for target shooting are atrocities to one who loves the lines of a graceful rifle. The buttstock is a chunk of wood, the forearm another chunk. To doll up one of these is the despair of the gunsmith who likes to have his work neat and trim. The unsightly sling-loop, with its pillows and horse collars, adds nothing to it. But that is what target shooters want; it is the vogue, so the gunsmith must trail along with the procession. The young marksmen who poke fun at the schuetzen rifles of pre-war days cannot see the ugly lines of their own muskets. Those old stocks, patterned after a fat sunfish, with their intricate spurs and hooks by way of trigger-guards, their clumsy palm-rests and outlandish Swiss butt hooks, were not so ugly, after all, compared with present trends.

We have walked away from double-set triggers—except

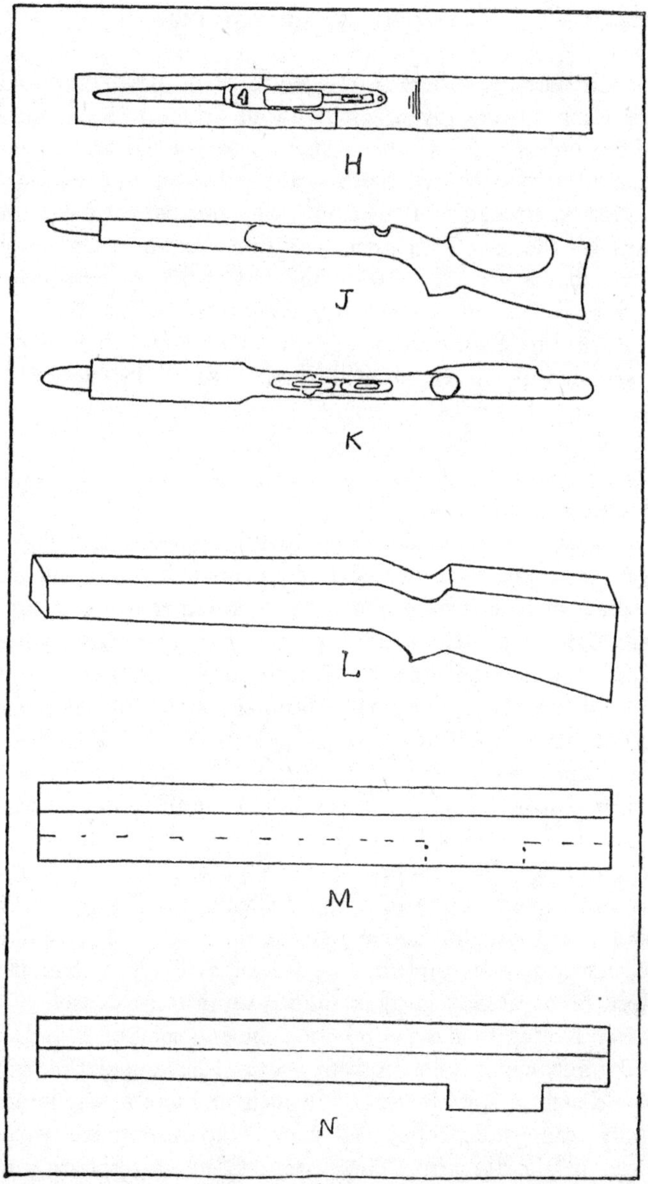

Figure 20. Stock blanks. H. Blank inletted for Springfield rifle. J and K. Rough inletted and shaped Stoeger Olympic Model 52 stock. L. Blank profile-sawed. M. Blank marked for center-line and sawing line. N. The same sawed out, leaving full-width section for cheekpiece.

for rest shooting—there is no need for them now, since some attention is being given *real* light-pull triggers. An example is the Model 70. Its pull is about five pounds as it comes from the factory, but if you want it lighter, no honing is necessary. Instead you turn up a tiny nut, adjust two other nuts, try the pull, then reset these three lock-nuts and forget about that matter. It is worth the cost of the piece to have a sweet, crisp let-off at about 3½ pounds. (See Fig. 27.)

Altering Stock Shapes. A lot of advice has in past years been given regarding the reshaping of rifle stocks like the Krag, Springfield, the old Model 52 Winchester, the Enfield and the Model 1887 Winchester single-shot. Of all these only two—the Enfield and the Springfield—are available in numbers now.

A stock that is too short may be lengthened by glueing on the butt a new piece of wood and shaping it up, but if only an inch of length be needed, it is less bother to use a thick soft rubber buttplate or build up the butt with plastic wood. This may best be done by either cutting a rabbet entirely around the butt, to provide a foundation for the plastic, or by setting a couple of dowel pins in the butt and building up around them.

If a pistol-grip is too far back or too short, it may be built up in similar fashion, and if it is checked, the patch will not be noticeable. This is best done by cutting into the curve, leaving its face rough to furnish a better anchorage for the plastic, or short dowel pins may be set in and built around. If such a grip be capped a neater job will result than if a block be dovetailed in, then shaped up in the old way.

For a comb that is too far back the end may be sawed off and a new comb built up from plastic. I have done this with old Model 52 stocks, adding an inch or more to the length and giving a much improved shape. One of these stocks had flutes in the forearm. These were filled with plastic and afterward checked, and as the filled portions are in the middle of the checked pattern, they are not noticeable.

Building up the comb is often done by planing the top from grip to butt, glueing a new piece of matched walnut on and reshaping the stock. Better practice, I think, is to fit on a metal or a walnut cheekpiece. The Westchester Trading Post, Mt. Vernon, N. Y., will supply metal cheekpieces, and A. F. Stoeger & Co., New York City, walnut ones. Richard Stamm, Presque Street, Rochester, N. Y., will supply a live rubber cheekpiece that is handier than some laced leather ones.

The 1887 Model Winchester single-shot rifle receiver is frequently used in making up a special rifle, particularly for .22-calibre target use, and for the Hornet cartridge. It is not worth while to try to build up that stock when a blank may be had at a low price, and the necessary fitting is not difficult. If the lower tang is straight, it can be bent to fit a pistol-grip, though a tang of that shape will be supplied by the makers. Before bending a tang the screw-hole midway should be plugged. While it is possible to bend the tang cold, this is not advised. Heat it dull red and bend it in the vise until the curve is approximately correct, then finish with a file. Part of the upper tang may be sawed off and re-shaped to permit carrying the comb further forward. The finger-lever, too, should be heated for re-shaping. The high sides of the receiver, if objectionable, may be altered by grinding, though the usual thing is to saw off the right side, to facilitate loading.

It is a pity that some firm does not make a receiver like the Sharps-Borchardt, the Ballard or the Winchester single-shot. These are all excellent for building up special .22-calibre target rifles, and the Sharps and Winchester receivers are strong enough for larger calibres. Some Ballard receivers have been used in this way. They are all right with the rim-fires, but not entirely safe for even the Hornet. It must be remembered in this connection that some of these old Ballard receivers are cast, not forged steel, therefore not adapted to high pressures. Only a few of these obsolete rifles are obtainable now, which is to be regretted, as not every hunter and target shot favors bolt-actions.

The single-shot Winchester receiver is better than the Ballard for rebuilding to hunting rifle use, as it is lighter. There is so much metal in the Ballard receiver, with its long stock-screw, that it is hardly possible to fit to it a barrel of medium weight and keep the finished weight under about nine pounds.

Lining Barrel Channels. If a customer has a stock with a beavertail forearm, then buys a heavy barrel and asks you to fit it into his stock, this is easily done by enlarging the channel to fit; but if he wants a thinner barrel put in his stock, different treatment is indicated. We hear stories about lining a barrel channel with plastic wood, scraping out enough of it to let the barrel in, etc. This can be done, but I prefer to treat this matter differently, and have finished up several stocks in this way that pleased the owners. The old stock was filled completely with a length of walnut, rounded and shaped to fit the channel, then after the glue had dried, the new channel was cut out, just as with a solid blank. Usually this piece of wood extends back only to the receiver mortise, and if the edges of the old channel were marred, cutting away enough of the edges to permit the new piece to be fitted closely makes a good job. Stain the surface of stock so the joint will not be prominent.

In cutting the barrel-channel in a blank, a piece of steel tubing a bit smaller than the channel will help a lot in smoothing lumpy places. Sharpen it by filing straight across the end, and keep it sharp in this way. A piece of a rifle or gun barrel will serve, if filed to a rough edge. The round scrapers mentioned elsewhere help in shaping the sides and bottom of the channel, and the receiver mortise, for with them one can avoid removing any wood from the upper edges, which must never be touched with anything, once they have been brought to a tight fit around the barrel. When the barrel channel is nearly finished, coat the barrel with lampblack and set it in, tapping all along with the wood handle of some tool.

When a barrel is properly bedded, it requires some effort to remove it from the stock after all screws have been removed, for it fits very closely along the top edges, as you will ascertain if you will blacken it, set it in the stock, then remove it and see how evenly the black is spread all along the top edges. Along the sides and bottom there will still be sufficient space to slip a piece of paper along without binding, as it should be, except at the muzzle end.

Fore-end Tips. Formerly tips for forearms were finished off with a schnabel, or, as we call it, snobble. One of the neatest of these was that of the single-shot Winchester, Model 1887. In that snobble a black piece was set, like B, Fig. 21. I like bakelite for a similar inset.

How to attach bone, horn, rubber or bakelite to the end of a forearm has often been discussed. Some workmen put the tip on with a wood dowel and two brads. It is difficult to cement or glue two glassy surfaces. A better method, I think, is shown at D. In this I cut off the threaded part of a quarter-inch machine bolt, tap the hole in the wood, turn the bolt down with thick shellac, bore a hole in the solid bakelite, thread the hole, then smear both surfaces with hot glue and turn the tip down. This is done before the barrel channel is cut, so block and wood are finished as a unit. There is little likelihood that a tip of this sort will loosen up, as the piece is held rigidly by the barrel, hence employing extra pins seems useless.

The tip E is prepared by leaving a tenon on the fore-end, then milling out a recess in a solid block of bakelite to fit and glueing all surfaces. This, too, is a strong attachment.

At F bakelite tubing was used. The tenon is flat on top but rounded below to fit a U-shaped channel cut down into the hole in the tubing, this hole being about ¾-inch in diameter. Of course the tenon extends entirely through the groove, so it is rounded off at the time the barrel channel

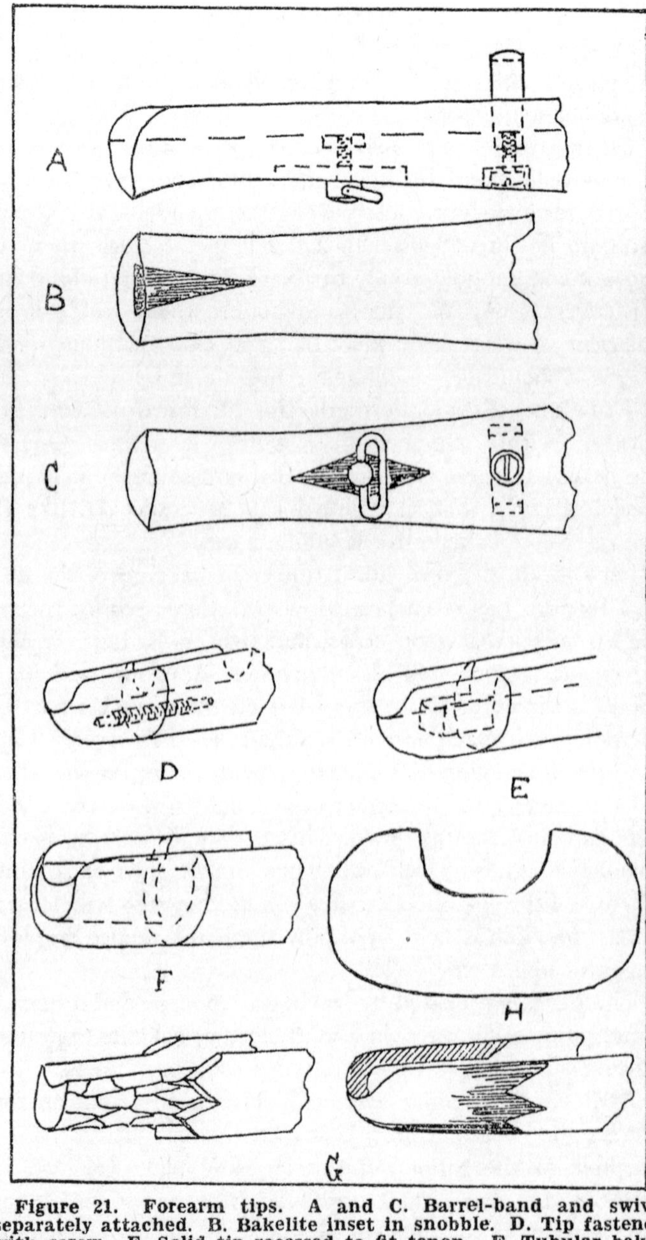

Figure 21. Forearm tips. A and C. Barrel-band and swivel separately attached. B. Bakelite inset in snobble. D. Tip fastened with screw. E. Solid tip recessed to fit tenon. F. Tubular bakelite fitted to long tenon. G. Tip built up with plastic wood. H. Sectional view of full beavertail forearm.

is cut. When finished the end is soaked with black alcohol dye, then black shellaced several coats, each rubbed and polished. It may be noticed if looked for; otherwise one would not see the joint. Similar tips may be seen on German rifles, but with them the black sleeve extends only part way up to the edge of the barrel channel.

In G a suggestion is offered. Ebony plastic wood is the material. The fore-end is finished roughly as a tenon, the plastic smeared on roughly until the mass is larger than the wood, then trimmed down to shape and finally polished. The design of this tip is "different." It is given merely to show how slavish we are about some things, and to give an idea of a pattern with oblique lines that match the points in the checking pattern on the forearm.

When tips were first put on, it was evidently done in the easiest way known—by sawing both wood and tip square, then joining them. But this right-angled joint is not in keeping with the curves that predominate in stocks, and anyway, a zigzag joint of some sort is stronger than a smooth one, as, if well done, it cannot slip or turn—a thing not likely to happen while the barrel acts as a support for the tip. However, whatever the material used, it seems to me it should be black, and not ivory or one of the variegated-color plastic substances available on the market. If contrast is wanted, set a piece of copper or aluminum between fore-arm end and tip, as suggested elsewhere for grip-caps.

Some day I mean to make a rifle stock from native juniper, or red cedar, as it is called. I have seen stocks made of this wood, and aside from its tendency to check, it is very handsome when finished with wax or lacquer, rubbed down. Jazz trimmings might set it off nicely!

"Trading" Stocks. Now and then a customer may ask you to fit his barrel and receiver into a stock made for another rifle. This I have done at times, and it works out nicely with some .22-calibre rifles but is not to be recommended for some high-power rifles. A customer had a stock made for a Winchester Model 60A single-shot rifle, then purchased a Model 69 rifle of the same make. After a few changes I adapted the stock to the magazine rifle, and fortunately there was no patching needed, so the result was satisfactory to the owner, though he could make no use of the factory stock that came with his Model 69 rifle. (See 2, Fig. 22).

The Model 70 Winchester rifle is another one that lends itself to a similar alteration. If a customer has a Model 54 special stock that he would like to have fitted to the Model 70, this may readily be done in a couple of hours, with only one place—a very small one—where the necessary alteration is visible. For the Model 70 parts the Model 54 receiver mortise will have to be enlarged slightly in two places; one is to cut back slightly to give more space for the trigger-and-sear assembly, the other is to deepen the left side in rear of the magazine. After these changes have been made, by blacking all the receiver parts and noting where the new parts bind, it is easy to see where a shaving must be removed here or there, and in a jiffy barrel, receiver and magazine will slip into place as nicely as if the stock had been made for the new outfit. (See 1, Fig. 22).

The cut for the bolt-handle must be deepened and turned further to the rear; the cut for the rear sight must be partially filled, to hide the cut formerly made to accommodate the elevating screw in the long slide of the Model 48 left-hand rear sight. The new rear sight is one of the stumpy affairs like the 48J, with slide cut off flush with the bottom of the base—but the main cut in the stock for this sight is the same as the one in the Model 54.

The rear end of the trigger-guard mortise must be deepened slightly. The plate is set in as a unit. The floor-plate is hinged on the forward end of what may be called a part of the trigger-plate, and it is about an inch shorter than in the older model, so a tiny piece of walnut or bakelite must be set in to fill the gap, and this is the only place on the stock that shows the alteration. This means boring a new hole in the forearm for the receiver-ring screw. At the factory this screw-hole is cut clean through the ring into the rear end of the chamber, but of course the screw does not protrude. I fill the small blank space in the old guard cut with a piece of black bakelite. The color matches blued steel closely and is almost unnoticeable. Gummy shellac holds the patch securely, as there is no strain on it.

The new Model 70 is said to have a full-floating barrel, but in all those I have handled so far the forearm screw is still used. In the Hornet rifle I have fired many test groups to ascertain just what effect leaving this forearm screw out or turning it down fairly tight might have on impact centers. There seemed to be little if any difference, but I fancy that there would be a difference if these tests were made on a hot summer day, and with the barrel heated from firing a number of shots. To forestall this possibility, with high-power rifles of this model I always turn the forearm screw down as far as it will go, then ease it two turns. This gives ample protection in the event the rifle be dropped accidentally, but does not put much if any strain on the barrel. In some of these stocks I have left the screw out entirely, and its lug as well.

In Fig 27 the mechanism of the Model 70 trigger and sear is given in a sectional view, at 2. Adjusting the trigger-pull must be done when the stock has been removed; but once set, there is no reasonable need for changing the adjustment.

There is just one thing about this superb rifle that I dislike—the bolt-stop release. This stands alongside the receiver at its rear end. To depress it and release the bolt one must press forward with the left thumb. The spring is quite stiff, and when it is pressed far enough to release the bolt, one is almost certain to lose part of the thumb, or at least the nail, when the bolt lugs and the bolt pass it. With cold hands a nasty gouge might be the result. Dismount the part by driving the holding pin out, anneal the release by heating with a soldering copper, then bore a tiny hole through the release and fit into it a short pin with a head ⅛-inch thick but only equally long. Rivet it in place after hardening it.

This gives the thumb ample support for depressing the release without danger of injuring it. This simple remedy improves the rifle.

Finishing an Inletted Blank.

Assuming that you have purchased for a customer a machine-inlettered blank, let us get to work on it. If it is for one of the Model 70 rifles, take out the bolt, remove the four machine screws from the receiver and forearm, take out the floor-plate, the magazine and the sear assembly, which is held by tapered lateral pins. Blacken all the parts and half the under side of the barrel, and try it and the receiver in their mortises. These will go down part way when you tap them gently with a wooden toolhandle. Remove them and pare away places in the barrel channel and receiver mortise that show black marks, then try the parts again. Continue until barrel and receiver will fit snugly, with no rocking when you press down on one end, then the other. The recoil-lug should be bedded solidly in its seat, its rear side bearing against the solid wood behind it. Taper the top of its edge slightly. With a bottom tool scrape the cut back to the tang until the straight lower edge of the receiver mortise will show black marks its entire length. See that the sides of the cut for the sear assembly are free of black marks and that the rear end of the barrel channel is clean. Mark the lower side of the bolt-handle with black, seat it in the receiver, turn the handle down, and relieve the cut under the shoulder until the bolt-handle will go clean down without impinging on the sides or bottom of its cut.

The barrel channel must be deep enough for the barrel to go down just half its diameter, and the barrel must be tight all along the top edges of the channel and a bit free at all other points save at the muzzle end, where the wood must fit the barrel snugly.

Fit the magazine into its seat, blacken it all around and try it in the stock. The rear end should be free of the shoulder behind it, to allow for recoil. The forward end and the sides may touch the wood lightly, but not enough to prevent you from putting it in and removing it easily. If there is a Model 48J sight on the rifle, the cut in the stock for it must be freed slightly along its rear side, but no cut is made in the stock under the sight, as was necessary in the Model 54 stock (to give free play for the sight-elevating screw.) The rear end of the tang should be relieved slightly, at the bottom, but not enough to leave a distinct gap, as in some of the Springfield stocks one sees.

Turn the stock over and try the trigger-guard, which in this model extends only as far forward as the rear end of the magazine mortise and is flush with the under side of the stock all along. The forward end, with the floor-plate hinge, sets deeper in the stock than in the Model 54, but it does not extend so far forward. The floor-plate when seated extends over the magazine mortise slightly, leaving no gap between the plate and the wood.

Fit the sear assembly into the receiver and try, being sure that no part binds on the wood alongside and behind it. Set the guard and floor-plate in, insert all screws and turn them down part way, meanwhile examining every possible place where metal and wood may be too tight. If all is well, turn the screws home then try the bolt, the trigger, the safety lock, the rear sight and its seat, the fit of the barrel-lug in the forearm, how close the tip of the forearm hugs the barrel, etc.

Now for the real bedding, on which accuracy depends so much. The lower contour of the receiver is almost straight clear back to the tang. Blacken these edges thoroughly, try the parts, then remove every trace of black from the receiver mortise. Assemble all parts. Turn the tang-screw clear down.

Press on the barrel at the fore-end, and if there is any tendency to spring when you release the pressure, remove all parts and work along the receiver seat with a bottom tool, removing high spots that show black with only traces of black at the forward end. Fit all parts and try the tang-screw again. If there is no rocking forward, turn the receiver-ring screw down and again try for rocking. Remove the parts and scrape all black evenly from the receiver seat. It should not bear heavily on the bottom now, for it will be pulled down a bit more when all screws are set, but it should just touch the bottom equally its full length. The barrel must go in snugly, with no binding at any point except at the tip, where it should touch but spring slightly if you pull it outward. Turn down the forearm screw its full depth, then raise it two turns, for it should not be snug enough to put tension on the forearm.

In the Model 70 rifle there are no bushings for the screws, but the rear guard screw sets very snugly in its hole in the stock. In the Model 52 stock the receiver-ring screw—the only anchor for barrel and receiver when no band is employed—has a bushing the top of which is rigidly held by an abutment plate set deeply in the wood, half in the receiver mortise and half in the barrel channel (E, Fig. 15). The rear guard-screw in the Springfield receiver has a strong bushing, and this is regarded at the arsenal as a very important feature in the bedding of the parts of that rifle. Accuracy suffers if the screw or its bushing is loose. The length of that bushing is important, too, for it must be exactly right—if too long or too short strain is imparted to the guard; in fact, a buckling effect which is bound to be communicated to the receiver and barrel when the piece recoils from a shot.

If all parts seem to be properly bedded, take the rifle out and fire it at least twenty shots, then remove all parts and examine minutely all important bearing surfaces for indications of too-tight fitting. Relieve these.

With all parts of the rifle assembled, lay out your guide sheet (1, Fig. 10) and place the rifle over it, the sights coinciding with the long horizontal line on the sheet, center of trigger just 13½ inches (more or less, as may best suit you) from the short vertical line on the sheet, then mark the heel for length. Move the muzzle down on the sheet until the distance from the front sight to the line is three inches (more or less, according to your fancy), the pitch for the butt. Draw a line from the mark just made at the heel straight across the blank to the toe, allowing ⅛-inch for thickness of buttplate, then saw off the surplus wood at the butt, being very careful to raise no splinters along the edges.

Now for the drop at comb and heel. The factory stock has a drop at the comb of 1⅝ inches and at the heel just an inch more—about right for all positions but a trifle too straight for a purely offhand stock. For this position much depends on the length of neck and breadth of shoulders of the owner; some men preferring that the heel drop be as great as 3¼ inches. If the stock is Monte Carlo pattern, like the Stoeger stock in Fig. 20, it will be well to shape up both the cheekpiece and the top line to butt before determining the drop at heel. In some cases it is as much as 3½ inches.

In fitting the buttplate, first make the V-shaped cut for the lip, using lampblack on the plate, curving the middle of the wood, working with the woodcarver rasp from the edge toward the center all around, and from end to end with coarse file—never across. This is a game of trying, cutting, trying, until the plate will set as smoothly as though it had grown on that bush. When that point has been reached, bore the screwholes, the one at the heel first, as it must set at an angle while the toe screw goes straight down. Start each hole with a drill the size of the body of the screw, then finish with a drill a bit smaller than the threads. Coat the screw with bullet lubricant or soap and turn it carefully part way, then the other screw, until both are down.

Three and one-half inches is the favorite distance from the front center of the trigger to the front edge of the pistol grip. Place the stock on your guide sheet, top of stock on the lateral line, and with an angle protractor lay off 20 degrees for the pitch of the bottom of grip. That point should be 4½ inches from the lateral line. The cap should be 1⅝ inches wide and 2 inches long. Fit it perfectly, set it with thick shellac, and fit the screw. The cap—and the butt-plate—are to be shaped up with the wood, and both are to be blued afterward.

As you are through with inletting, oil the mortises now—two coats half linseed half turpentine—then start on the outside with a half-round rasp, cutting first behind and parallel with the grip on both sides. Keep in mind the fact that the thickness of the buttstock will be 1⅝ inches at the plate. Taper it, then, to 1⅜ inches at the center of the grip—a perfectly straight line on both sides (theoretically on the left side, of course, as the cheekpiece will break that line). This will, if the curves in the grip be correct later on, give a grip circumference of 5 or 5¼ inches. Now plane or spokeshave the right side of the stock, rasp from butt to grip under the cheekpiece outline, around the grip and behind the cheekpiece. This should be shaped very much like a Bartlett pear sliced lengthwise, the edge to be the top line of the comb (P, Fig. 24). This brings the forward curve a half-inch further forward than the point of the comb. This will be seen in the top view of a Model 70 stock, in Fig. 22. In that stock the forward face of the cheekpiece is not saucer-shape, as in some Swiss patterns. The only concavity is from the top line toward the lower edge, but the comb bears a half-inch to the right of the center line of the stock—giving a very comfortable form for either iron or scope sight use in all positions. The comb is under-cut considerably on the right side, leaving a hollow there for the heel of the thumb.

Some men will tell you that they like a good thick comb.

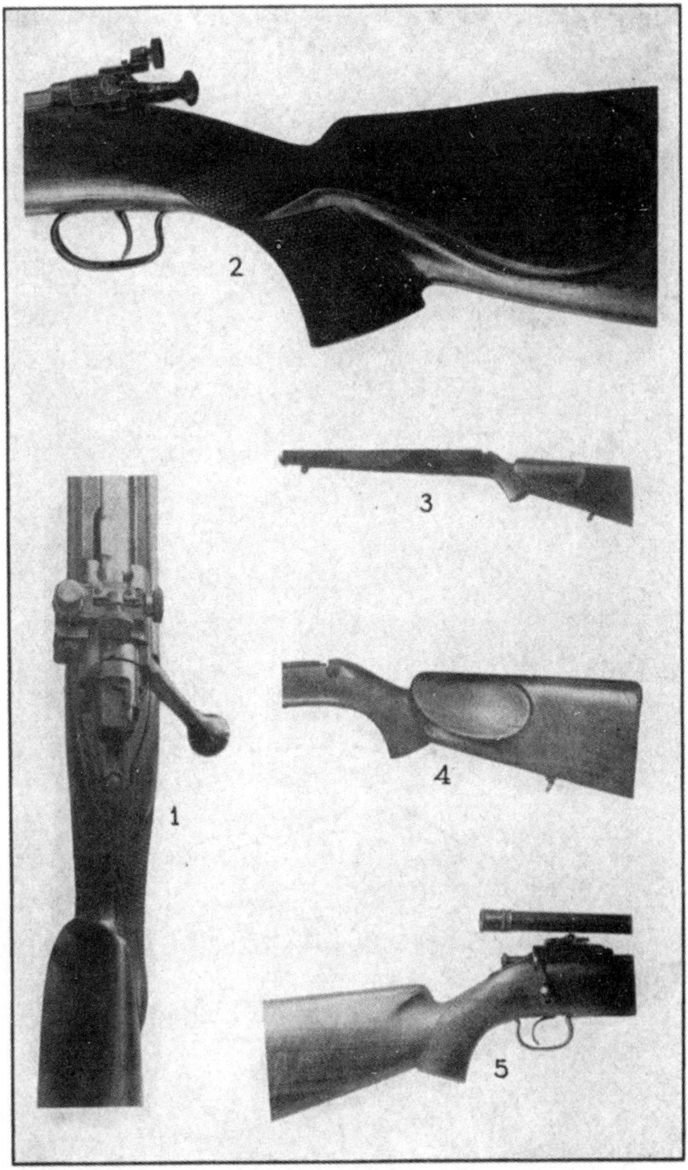

Fig. 22. 1, stock originally made for Model 54 rifle, adapted to Model 70 rifle. 2, Model 60A target stock fitted to Model 69 rifle. 3, 4, and 5, Model 52 stocks of French walnut.

Very well, finish the stock but leave the cheekpiece full and round at the top. Let the customer try it at the range, then suggest thinning and curving the hump and let him try it that way. Eventually he will concede that the overhanging comb will be much more comfortable, particularly with scope and heavy recoil. And with it the comb may be higher but still not too high for iron-sight use.

From point of comb to heel must be a straight line—the Monte Carlo pattern excepted, of course. Draw a straight line from the toe to a point about one inch forward of the trigger cut and remove wood to agree, but this line should stop at the rear side of the grip in a neatly curved fillet rather than an angle. The lower edge of the butt should not be thick and clumsy in appearance, but care must be used to keep the lines there parallel with the center line of the butt.

From the point of the comb forward to the tang great care must be taken to avoid cutting down too far in order to bring the grip circumference to the figure already named. This had better be done alongside and under the grip, where a deep curve is permissible. A quarter-inch can be taken off the sides of the grip, and this, with the deep curve underneath, will give the flaring effect to the grip that is so satisfactory when one is shooting right along and the hand tires if the grip is of too great circumference. If a Wundhammer effect is sought, leave a slight hump on the right side of the grip—some men like it, and it surely fits the palm, even though it gives a cockeyed outline when the grip is viewed in profile.

Now work forward, rounding the stock under and alongside the receiver. If the forearm is beavertail pattern, curve sharply on the sides, round inward toward the top of the stock, as in H, Fig. 21, so the edge there will be neat and trim rather than blunt, as in some stocks one sees. Keep the width of the beavertail at least 2¼ inches as far as the location of the swivel-stud, 16 to 17 inches from the trigger, then taper sharply on all surfaces to a neat rounded end.

This is a problem, too, for if it is not neatly shaped, the end of the forearm will look decidedly clubby. In the new Model 416 Stevens target rifle the sides of the tip are hollowed, as will be seen at M, Fig. 14, and this gives a neat effect to the forearm. In the new blank (L, Fig. 14) bakelite arrow-heads were set in instead.

If the swivel-stud is set about two inches back of the end (A and C, Fig, 21, and D. Fig. 14) a long bakelite diamond swivel base makes a nice finish for that part of the stock, but if this be used, a similar diamond should be set in the buttstock for the swivel there, to match.

So far the work can be done with a rasp, a small plane and a spokeshave. The stock should take on form. Sanding comes next. Use coarse sandpaper, rubbing thoroughly but with ever lessening pressure, and eliminate all marks left by the rasp. Change to finer grades, finally very fine, then wet the stock with a cloth, let it air dry, and resume rubbing with very fine paper; wet again, and so on until all marks are gone and the wood takes on a bone-like smoothness—and you will be approaching a real finish. With very hard dense Circassian walnut this wetting and rubbing the raised grain may be completed in about seven sessions, but with softer woods I have carried the work to thirteen or more times, still raising some grain at the last. Usually half-a-dozen times will answer, provided *all* the final rubbing be done across the grain with fine steel wool rather than sand-paper. After this rubbing examine every part of the stock minutely for scratches. They show most plainly on flat surfaces, like the sides of the butt near the plate. Stubborn ones may be removed with a convex-edged piece of glass or a flat scraper.

At this stage it would be well to ask the owner to shoot the rifle as it is, one day at least, then suggest changes, if any, as this is the time for final alterations, especially in the shape of the cheekpiece. If the stock is satisfactory, give it a partial surfacing of linseed oil, wax or lacquer, as will be mentioned in detail further on. Just here I do not, in my own work, follow the rule of some stockers—I prefer to complete the checking of a stock before oiling it at all outside of the mortises; or, if it is oiled before checking, the areas to be checked are left bare until that work is finished. Take your choice.

Another thing: If your stock is more or less curly but without contrast in the light and dark areas, do this just before you first start sanding: with an ordinary steel pen and India ink trace the edges of all dark areas, merely to relieve them and make them stand out more prominently when the surface is finished. At first the effect will startle you—the dead black lines will seem to be out of place alongside the light brown of the lighter portions. Do not mind that—the wetting and sanding will remove all but faint traces of the ink and you will have nice mild contrasts instead of a uniform brown with the merest traces of grain. After the oiling and rubbing the black markings will be slight but the general effect will be pleasing. And if you prefer, use brown instead of black, or any stain.

Checkering or Checking.

Some of us call the cross-hatching of metal or wood, to produce a non-skid surface, checkering; others use the simpler term, checking, and as both are fully understood by shooters, it seems the shorter word may fully convey the intended meaning; so let us proceed to do some checking on our partially finished stock.

Checking may be put on a stock merely for ornamental purposes. That is something that will not interest you at first; you want utility—a surfacing of the hand-holds on a gun that will make it less slippery, easier to grasp firmly in any one of the four well-known shooting positions. This narrows down to two areas, the grip and a part of the forearm about a foot forward of the trigger. Very well. If needs must, this can be done by any boy with a piece of hacksaw blade—in fact, many jobs have been done with no other tool. Possibly this may suit some boys, but not others; no one would be proud of such a job. And while about it, why not make the thing more or less ornamental? So special tools are suggested, simple though they may be.

With a strip of celluloid, two groove cutters and a bent-end three-square file one can do all the checking needed on a stock. How to make these tools has been described in Chapter IV. Look up all the stocks and pictures of stocks you can find, then with a pencil lay out a pattern that will be quite simple, involving the least possible amount of work. Of course you will want to start checking the grip, but if you will start with the forearm you will get an idea just what checking means, and by the time you are ready for the grip you will have learned some of the rudiments of the work, and may not spoil the more difficult pattern on the grip.

Decide on a certain pattern and measure from point to point until you are sure how long it will be. Say it is seven inches fore and aft on the center line of the forearm. With your flexible straight-edge and pencil mark a line entirely around the forearm, another one seven inches distant, a third one exactly half way. These are the guide lines. Now draw a line a quarter-inch below the top line of the forearm, one on each side (A-B, Fig. 23). Both will be theoretically parallel with the center line. Next draw a line obliquely around the stock, from the extreme right forward to the extreme left aft, this line (C-D) passing exactly through the center mark on the center line of the forearm. Draw another line from the opposite side. Your pattern will now consist of a boxlike design with two lines running from corner to corner obliquely. Draw another line on each side from the center line at one end to the line encircling the forearm half-way of the pattern; same thing at the other end. Stop these lines where they intersect the original oblique lines; result, three sharp points at each end of your "box."

Half way draw a long diamond straddling the center line

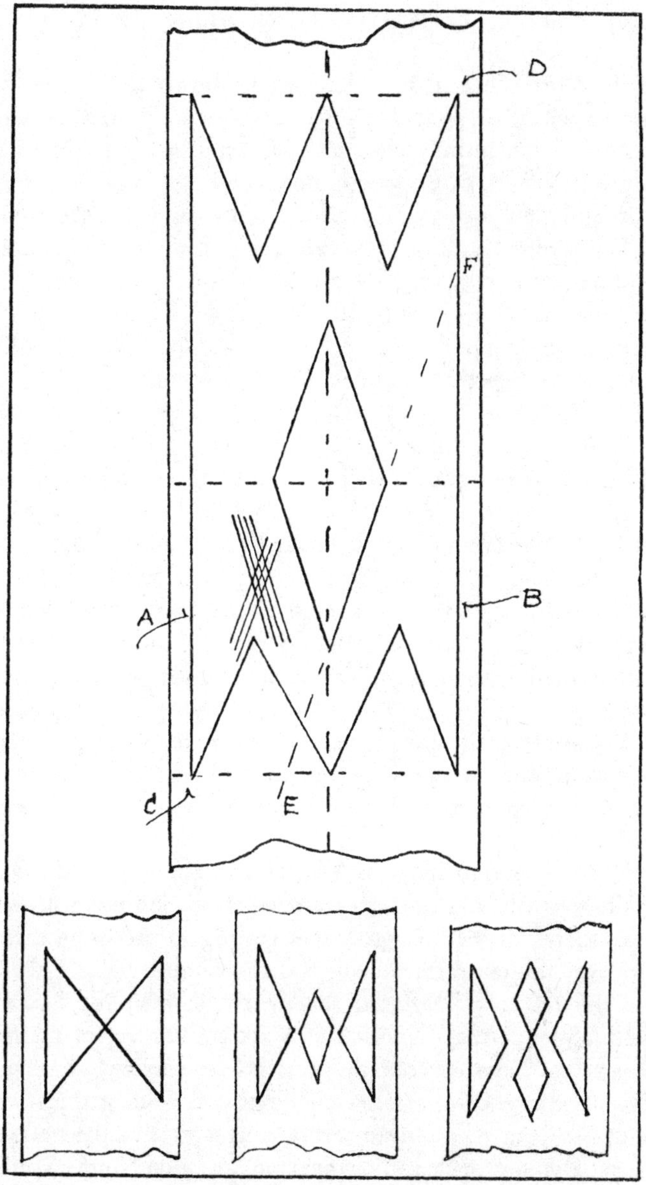

Figure 23. Above, an outline for forearm checking. A-B. Border line at top edges of forearm. C-D. Master line. Broken line E-F, first line for starting the checking tool. At bottom, three simple designs for forearm checking.

of forearm. That is all. The idea is shown in Fig. 23, together with three patterns for the beginner to practice with. If this is not entirely clear to you, make a pattern like the illustration, on paper, cut it out, bend it around the forearm and view it there, then pencil your pattern on the wood.

With your single-edge V-cutter and straight-edge cut the outline of the pattern, making the grooves quite deep; trace the diamond; then, with the V-tool and straight-edge cut one of the diamond lines clear to the border (E-F). See that the angle is exactly the same as all oblique lines. Set the two-edged spacer in this groove and cut a second groove from end to end. Set the spacer in the second groove and cut a third one. Continue in this way until the wood from diamond to border has been scored in one direction. Go back to the initial cut and work toward the opposite side of the pattern. Some men do better work from left to right; if preferred, reverse the stock and make all cuts from left to right—the only thing that matters is to cut against the grain rather than with it, as must be done at times in checking the grip.

When the entire pattern has been scored in one direction, brush out the dust and start in the opposite direction. The method is suggested by the broken lines in the sketch (Fig. 23).

Keep all outline grooves deep and clean, and make every effort to avoid running over one of these outlines with the tool; there will be no border-tool cutting to obliterate them. Go over the entire area with the spacer and you are ready for the real checking. Do this with the bent file, correct inequalities in depth with the V-tool. Cut deeply, so that when you have covered the area to be checked, you will have, not a series of shallow cuts, but real 60-degree grooves with clean-cut diamonds at every intersection of the oblique lines. Use a stiff brush right along as you work. If the light is not good, place your work so that the shadows will fall on the far side of each groove, giving contrast. Cutting directly toward the light will give you no contrast to prevent slopping over. This work is tiring on the eyes. Do a little at a time, but do not call it a day until the entire pattern is evenly scored and all diamonds stand out prominently. That is real checking.

If you have any doubts as to your ability to do good checking, start with some old stock you do not care about.

Checking the grip is another story. If the stock is for a shotgun or a hunting rifle, lay out a pattern on each side that will not come within an inch of its mate, but for a target rifle or any rifle that is to be really ornamented in this way, have the pattern on each side almost the full half of the grip —just so the halves will not meet at the center lines on top and under the grip. If a space half-an-inch wide be left bare underneath, the fingers of the right hand will never miss roughness there; but if the top surface of the grip be left bare, the thumb will not have the support it needs, if one shoots with the thumb crossing the grip.

No paper pattern will aid you here. Depend on the eye instead, but if you make a mark on one side, match it as exactly as possible with a corresponding mark when you are working on the opposite side. All diamond points must coincide wherever located.

For a grip on a plain stock, sketch the first line slightly above the line of the cap, and let the grip line curve just as the under line of the grip does, though it may be a shade wider at the bottom at the rear end of the grip. If a cheekpiece stock, the lines may be run somewhat like those in Fig. 24; follow the grip under-side line on the right, but curve upward to the left, then recurve around the end of the cheekpiece on the left side, extending almost to the center line atop the grip, to leave a bare space there at least one-quarter-inch wide. Underneath the grip there may be points, or the bare center line my curve upward wider to the point of the first diamond there, alongside the trigger. On the side of the grip the points may be two, three, or four in number.

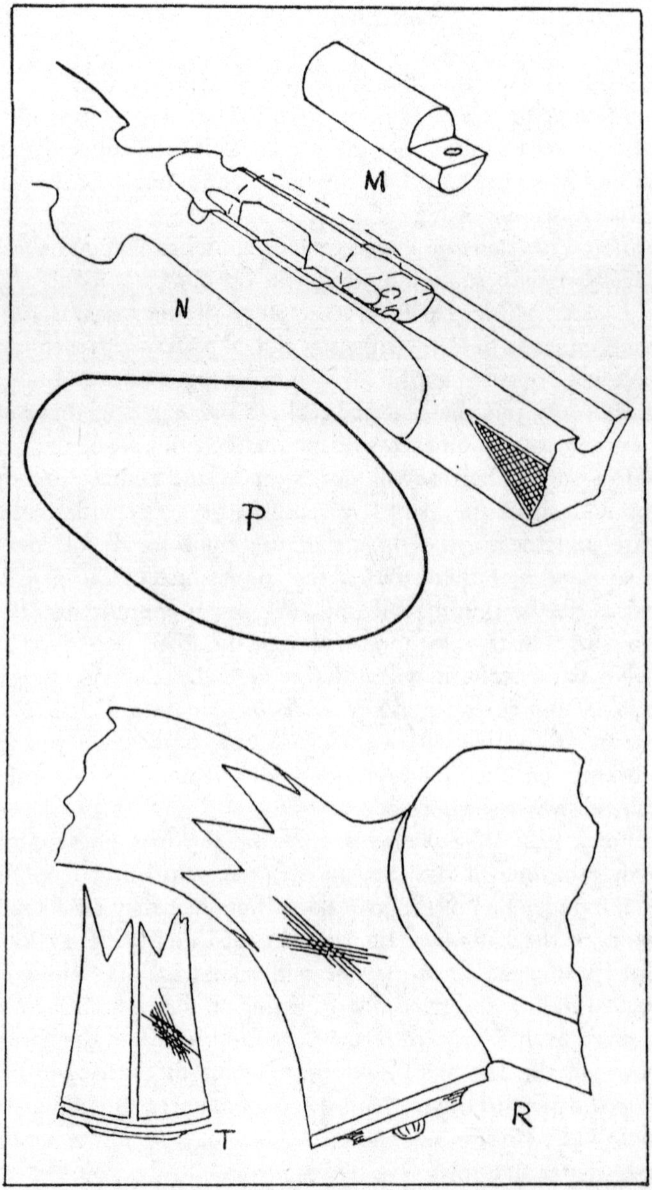

Figure 24. M. Mortise gauge and (N) method of using it in a Model 52 stock to spot receiver-ring screw-hole. P. Pattern for cheekpiece. R. A sketched outline for grip checking pattern. T. Under side of grip with parallel checking borders.

Sometimes a bare diamond may be left at the middle of the pattern on the side of the grip. There are so many patterns possible that no set rule applies. I make a different pattern for nearly every stock, as fancy at the moment dictates, though all are more or less similar, and nearly all extend over the grip, forming a very comfortable hold for the right thumb.

A checking cradle is very useful in all work of this sort, but especially so in grip checking, as the work must be turned this way and that as one proceeds. Here one's hand must be very steady, so that one can drive a comparatively straight line around curves and compound curves, some places with, others across very brittle grain.

While it is well to cut a groove from one side to the other without shifting from end to end of the stock, on a cheekpiece stock this is not always possible, so some grooves must be cut part way from one side, then extended or completed from the other side, as the cheekpiece interferes with the hand and tool in some instances.

Although it is very difficult to do so, try to keep both edges of the spacer the same depth in the grooves, else one edge will have a tendency to ride out of the groove and form curves where straight lines are wanted. The brush should be used right along here. And if checking the forearm tired your eyes, take things easy on the grip, and never continue the work when you begin to lose interest or be careless. It does not pay, and at best this grip checking is slow work. For that reason never promise a checking job in a time too short for you to do full justice to it.

Inletted Stock Blanks Available. If a customer asks you to buy and finish for him an inletted blank, of course you can readily obtain one from any of the firms that supply these. The Winchester Company will supply an inletted blank instead of a finished stock for any one of its rifles. Then there is the Springfield rifle that so many young men fancy—partly from sentimental reasons—and which any member of the National Rifle Association may purchase through the Director of Civilian Marksmanship, in Washington. This rifle may be had in either .22 or .30 calibre. The latter is supplied in the pattern known as the service rifle and for a slightly higher price the Type C pistol-grip stock will be supplied instead of the military stock. It may also be had with Lyman 48 rear sight fitted. This is an outfit that lends itself to reshaping and refinishing as a sporter; and it is an elegant thing to practice on. The pistol-grip stock is full and large, so it may be fined down, the front band removed and an inside band (or no band) fitted; a fore-end tip put on, a cap added to the grip, a Model 1897 buttplate used, and the grip and forearm checked.

The barrel will need working down after the service rear sight has been removed, for this sight is mounted on a tube several inches long, and that part of the barrel must be draw-filed and blued before the job is finished.

The Model 1917 service rifle, the Enfield, may be had from the same source for $12.50. It is .30 '06 calibre. For $6.00 a rough-inletted blank can be bought, and after the clumsy receiver has been altered and better sights put on, it may be shaped up into a neat target rifle at low cost.

The .22 Springfield is sporting type, has an improved so-called speedlock, and the pistol grip stock may be shaped up to suit the most fastidious owner. The bolt in recent models has a shorter throw than in former issues. Older .22's, having the long throw, may be improved by putting a stop in the receiver.

The Good Old Krag.

All the Krag-Jorgensen rifles left over in the hands of the Director of Civilian Marksmanship have, I believe, been sold, but there are a large number of these excellent rifles in the hands of various people, and these can be purchased at very low prices. The original barrels were thirty inches long, but in reshaping the rifles the barrels were usually cut down to 24 inches or less and a Springfield front-sight assembly put on. New barrels of various calibres were put in, and lately the Hornet cartridge has been adapted, either by means of a Springfield .22-calibre barrel rechambered, or by relining and re-chambering, to Hornet cartridges. To this end the old magazine was removed and the rifle used as a single shot, or the box magazine was cut off, a new magazine to hold three or four cartridges installed, and the action restocked like other bolt-action rifles.

If work of this sort be done with the Krag an additional screw should be put in the receiver ring. The Springfield receiver has two machine screws, spaced 7¾ inches apart; the Model 70 Winchester has three receiver screws, the front and rear one being 7½ inches apart. In the original Krag receiver the two screws are spaced only 3 inches apart, but by putting another screw in the receiver ring, the spacing of screws can be made 7⅜ inches. With proper bedding and this extra screw, the Krag makes a fine hunting rifle. With this arrangement no barrel band is needed, though one of these is sometimes used on hunting rifles, attached, sometimes, to the swivel stud.

Cutting a new screw-hole in the Krag receiver ring should be attempted only if one is willing to make a long job of it and be extremely careful with drill and tap. The ring is case-hardened, the hole to be bored can be only about 3/16-inch deep, if one goes down no further than the width of the receiver ring, and the screw will go down only about three turns. It is best to locate the place for this screw hole very accurately, then spot it with a center punch and spot anneal this with a blazing hot soldering copper. Try a drill smaller than the one to be used later on, and if it does not cut, use the copper again. In the Hand-ee set there is a grinding stone about ¾-inch in diameter, and this may be used to grind away the surface just over the screw hole, then by using the copper again, you may get under the hard skin with a drill, or failing with it, with a piece of broken rattail file ground to a four-sided point. For a hole ¼-inch in diameter the hard skin must be worried away over a trifle larger area, else drill or tap may be broken. And when the proper-size hole is deep enough, grind the drill used, or a spare one, to a very blunt point and square the bottom of the hole with it, so the tap can go down almost to the bottom. Taps as they come are usually tapered too much for work of this sort, or they are sold in sets, one tapered, the other one blunt, called plug. If two are at hand, start tapping with the taper tool, then, when it will go no further without dangerous pressure, use the plug tap and go down until it binds, then try the screw and be content if it will go down three turns, for the screw to be used will be only a reinforcing one.

To spot the hole in the receiver channel without fishing for it, turn up a piece of steel tubing and shape one end to fit snug but not tight in the screw-hole. Cut off the other end and shape it. It should protrude not more than $\frac{1}{16}$-inch. Assemble the parts and tap the barrel with a tool handle, then remove and you should find a neat ring in the wood, corresponding exactly with the plug used. Lift this plug out with the end of a rattail file, square a drill with the stock after various measurements to make sure the spot to be pricked on the outside of the stock is true, then if in doubt, bore a very small hole clear through. You can ream this hole or follow with a drill of the right size, correcting small errors, if any. Make a steel bushing for the screw-head, and set the screw down in oil. Black the under side of receiver and barrel and try the parts with the three screws. Remove excess blacking if there are signs of binding at either end of the mortise, so the parts will go down without any rocking fore and aft. Then try the rifle for groups.

In testing rifles for groups, the ordinary round bullseye is not so efficient as a cross, provided the lines in the cross be proportioned to the apparent width of the cross hairs in your rifle scope. At Springfield Armory a manila card is used. It has a vertical bar about three inches wide and eighteen inches high. At its right center a shorter horizontal bar a foot long is attached. Used at 200 meters, this device is quite clear when viewed over service sights, and it is fine for scope use. On Cape Cod this device is placed alongside the roads to warn motorists that a side road is just beyond. If the horizontal arm points right, the side road joins the main one on that side; if left, a road coming in from that side is indicated. For a cross road a plus sign is used. As you drive along those roads, you can't help wishing you could try the board with your pet rifle. In shooting for groups only, using a spotting scope, it is good practice to align the sights vertically, then set the scope so the group will print to the left of the vertical bar, in the white, where it will be distinct. Satisfied with the way the rifle groups its shots, move the scope over for center. In muzzle-loader days one always fired at a cross, and usually the distance of each shot from the cross center was measured, the total, in inches, for all shots, giving the score; string measure shooting, it was called. If you keep a record of groups, give the height first, then the width. The rifle that will group its shots on or close to a vertical line is a good one. Slight changes in light may cause the shots to string up and down, but if the dispersion is wide right and left, and there is no wind, improvement in loads or holding is indicated.

Bore sighting a .22-caliber rifle helps materially in aligning sights, but firing a few shots helps more. If you have no place outdoors to shoot a rifle to sight it in, do this in the shop. It can be done with perfect safety if you will get a short cut from a thick, sound log and fire at a target tacked on one end. The distance is not so important as the fact that the sights can be aligned perfectly at any distance further than twenty feet. After a few shots have been fired from a solid rest, it will only be a matter of altering the elevation when the rifle is later fired at 25 yards or further. Black cherry makes a perfect backstop, but any wood will do, hardwood preferred. Of course after considerable firing the end used will be cut up a lot. Dig out loose stuff, pour a small quantity of thin glue in the holes, stir fine sawdust in with a stick, then tamp the mass down and let dry. A piece of log a foot thick can be used for a thousand or more shots and still be safe to use. Bullets fired into the end grain of a log stay put, so there is no danger of a bullet glancing or going astray.

Rifle stocks that have been subjected for a long time to alternate heating and wetting in matches may well be expected to warp away from their barrels. Those fitted when new with cross-bolts are not so much affected by warping, but no one loves these ugly things. If one or two bolts must be put into a stock, however, conceal the ends as best you may with walnut or bakelite insets. If walnut, cut plugs to fit and glue them in, cutting these plugs across the grain, for a better match. If bakelite, use a diamond shape.

Chapter Fourteen

MAKING STOCKS FROM SOLID BLANKS.

Walnut is conceded to be the material par excellence for gun and rifle stocks. It is not my intention to give a long list of all the varieties available. One reason is that nine out of ten men, in buying blanks, obtain them from a distance, and must either accept or return whatever wood is sent them. Usually they accept and make the best of their bargain, be it good or bad. Dealers sell blanks under trade names—American, plain or fancy; English, French, Italian, Circassian. Their supply is limited and so is one's choice. The buyer often if not usually sends a certain sum and asks that his money's worth of walnut be sent him. A better way—and no dealer will refuse if bank references be given—is to ask that a blank be sent on approval, the return charges to be prepaid if the prospective buyer is not satisfied.

What Sort of Walnut? I like Circassian walnut, it is so dense and hard, and when a stock is finished carefully, one can be proud of it; but when all is said, there is no handsomer walnut than a piece of burl or crotch walnut from one of our Middle States, though I must admit that I like the blanks that come from California, taken, we are told, from trees grown from the English walnuts we all love to eat at Christmas time.

Plain plank cuttings are generally soft and do not give the results we seek, especially in checking and oiling, but the better pieces of curly walnut are so satisfactory that they can be recommended for the finest stocks. And if imported walnut is wanted, reliable firms supply it at reasonable prices. One of these is Mitchell Bosly & Co., Ltd., Birmingham, England. There is no duty to pay on blanks.

As a lad I served as apprentice to woodworkers in a large furniture factory, and handled tons of the most beautiful walnut ever grown; and I regret that some of the pieces we threw into the factory furnace could not have been saved until now. Farmers made fence-rails from equally fine material, while the crotch lengths—wonderful stock material—were burned in fireplaces. Nice blanks of such walnut sell now for about the same prices as plain Circassian, say $10.00 to $20.00, and they are worth it.

California walnut—and similar material comes from other dry-land States—if it is grown from the nuts of the English walnut, is very good stock material. The blanks I have worked are lighter brown than Middle-state walnut, denser but not so heavy, and the ribbons are quite dark, almost black in some pieces, hence their resemblance to Circassian walnut. Whereas the ordinary factory rifle stock weighs more than 2½ pounds, this California wood may be brought down to nearly two pounds. By way of contrast, a full beavertail-cheekpiece target stock of Circassian in my shop weighs 2 pounds 13 ounces, and a curly domestic walnut stock, with oval forearm and Monte Carlo cheekpiece, weighs 3 pounds 11 ounces with buttplate.

In passing, it may be well to warn the young gunsmith that it is hopeless to try to reduce the weight of a completed stock by boring holes in the butt or cutting narrow mortises in the barrel channel. A three-quarter-inch hole four inches deep will remove just about one-half-ounce of wood, so it will be readily seen that very little more weight can be taken out by cutting a pocket in the butt, since the usual trap buttplate is heavier than a plain one, so in the end the matter of weight cannot be altered enough to warrant the labor involved. To offset this, however, the trap butt is a handy place to keep small articles needed in the field.

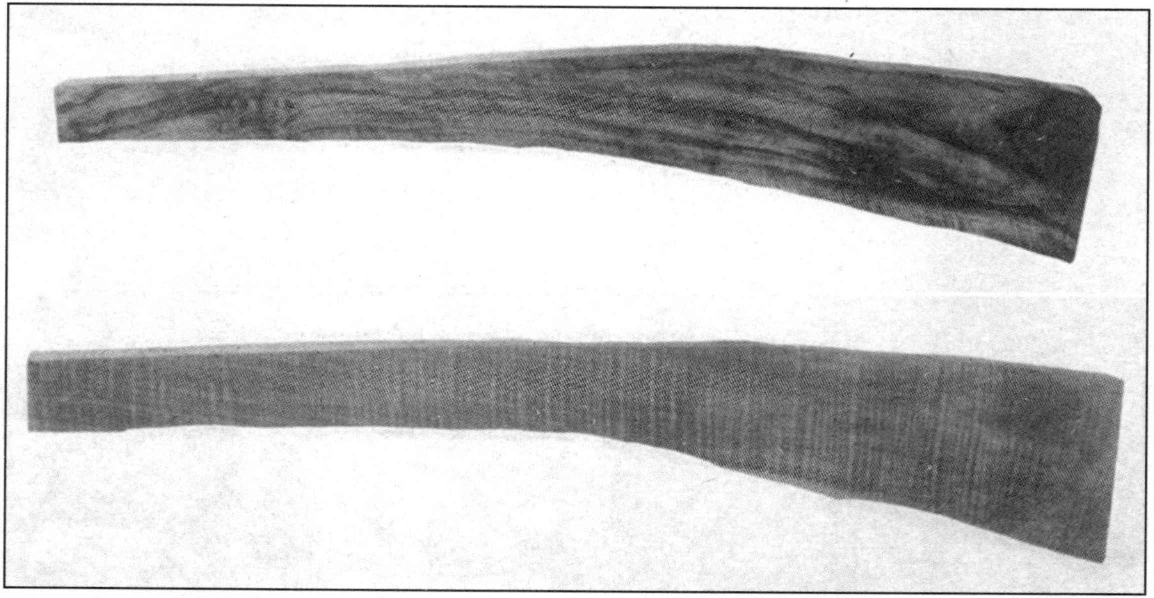

A pair of full-length rifle stock blanks, not inletted. Both are Circassian walnut and with excellent figure. The bottom blank shows the rare "fiddle-back" grain—a blank with such handsome figure may cost up to $50.00.

Does Hand Work Pay? Why go to all the trouble and care to make a stock from a solid blank when all the inletting and shaping may be done by machines? Just this: Machines have limitations. They cannot cut as closely in restricted places as a good workman can do with hand tools. They cut away some wood that the hand worker leaves intact. Sometimes it is necessary to reinforce these machine inletted blanks with cross-bolts, unsightly though they are.

These facts the young smith should keep in mind. In copying an old stock, he should not be slavishly guided by the cuts in it. It is better to make his own minimum measurements from point to point, and compare these with the pattern; try his cuts, and if they are adequate, let them stand.

In inletting a blank the receiver is stripped of all parts and it and the barrel bedded, then the parts are replaced as needed and cuts for the sear and trigger made. No wood is wasted; just enough is removed to let the parts function freely and to anticipate the effects of recoil on parts that taper and must be allowed for by removing just enough wood behind them.

Rifle stock blanks come in three-foot lengths six inches wide and a scant two inches thick. They are unfit for cheekpiece stocks and for full beavertail forearms. If you insist that a blank be 2⅝-inches thick—it must be for a real cheekpiece—you will probably get it a quarter-inch less. Trying to make a cheekpiece from a thin blank is a waste of time, for the best you can do is get a tracing of its outline, and the forearm will not be thick enough for a beavertail effect.

Accept no blank in which there is cross grain at the grip. If the grain runs across the forearm, upward, well and good; it will work out well, but never at the grip. A customer brought me two pieces of Circassian walnut that he had bought from a maker of "antique" furniture. One was a handsome piece, but for the other one the pattern had been placed in an opposite direction, to save waste, and the grain in it ran directly across the grip!

Inletting a Stock Blank.

Before our young gunsmith progresses very far, he will want to inlet and finish up a stock for the Springfield rifle, starting with a blank. This I would not advise. We teach boys to shoot with .22-calibre rifles first, then, after they have become accustomed to these light rifles, we let them have service rifles or hunting rifles of high power. And it is a good plan to start stocking the comparatively simple small-bore rifles before taking up high-power arms and their more intricate fitments and adjustments.

Start with a rifle like the new Model 416 Stevens, noted for its simplicity. And a black walnut blank 2½ inches thick from Indiana, let us assume. Look it over carefully and note that in the butt there are whorls running in all directions, but toward the grip these straighten out, then run quite straight toward the forearm tip. This is as a stock blank should be; it was cut by a man who knew his onions. Put it on your bench, left side up, and on top place the factory stock, on which you mean, if possible, to make such improvements as you have already decided on. This factory stock is 32 inches long, the blank about three feet, so there is space for shifting about until the lines suit you. Try other stocks on the blank, and when you have one that seems about right, adjust stock and blank so the top lines will coincide, then trace with a black pencil entirely around the selected stock, being sure the blank is wide enough for the grip, and long enough at the butt to admit of some shifting of length lines, as you come to them.

With square and pencil lay off a line across the blank at the tip, and saw across. Turn the blank up and plane the top surface until it is absolutely true and straight a distance of 19 inches—a shade further than the finished top line will be. With a sharp ripsaw cut just outside the lower forearm line another 19 inches, which will bring you almost to the place where the curve of the grip is to start. Use a narrow

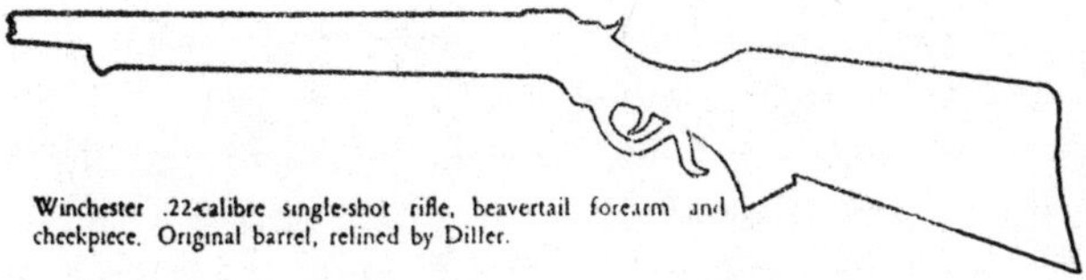

Winchester .22-calibre single-shot rifle, beavertail forearm and cheekpiece. Original barrel, relined by Diller.

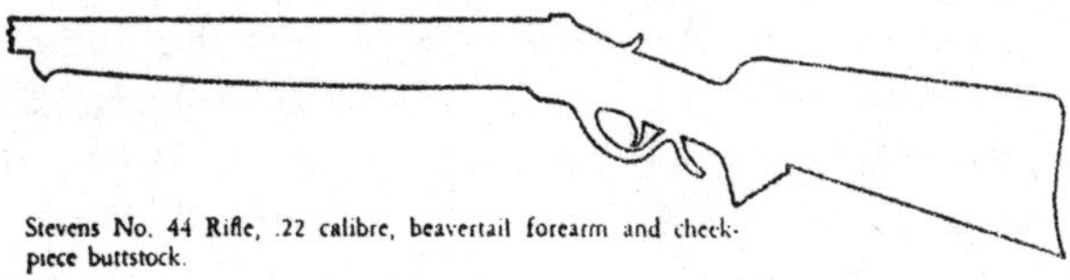

Stevens No. 44 Rifle, .22 calibre, beavertail forearm and cheekpiece buttstock.

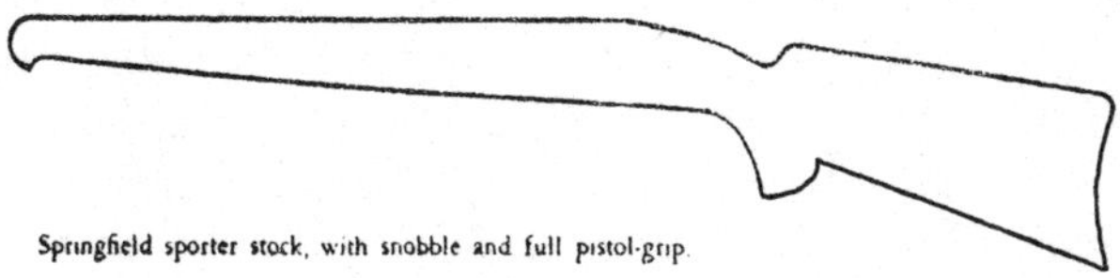

Springfield sporter stock, with snobble and full pistol-grip.

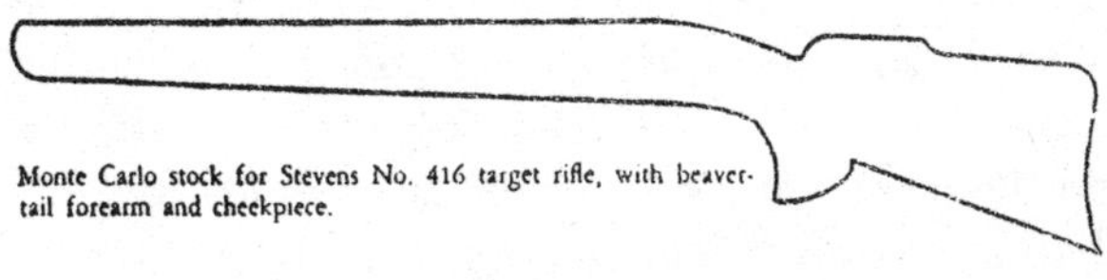

Monte Carlo stock for Stevens No. 416 target rifle, with beavertail forearm and cheekpiece.

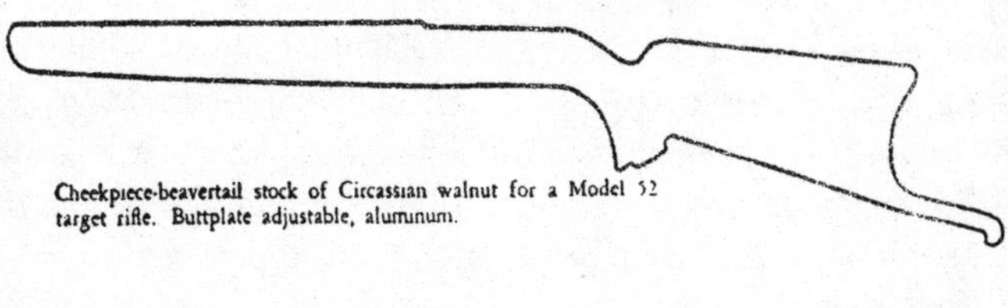

Cheekpiece-beavertail stock of Circassian walnut for a Model 52 target rifle. Buttplate adjustable, aluminum.

Reproduction of paper tracings of various popular rifle stocks. In many instances, it will pay the workman to make templates from these patterns for use in laying out the stock outlines on the blank.

keyhole saw to cut the curve up and out of the blank—the forward part of the pistol grip.

Make the next cut from the butt to the rear of the grip (M, Fig. 20). Saw off the bottom of the grip at an angle of 20 degrees from top line of blank (indicated by the broken line in the sketch).

As it is customary to keep the drop from sight line to comb as high as may be to let the bolt clear the comb, this makes the drop at heel about 2½ inches, so rip from heel to comb accordingly. In the stock before us the actual drop from top line of blank is ½-inch at comb and 1½ inches at heel. (The finished stock figures are 1½ and 2¾ inches below the line of sight.)

Nineteen inches from the square end of the forearm mark across the blank. Mark again four inches back to the point of the comb. Back again 10 inches for the tentative distance from comb to heel. Saw out the hollow for the grip. You now have a rough, generous outline of the stock from the side, but with surplus wood at the butt. (See L, Fig. 20.)

It is assumed that the right side of the blank is straight. Square it with the top line. With a scratch gauge set at ⅞-inch, run a line entirely around the blank, deep enough so you can see and refer to it as you work, right up to the time you finish rounding the stock before sanding. Set the gauge over to the 1¾-inch mark and scribe another line all around the blank—the greatest thickness guide. Just outside this line start ripping (M. in the sketch) and stop at the forward end of the cheekpiece, or just 21 inches from the end of the forearm. Rip on the same line from butt, about six inches, or to leave about six inches for length of cheekpiece, then saw across, leaving the blank like N. Plane all along the left side, except at the cheekpiece, to leave the thickness full 1¾ inches. This left side of the blank is not to be taken as anything more than a rough guide, as all measurements are to be made along the top and right side of the blank.

Eleven and one-half inches back of the fore-end tip scribe a mark across the top of the blank—the location for the forward end of the receiver. Go back 7⅝ inches and scribe another mark across the top; this space to be a snug fit for the receiver, when it is let into the blank. As the diameter of the receiver is $1\frac{3}{32}$-inch, draw parallel lines on the top of the blank a shade further apart than one inch, or each one a half-inch from the center line on the blank. From the mark locating the forward end of the receiver mortise run two lines forward to the fore-end tip, where the two lines should be a scant ⅞-inch apart—the barrel at that point being a shade thicker than ⅞-inch.

Make a cut the full length of the barrel-and-receiver mortise—19 inches—and work this out to two-thirds its finished width, or well within your pencil marks. Use a depth gauge, remembering that the rear end of the barrel is to be sunk just ½-inch and the front end ⅜-inch. The receiver depth is to be only $\frac{1}{16}$-inch greater, but unlike the barrel, it must not taper at all.

At this stage it will be easier for the beginner to strip all parts from the receiver assembly except the safety slide, if he has not already done this. Remove the bolt and slip the rear sight out of its seat by depressing its spring. Place all parts in a row on the bench, so they may be replaced readily. Back of the fore-end tip 13¼ inches bore a ½-inch hole, being very sure it is precisely in the center line of the blank. Back of this hole 1½ inches bore a second one the same diameter and connect them by routing out the separating wood with a ⅜-inch flat chisel and smooth the hole with rasp and file. This is the magazine mortise. Start the trigger mortise 3¾ inches further back, making it 1⅜ inches long and ¼-inch wide. It will be just ⅛-inch short of the rear end of the receiver mortise, which I prefer to cut out square at that end, although the factory stock is tapered out on to the grip—an easier but not a pleasing method.

In the receiver mortise cut away the wood between the two

holes just bored, depth full 1¼ inches, width ½-inch, the bottom parallel with the top line of the blank. Coat the under side of the barrel and receiver with lampblack and oil and lower them into the mortise as far as they will go—the safety slide and the rear-sight base interfering. Mark the location of the rear sight base carefully, then cut out a piece of the wood on that side to coincide, so you can lower the receiver further into its mortise. When part way down, tap along the top of the barrel and receiver with a chisel handle, remove the parts and pare away gingerly the places in barrel channel and receiver mortise that show heavy blacking.

At this stage the barrel and receiver should rest in their cuts about half way down, both exactly centered on the blank. If you have an old barrel or piece of tubing, slide it along the channels as a guide in keeping cuts round and even. Work down with a flat chisel, reducing the sides of the cut a little at a time, trying the parts frequently, keeping in mind all the time that the top edges of the channel must hug the barrel when both are fully bedded. The safety slide will stop this until a shaving is taken off the right side, to permit it to function, and the sight-base cut must be deepened gradually until the base will go clear down on the wood; then file away a trifle, so it will all but touch bottom. The parts should now rest in their mortise, with no rocking fore and aft, and the forearm should touch the under side of the barrel for an inch.

In the center of the square cut at the rear end of the receiver mortise, with a rattail file cut a tiny channel for the head of the striker, to be fitted later. Saw out a portion of the right side of the receiver mortise and round the cut, to let the shoulder of the bolt function smoothly. Black the shoulder and try it in its seat; if it is not quite free the safety will not function. This you can determine by trying the bolt several times.

Now replace all the receiver assembly parts. If the long cut in the center of the receiver mortise is just deep enough to permit the parts to clear, you can spot the location for the hole to be bored for the main receiver screw by turning up a hardwood plug, pointed at one end, and slipping it into the screw bushing. Tap the barrel over it to make an impression. Bore a ¼-inch hole for this screw, and try it before going further.

Now for the lower side of the blank. With your outside caliper measure the thickness (depth) of the blank at several points, using the factory stock as a guide. Plane off the surplus, tapering gradually from the forward under side of pistol grip to tip of forearm. At that point the total depth should be 1⅛ inches. Square all surfaces neatly. It will be noted at this stage that the trigger guard is merely a strip of metal laid flush on the under side of the stock and secured with three screws and the receiver-ring machine screw; and that there is no trigger-plate, so the trigger wabbles about as you test it with your finger. To remedy this, select a piece of flat steel four inches long and ⅝-inch wide, round one end and bore a hole the same size as the rear hole in the guard, under which it must lie later on. Bore a hole further forward to coincide with the middle wood screw through the guard. For the trigger bore two holes and connect them, using first a needle knife-file, then a hacksaw blade, filing the edges smooth. This trigger-cut should be 1⅜ inches long and just wide enough for the trigger to slide freely.

With the guard in place on the blank, scribe all around it with a sharp pencil, then cut out a bed for it $\frac{1}{16}$-inch deep. Remove the guard and fit in the trigger-plate after bending it so the middle portion—inside the guard, will be flush with the surface of the blank when the screws are all down. Make this bend in the vise, using a flat piece of metal alongside the plate on one side, and a piece at each end on the other side, then close the vise-jaws until the plate is bent up slightly one-third its length on one side, with the ends depressed slightly for the other side. (See G, Fig. 15). The forward end of this trigger-plate is purposely left long, in case one wishes to use a palm-rest with the rifle—which weighs more than ten pounds in its heavy native walnut stock, and is therefore nicely adapted for offhand, palm-rest shooting.

A palm-rest similar to 3, Fig. 18, may be used on this Stevens rifle merely by boring a hole through the guard and trigger-plate and threading it with a ¼-20 tap. It may then be used in this rifle without the magazine dummy fitted to it for the Model 52 magazine slot. There is a wood screw in the Stevens guard just forward of the guard-loop, and the hole for the palm-rest may be bored an inch further forward, with the support of nearly ¼-inch of metal, so it will be amply rigid.

While we are about it, let us look at the Stevens trigger. As it comes this trigger wabbles sidewise and has an unpleasant backlash of ½-inch. We have already stopped the side play by inserting a plate. Now bore a hole in the guard just back of the trigger and thread it with a ⅛-40 tap. Taper a piece of drillrod, fit a tiny bakelite head on it, thread it and turn it into the guard from the outside. It should project just ¼-inch inside the guard. When the trigger is pressed, it will move ⅛-inch and stop against the screw point. In this way you can, in a few minutes, transform an ugly trigger-pull into one that is short and crisp.

An adjusting screw is integral with this action, lying just behind the trigger. Try the pull, using the sandbag weights mentioned in Chapter V. If the trigger will barely support three pounds, well and good; but if it will lift more, adjust the screw so it will pull just three pounds. It should be added here that the trigger-stop-screw just mentioned must be turned out to the guard for the removal of the bolt, since, in releasing the bolt the trigger must be depressed to the guard.

Now look over the work done so far. In Fig. 14 the reference letter M shows the factory stock after some refinement of lines, the addition of a cap to the grip and undercutting of the comb on both sides—making a much trimmer stock. Checking is to follow. At L will be seen the inletted blank we have been working on. It is still square, though the cheekpiece lump has been rounded a bit and the top line rasped, ready for rounding. The next step is to measure from the center of the trigger to the middle of the butt 13½ inches back, try the rifle on the guide sheet (1, Fig. 10), scribe a line across the butt that will give a pitch of about three inches, then saw off the butt and fit the plate. The method has been described in Chapter XIII.

If a customer has decided ideas about cast-off or cast-on, now is the time to decide this matter. Usually a buttplate is set on the center line of the blank. If cast-off is wanted, the plate is set ¼-inch or more to the right of the center line; or the toe may be set over and the heel left on the line. It depends on the way a rifle is held by the man who owns it, the contours of his face and jaw with relation to the fit of the cheekpiece. If in doubt, do not put the plate on just yet but fix it with a thick piece of leather and brads and ask him to try it with the pad set first one way, then the other. Cast-on, of course, means setting the plate or its heel to the left of the center line of the stock. The letter Q, Fig. 14, shows a Springfield-Niedner heavy-barrel .30 '06 rifle with a Minarick pattern aluminum adjustable buttplate. Figs. 13 and 14 show several checked steel shotgun buttplates such as we will fit on our sample stock. The shape of the cheek-piece contemplated will be seen at P, Fig. 24. The forward end of the cheekpiece curves forward from the point of comb, then downward, its surface being almost straight fore and aft but concaved slightly toward its lower edge. An exception is the stock K, Fig. 14, made from a three-inch blank and with a slightly concaved surface. In all these examples the common tendency to make the cheekpiece saucer-shaped has been avoided. In that form rifles with heavy recoil punish one unduly, and there is a tendency to throw one's aim off the object fired at. The stock R, Fig. 14, was made for a speedlock Model 52 rifle. The mortise for the housing of that lock differs markedly from that of older models of that rifle.

The letter S, Fig. 14, shows one form of snobble and the checking is similar to the patterns suggested for work of that sort in Figs. 23 and 24.

The next step in our work is to fit a cap on the pistol-grip. Normally the forward edge of the cap should be not more than 3½ inches from the forward center of the trigger. From top line of blank to point of grip our stock measures 4$\frac{3}{16}$-inches, but from rear end of receiver to comb the distance is full three inches, whereas in other models it is quite a bit less from comb to tang—but in this model there is no tang, the rear end of the receiver ending abruptly—we set it down in the grip in a right-angle cut, it will be remembered.

The grip cap should be rather long and narrow as opposed to so many nearly round grips one sees on shotguns and some rifles. Make it two inches long and not to exceed 1⅝-inches in width. And as we are "dolling up" this stock a bit, set under it a bit of copper or aluminum about $\frac{1}{32}$-inch thick; it adds to the neat appearance of the work.

We have already discussed tips for forearms, but as the cross-section decided on for this stock's forearm is neither U-shaped—hunting-rifle style—nor beavertail, the end will look rather stubby if a tip is put on; so instead we will set in on each side just back of the end a bit of black bakelite shaped like an arrow head or just half of a long diamond. Make the rear vertical end a half-inch, the two other sides one inch. Cut into the wood $\frac{3}{16}$-inch, bevel the piece of bakelite slightly, making a tight fit, then set it down with thick shellac, fit the other piece, then clamp both until next day.

This will remind you that a base for the screw-eye or swivel is to be set in the buttstock about four inches above the plate. Cut a bakelite diamond 2¼ inches long and ⅝-inch wide, bevel it, cut out a mortise for it, set it with shellac and clamp it. Bore a ¼-inch hole in its center, and when the cement is dry, file and sandpaper these three insets down flush with the wood.

From what I have said about bakelite, you will infer that

I favor it for ornaments. I do, for the reason that it finishes up nicely, does not change color like hard rubber, nor split like horn, and it is so near the color of blued steel that it harmonizes well with the steel parts of a rifle.

Turn the blank bottom-side up. One and one-half inches from the end scribe a line across it, and another line four inches further back. From a piece of flat steel $\frac{3}{16}$-inch thick and 4 inches long cut out a piece ⅝-inch wide, round the ends neatly and bore a $\frac{13}{64}$-inch hole close to each end, countersinking both. Bore three other holes and thread them for a swivel-stud, say with a ¼-32 tap. Lay this plate on the blank between the lines already scribed, mark around it, then cut away the wood inside the marks and let the plate into the blank. At the rear end cut a hole for a wood-screw and turn it down. For the screw-hole at the other end we must prepare in a different way.

When you looked this Stevens rifle over for the first time, you were probably horrified to find that a machine screw secured the forearm to the barrel. And you threw this screw into the junkbox *pronto* and filled the shallow hole in the barrel with a dummy, then removed the high front sight, slipped a barrel-band over the muzzle and back to a point just over the dummied screwhole, fitted a short machine-screw into the lug in the band, relieved small sections of wood at the edge of the barrel-channel to let the band down, and counterbored the screw-hole in the channel, then turned the machine-screw up fairly tight.

This thing works out beautifully—I have referred to it before—leaving the barrel snug in its channel but with a husky bolt and band holding it, to prevent accidental splitting of the forearm should one happen to drop the rifle or fall with it; this fastening supplemented by the receiver screw, a foot further back. And the three threaded holes in the swivel-plate permit you to shift the position of the forearm swivel 2½ inches forward or backward. This is all one will ever need in four-position shooting, and it does away with a whole flock of holes in a long plate—nine, for example, in the factory stock. The pull on the swivel from a tight sling-strap is communicated, not to the barrel-band direct, but this strain is absorbed by the four-inch plate, and by the stiffened forearm. The barrel-band is just tight enough to fit snugly around the barrel—an ideal arrangement, in my opinion.

This blank we have been working on was shaped up so that a Monte Carlo cheekpiece could be worked out, or removed, as might be decided, later on. I like to take a newly restocked rifle to the range and shoot it awhile, then rasp a bit here and there, trying it for fit, rasping, shooting, with the result that toward the end of the day the stock seems to fit perfectly; but if not, the cheekpiece may be altered at any time without touching the other surfaces of the stock, for it is a separate unit.

Rounding the Blank. Remove the metal parts, set the blank in your padded vise and start cutting corners. For this a short drawknife may be used at first, then a small plane, followed by a spokeshave and a half-round rasp. Make a pattern for the cheekpiece (P, Fig. 24) and rasp around the edges until it is roughly shaped, then cut the block down on a long bevel until its top extends a quarter or a half inch to the right of the center line. Rasp across the right side of the butt with long diagonal strokes, first one way, then the other. With a bit of practice you will be astonished to see how smooth the result is. With a half-round gouge undercut the comb, cut from the under side of the grip up toward the top of grip, around under the grip, rasp around the heel and the toe, then turn the blank over and work under the cheekpiece, alongside and up across the grip, and continue this rounding until the wood is almost down to the buttplate. The buttplate. remember, must be your guide for form, and by sighting along one side, then the other, making cuts on both sides uniform with the center line, you will progress famously. If the plane is used, cut against the grain on the butt, as otherwise you will dig in and leave holes you cannot work out. The rasp

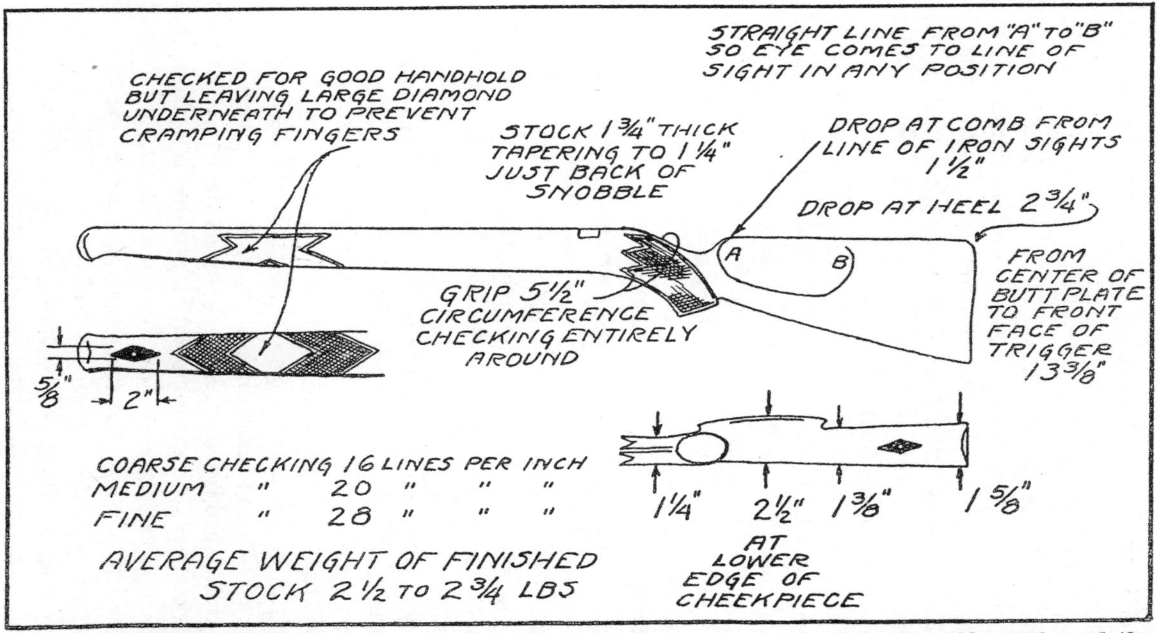

Pattern intended to assist the beginner in laying out the form and dimensions of a rifle stock, and the principal points where careful measurements should be made as the work progresses. After stock is completed, all such patterns should have complete dimensions and other pertinent data written down and then be laid away for possible future reference.

is the thing for awhile here, but reduce pressure on it until it cuts quite smoothly.

Rasp until the wood is nearly down to the buttplate, then follow with a 12-inch double-cut file and continue cutting all around the butt until the file removes a bit of metal at every stroke. Cut away on both sides until the thickness of the stock just behind the cheekpiece is a little less than plate width—remembering that after the stock is finished all metal parts are to be polished and blued.

If the grip is to be finished with a flared edge, rasp and file it until its width at the cap is 1⅝ inches, at its center 1⅜ inches, and the circumference 5 or 5¼ inches, depending on the length of your fingers. This is to be a target, not a hunting stock, remember, hence it can be a trifle full.

Reverse the blank and shave off the corners from the grip forward, then round them gradually with the spokeshave. Keep in mind the form of the cross-section of a cruising canoe, and imitate it. From the keel the lines of a canoe slope upward slightly to the smooth round bilges, then they "tumble home;" that is, describe a sharper curve to the gunwale lines—in your case to the barrel channel. Beavertail forearm curves are merely an exaggerated form of the canoe cross section. Formerly target stocks were often finished up with hard shoulders instead of rounded ones; then came the beavertail craze and its exaggerations, followed by the semi-beavertail, and even these are often made with hard curves. These rifles are shot with the left hand and forearm insulated from body tremors with a thick mitt extending half-way to the elbow, with a soft rubber pad behind the upper arm on the strap, and with a thick sheepskin pad riding the loop of the strap, so there is no need to grasp the forearm. Instead it lies free in the palm of the left hand, and if the shooter cants the rifle after all these precautions, it is just too bad.

Wetting, sanding, and preparing the stock for waxing or oiling were covered in the last chapter, as were also the operations of checking and finishing.

Waterproofing Stocks.

Just what to use in waterproofing stocks depends on the variety of walnut to be treated. For the soft domestic walnut, which will soak up linseed oil until the cows come home, some filler is indicated. I have used so much tung nut oil in various ways during the past twenty-five years that I have great faith in it and some of the wood finishing mixtures of which it is the base. As it comes this oil is quite thin and colorless. It will jell when very cold, and it will also thicken greatly when heated toward the boiling point. Unlike linseed oil, which of itself never really dries, tung nut or chinawood oil, as it is called, if spread on a sheet of glass will dry hard over night. It then resembles the substance called ground-glass substitute—a frosty-like rough surface. Used raw on walnut, after several coats tung oil gives a whitish surface, so it is not good for use until it has been mixed with gums that will help set up a smooth, colorless gloss.

This brings us to spar varnish, in which tung oil is used, and to waxes for fine furniture and hardwood floors. One of these that is made up from tung oil is Minwax, made by the Minwax Company, at Delawanna, N. J. There is a wood stain that is used first, then waxing follows, and the result is a dull, smooth surface that wears well but may be touched up at any time by rubbing with the wax on a wool cloth. Hot water, grease, common fruit acids and similar things do not affect this finish. If a soft walnut stock be warmed until it is uncomfortable to hold, then rubbed with warmed Minwax, the wood will absorb the now fluid wax as readily as it would linseed oil; then, after it is left awhile, the stock may be rubbed thoroughly with felt and pumice flour, and the surface will be smooth but not glossy. At first rain water, if left on the surface until dry, will discolor the wood slightly but may be rubbed away with a cloth. After waxing a few times this fault does not recur. I am not positive that this Minwax finish is the best one for all sorts of stocks that are dark in color, but for porous walnut it is at once a filler and a finish.

Rub it down with pumice and crude oil on a strip of rough duck and the surface is matte but beautifully smooth, while every trace of grain contrast stands out clearly. Whereas linseed alone, or linseed and spar varnish, darkens the wood and breaks your heart at the same time, the wax improves contrasts and adds only a shade to the dark color. Repeat waxing to your heart's content; a good wax body furnishes a splendid ground for the hardest sort of rubbing, and a stock, waxed and rubbed a few minutes monthly, will always look like new.

Dense walnuts do not lend themselves to this treatment. Their color is too light, darkening improves their appearance, hence linseed is indicated for nearly all imported stocks and California walnut. When the wood is smooth enough, soak it with all the boiled linseed and turpentine (half and half, with a little spar varnish added, if you are seeking waterproofing first and appearance afterward) the wood will absorb. Give it four or five liberal coats the first day, let these soak in and dry for a few days, rub across the grain with pumice and crude oil until bone dry, then every other day for a fortnight moisten the surface with oil on a cloth. When dry rub down each time and call it quits; very little more can be done, as the wood will not absorb more oil for a long time.

We are outgrowing the old prejudice against varnish for stocks. And we are forgetting that other ancient pipe dream about kettle-boiled linseed oil. I still have a bottle of this stuff that I picked up before the World War. It is so dark that no one would think of putting it on a nice stock. After all, spar varnish is merely another name for what was called hard-oil finish a generation ago. Gold size, copal gum and linseed oil mixed were commonly used. All such mixtures are best when warmed until the rosin content is rendered more fluid than when cold. Flowed on warmed wood, such substances penetrate nicely and dry rapidly without gumming. Linseed thinned with turpentine, with the trace of rosin supplied in the small portion of spar varnish used, dries with a hard gloss which of itself is objectionable. Rub this gloss down and you have a hard waterproof surface that is flexible enough to absorb hard knocks without discoloring. Elbow grease is the main ingredient. Do not expect to improve by rubbing a stock that is fuzzy; it cannot be done. The secret of a fine finish is in the amount of wetting and sanding given the wood before oiling. Wood that is rubbed when dry until it has a sheen like a polished bone will require much less rubbing after oiling.

And if you must use linseed on dark wood, use clear filler first.

At this stage blue all fittings and replace them on the finished stock. It is ready for use.

Scratches and dents in walnut. Walnut stocks that have been damaged in a fall or otherwise may be repaired in various ways. A dent can usually be treated by covering the place with a drop of water, then by holding just over it a piece of hot metal until the water turns to steam and disappears. When dry, rub the place with old crocus cloth, then rub in with the finger a little wax, linseed or spar varnish, and when this is dry, rub with an oily cloth.

Gouges must be filled. Plastic wood will serve, but the clear substance is too light in color, so it is usually best to fill the place with walnut dust and DuPont cement applied with a knife blade and packed smoothly, then rubbed down when hard.

Springfield sporter stocks usually have a mortise for the huge service swivel base. This is usually filled when a stock-eye or ordinary screw swivel is put on. The old mortise may be filled with ebony plastic, rubbed smooth, then a hole bored for the swivel stud. This long oval is not neat, however, so it may be cut out to diamond shape and an inset of bakelite used. This applies, too, to forearms in which a long swivel base with two screws was put in.

Insets of metal—oval, shield or diamond shape—may be set in with ebony plastic. For this a blob of solder, if put on the back, will give the plastic a good grip on the smooth metal.

Restoring the finish on a much-worn stock depends on what was originally put on it. Varnish can be sanded off, or scraped with thin glass then smoothed with fine sandpaper and pumice until no scratches show, and surfaced with spar varnish, or boiled oil with a little spar added, followed by rubbing when dry with crude oil and pumice on a piece of coarse duck. Stocks that were oiled originally may be rubbed with crude oil and pumice, scratches scraped out with glass, then sanded, with two or three coats of linseed, rubbed dull. Gummed checking should be cleaned with a three-square needle file, then given a coat of oil on an old toothbrush and this oil rubbed out as it dries. Quite nice repair work may be done with clear Duco, especially when only a small area is to be treated. When a new buttplate is put on a stock and the wood next to it reduced to fit, restoring the color of the wood affected should be done gradually with a piece of wool and a little oil or lacquer, then, when the new work matches the old in color, go over the butt with oil and pumice. When linseed is used, set the stock in a sunny place and turn it frequently. Sunlight darkens the oil. For jobs of this sort use a little dryer with the oil.

To polish wood, according to Haswell, rub the surface with pumicestone and water until the raising of the grain is removed, then, with powdered tripoli and boiled linseed oil, polish to a bright surface.

Future Gunstock Material. Apparently there is only one way in which the stocker of the future will be able to obtain good material, and that is to find something that will take the place of good walnut. Eventually there may be a limited supply from trees now growing, and that means trees from climates like that of California, where everything grows rapidly. Walnut as we know it now cannot be grown to order for the near future; and after it has been grown and cut, the wood should be seasoned slowly for a long time. For target stocks, which do not need to be so strong as those used on hunting rifles, there is black cherry, curly maple, tropical mahogany and its softer cousin, baywood or bay mahogany, all good, but most of it rather too straight-grained for nice stocks. For strength we have hard maple, used for many years before walnut came into general use. It is plentiful and costs much less than walnut. Its light color calls for staining, until customers get used to lighter colors in stocks. It is heavy but very dense, hence it takes checking nicely, and staining is not difficult. A customer has a pair of old Kentuckies, one flintlock, the other altered to percussion. Apparently one stock had been broken and a new one made. One stock is beautiful fiddleback maple, the other one a good match, when viewed from a distance of five feet. I took that stock off, and found it was made from a piece of straight-grain birch, but it had nice markings, and these were made with pieces of bent wire, heated and held close to the wood to scorch it in a pattern closely resembling cross grain. It is possible to do this with a torch and a piece of metal cut out to produce odd curlecues—a sort of stencil, in fact.

Laminated wood is used so much now that it is probable it will be material for stocks before very long. There is no reason why it should not be. Modern glues are so efficient that pieces of wood put together with it will withstand anything short of soaking in hot water. Take, for example, the glued strips of Tonkin cane used in fly and bait rods. If anything must withstand more stresses and strains than a fishing rod, I am not familiar with it.

Let us indulge in a pipe dream about the possibilities of laminated wood stocks. You know how ship models are often built up—I have done this sort of work on canoe models. First there is a piece for the bottom, cut to pattern, with a portion of the inside hollowed slightly. Glue to it another piece previously sawed out, to save work with a gouge; then another layer cut out still more—and you have the inside of the hull. Shaping the outside is simple. Following this notion, take a paper pattern of a stock and make a tracing on a piece of walnut seven-eighths of an inch thick. Saw around the tracing. Saw off the top half-inch from tip to tang, representing the barrel-channel. On each side glue a strip the full size of the pattern. When dried under strong clamps, you will have a piece of material all cut out for your stock (profile, side view), the barrel channel straight and true but still square, ready for rounding and deepening. The thickness will be 2⅝ inches, plenty thick for a cheekpiece-beavertail stock. And one-third of the work of making a stock will be saved. Use curly walnut for the outside pieces, plain stuff for the center piece. Viewed from above, there will be two joints visible along the tang and back to the butt. Underneath the joints will show more plainly, but the underside of a stock is not seen enough to be objectionable. The three-piece stock will be stronger than a solid blank. And as for appearances, one soon gets used to such things, so possibly it may become the vogue to have stocks made from four or five layers of woods of different varieties and colors.

Scraps of walnut or other woods might be used, to give greater contrast. Think of the saving of good walnut!

If stocks are ever made from three pieces of wood, as suggested here, it would be a very simple thing to cut out a portion of the central strip at the rear end and shape it for a pocket over which the buttplate might be set on at the proper time. Trap butts are handier than one would think until after he had made use of one for awhile, in hunting. In one there should be kept an oily rag, a metal tube of oil, a short but stiff screwdriver, and even a few cartridges, if you like.

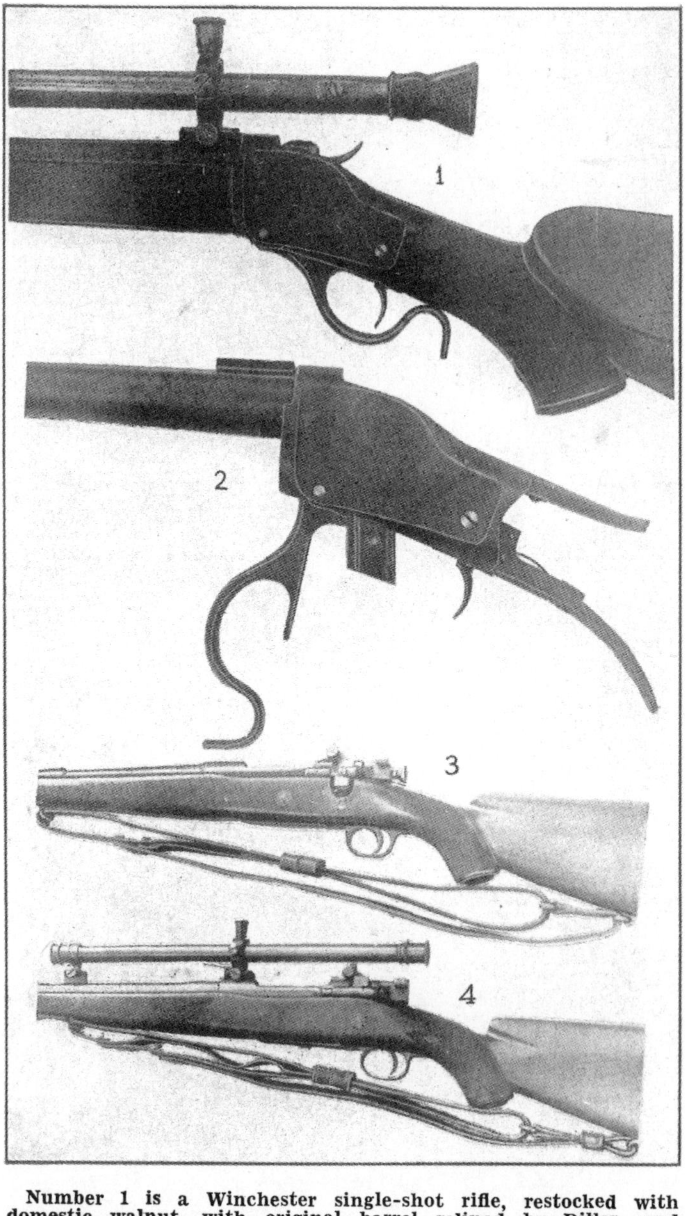

Number 1 is a Winchester single-shot rifle, restocked with domestic walnut, with original barrel relined by Diller, and with Malcolm scope. 2, the receiver of this rifle, with both tangs bent for better shaped pistol-grip, and finger-lever shortened. 3, a .30 '06 Springfield sporter, with stock re-shaped; and 4, a Springfield .22-caliber rifle, refinished to match 3.

CHAPTER FIFTEEN

"WARMED-OVER" RIFLE WORK

There is one line of work the young smith can prepare for as he gains experience and can afford machine tools of the simpler sort. This is making up rifles from parts of proved merit. Although the manufacture of the Ballard rifle was discontinued longer ago than most of you can remember, the splendid receivers of those old rifles may still be picked up now and then. The Sharps receivers, last made about 1878, may also be had by trading or purchase occasionally, and the equally good Winchester single-shot receivers, rifle and musket, are still supplied by the manufacturers, although the rifles of that pattern are no longer made, more's the pity. Try to collect some of these receivers, refinish them, send them to the makers to have barrels fitted, restock them, and sell them to customers who want a rifle of superb accuracy, even though it is old-fashioned in appearance and mechanism.

I do not write this because I am an old fogy and believe the old rifles were superior to the modern ones. Proof of this is found in the fact that whenever a new model bolt-action rifle is put out, I go hungry, almost, to save up enough money to buy one. But I know scores of men who cannot afford the extra-fancy prices asked for these new beauties, and they are glad to get a rifle of an old model, provided it will shoot accurately. They want good barrels, of course, but a sweet, crisp trigger-pull appeals to them almost as much.

Of the receivers available from manufacturers now the Winchester single-shot is one of the best. You can buy it for about $15.00, new and complete, in three patterns, heavy, medium, and light, and the skeleton pattern called the musket. It comes with lower tang for straight grip, but a pistol-grip lower tang is optional. Stevens receivers, are furnished in several weights, the old 44½ being a favorite for rebarrelling fine target rifles.

To make up a rifle on order for target shooting, it is best to have fitted to the new receiver one of the regular musket barrels, which is the same, outside, as the more modern Model 52; or a still heavier barrel, if that is specified in the order. If the work of a private maker is preferred—Niedner, Eric Johnson, Pope, Sedgely, Peterson—send the receiver to one of them for fitting and chambering the barrel, then restock it, put on scope-blocks and sights, and sell it at a profit for much less than one of the fancy bolt-action rifles would cost. Keep in mind all the time that, some day, you will be equipped to do this work yourself, in which case all you will need to buy is the barrel-blank and the jewelry. Thread-cutting means owning or having access to a good lathe, chambering reamers cost a lot, but only a few will be needed, anyway, and the expense of getting tooled up may well be taken care of through the sale of a few rifles, leaving you equipped to take care of similar orders right along.

Receivers bought cheaply, or traded for, usually need cleaning, polishing and blueing, the lower tang bent to fit a pistol-grip or a new tang purchased. The Winchester lower tang may be bent quite a lot, the upper tang cut off, to allow for a comb further forward, and new screwholes cut. If a straight tang is to be bent, remove and strip it, then plug the screwhole midway, heat and bend to the desired curve. The finger-lever is often reshaped, too. Do not try to bend these parts cold. The old Stevens receivers require different treatment. The lever may be successfully bent, if heated red hot and treated gingerly, but do not attempt to bend the lower tang.

Instead, set in a piece of mild steel just back of the body of the receiver, by welding or brazing, bend to form, then saw off the old lower tang just back of the mainspring stud, blue and send to the factory to have a barrel fitted. Some of these old-timers come out real cocky after being warmed over, and they are fine for .22-calibre use, though it may be wiser not to expect them to stand the hammering of some of the high-power .22's. The Winchester and the Sharps receivers, however, are strong enough for almost any cartridge, but in the case of the former, it is safest to have the old firing-pin bushed and a new one of closer fit substituted.

Almost any one of these mechanisms is ideally suited to target work. They are simpler than bolt-action mechanisms, plain, single- or double-set triggers are to be had, and the pull can be made as light as may be safe, by honing. The best bet is the action which leaves the hammer at halfcock when the block is closed—this being the only safety-lock inherent in these mechanisms.

Another advantage in a rifle of this sort is the smaller quantity of walnut needed for buttstock and forearm. In the yards forearms are cut from waste stuff, and the buttstocks cost less than half the prices of bolt-action stocks. For example, Oregon myrtle full-length stocks cost ten dollars and up, but for a two-piece stock you can lop off a third and still have nice material. I have worked up very nice pieces of domestic walnut for Stevens 44 and Winchester single-shot stocks that cost less than $3.00. One of the important items inherent in restocking these one-shooters is to have the parts fitted solidly, so that the finished rifle will be just as stiff as any bolt-action rifle. Another thing is that, with a mere shell of walnut for a forearm, atmospheric influences will have no effect on group-centering. Hot sun and rain will not affect the rifle, since there will be no stiff stock to work against the natural vibrations of a light, or any, barrel.

Of the three receivers mentioned, the Ballard is one of the sweetest, though they are very scarce. But the shape of the receiver is not nice. It is so long that it is difficult to work into it a stock with comb and grip as close up as in bolt-action rifles. Offsetting this is the better position of the rear sight—one of the old-time folding tang sights set close to the eye, where a sight should be put, and with a sighting-disc an inch or more in diameter—the whole thing foldable when a scope sight is being used. Either a plain or a wind-gauge tang sight may be used, and the cost of one of these is less than half that of receiver sights. By making the forearm fairly long, and by setting into it a plate with several holes for shifting the position of the front swivel, this jigger will have "everything." Instead of a screw and lug to secure the forearm, use a band forward, the rear end being secured to the receiver.

Fancy and special barrels by private makers will cost $30.00 or $35.00, especially the very heavy ones some target shooters insist on—one of these, made for the Springfield, being 28 inches long and with a diameter throughout of about 1¼ inches. Factory prices are a bit less, but the standard Winchester .22 musket barrel costs $15.00. Savage and Stevens barrels, both accurate, cost somewhat less.

For a hunting rifle the net cost of warming over an outfit may be cut down. For example, unless I am misinformed, the Winchester Company will put into a receiver any one of its barrels at reasonable cost. One of these I like because its accuracy is excellent is the Model 60A Target barrel, tapered, 27 inches long, and made for the .22 long-rifle cartridge, list price $3.50, chambering and fitting about $4.00. Other light barrels are the Model 57, 22 inches long, the Model 63, 23 (20 inches optional) inches; the Model 69, 25 inches, $6.00.

REFINISHING OLD RIFLES

It would be interesting to know how many discarded rifles are lying in closets, attics and barns—discarded merely because they *are* of an older type than other rifles of a more modern pattern—really more stylish. Prices of rifles and ammunition have advanced so much in recent years that it is not a bad idea to look up some of those old-timers, and see if a bit of work expended on them will not be worth while. This is being done right along, as witness the fact that parts for the old-timers are sold or swapped every day, to appear later on with new barrels, fancy sights, and all the fixings really needed on a good target rifle.

Take, for example, one of the single-shot Winchesters. There are lots of these to be had—and of all the single-shots, this is one that may be refitted easily, as all parts are still made. The receiver may be rusty, the barrel ruined. Good. Unscrew the barrel and junk it (or have it relined). Take the receiver apart and go to work on it with emery and crocus cloth until all surfaces are smooth and glossy. Stone all parts, angles, curves, remove all rough edges, scrape and polish the springs, smooth up the hammer, trigger, sear, and if the extractor is rough, order a new one and fit it. It will not pay to use old parts that are badly worn, when, for small sums, new parts may be installed instead. When all working parts have been cleaned as bright as a new dollar, blue them, then send the receiver to the factory and have a new barrel put in. This will cost much less than you would expect, and when the outfit comes back to you and you make a new buttstock and forearm for it and put on your favorite sights and scope-blocks, you will have a good outfit that will cost very much less than one of the more fancy bolt-actions.

If the rifle is .22 calibre, and it is to be shot at target indoors, just why must it be a bolt-action, when you do not use the magazine at all? Simply this: Bolt-action rifles are stylish, just now, so, sheep-like, we must have them. On the outdoor ranges the magazine rifle is the thing, of course, for some matches are shot rapid fire, and there are running-deer matches, too, so we will consider here the individual who favors the smallbore rifle, and it lends itself beautifully to reshaping, refitting, and all sorts of changes—all at very moderate cost. There are several patterns of receivers. The lighter ones are better adapted to use with new .22-calibre barrels than the heavier high-wall actions which were originally made for barrels from .32-40 to .38-55 and .40-calibre, but for the .22 long-rifle cartridge it is perfectly safe to saw off or mill away a part of the right-side of these heavy receivers, as in this shape they are handier for loading but still amply strong.

Barrel cost is not so important as one might think. There are numbers of light barrels that may be fitted to these actions for just about what a relining job would cost, but for extra heavy or long target barrels, the cost will be higher, of course, Relining jobs cost nearly as much as new barrels, except that it does not cost any more to reline a heavy barrel, already in a receiver, than to do this work on a light barrel. This is true of the now obsolete Winchester musket, the barrels of many of which have been shot out or are rusted. Relining to .22 calibre is a simple improvement, since there is no rethreading to be done, and rechambering and finishing off the barrel at both ends is about all that is needed.

If a firing-pin is rough or has been battered by careless snapping, hone it carefully with a slipstone, or remove it and put in a new one. This will cost less than one dollar, and a few cents more will buy an extractor, so it is not economical to try to make old parts function when they are badly worn.

While very few Sharps-Borchardt receivers are to be picked up now, if you are lucky enough to buy one, hang on to it. Like the Ballard, this receiver is heavy, and has a long stock-screw, but for a target rifle, or for one of the popular high-speed .22-calibre cartridges, like the Lovell, it is a splendid receiver to start with in building up a special rifle. The better ones were made with the sides of the receiver milled out and fitted with panels of hard rubber or walnut matching the buttstock on the rifle it came with. The hunting rifle receiver was a plainer pattern, and, of course, a bit heavier. Some of these receivers have been equipped with double-set triggers, and of course no safety, as this device had been removed and the rear trigger of the set put in its place.

If you contemplate making up a rifle, using a Winchester single-shot receiver, and buy it from the factory, specify whether it is to be used with a rim-fire or center-fire barrel. If for .22 long-rifle, a receiver for that cartridge will be furnished, so there need be no altering of the firing-pin. The factory will alter a used receiver from central to rim-fire, of course, but for high-speed center-fire cartridges it is better to start with a center-fire block in the beginning. While breechblocks are often bushed and altered from rim- to center-fire, I for one would prefer not to use high-speed ammunition in such a receiver, if it be possible to start with a solid block in the first place.

If one of the old-time high-wall Winchester single-shot receivers is used in making up a rifle with a .22 long-rifle barrel, it is customary to saw off the right-hand side of the receiver, as it is very awkward to insert a .22 long-rifle cartridge in the chamber of a receiver made for longer center-fire cartridges. This cutting can be done with a hacksaw, and the receiver will be amply strong, but a workmenlike job can be done with just a little more labor by grinding or filing the top of the receiver just back of the chamber. The abrupt shoulder can be rounded quite a bit without altering the neat lines, and when the part has been blued, only an expert will notice the change in form. But after reducing the height of the receiver, all sharp edges should be rounded neatly with a small needle file; then, in inserting one of the small cartridges in the chamber, usually in the dark at indoor-range firing-points, one's fingers will not feel like thumbs.

I may be mistaken, but signs point toward single shots just now instead of bolt-action rifles for target shooting indoors. One reason—and possibly the main one—is that any young gunsmith can build up a nice single-shot rifle for about half the cost of the newer model bolt-action rifles; and as I have said before, in some ways the single-shot is more efficient, certainly more simple, for nearly all clubs prohibit magazine loading indoors, anyway. For such rifles as these the Winchester single-shot receiver is one of the best bets, since new receivers and parts for old ones may be ordered by mail and installed by our young gunsmiths.

There is one thing about these two-piece single-shot rifle stocks that it will be well to consider: The inletting and shaping look simple, compared with this work on a bolt-action outfit. This is true in a way, but still there is quite a bit of real fussy work work involved. The main thing is to get the buttstock bedded so solidly that when the screws are turned down finally, there must be no wabble whatever, for this is a job that cries out for the utmost solidity at both ends of the receiver, as otherwise close grouping will not be possible.

In another place I referred to the trick of reassembling the parts in a Winchester single-shot receiver after having taken out all parts for cleaning. A beginner is always stumped, for there is a certain way to do this, and he will generally try everything else first. One way is to use a drift-pin made on a slight taper, of the same size as the finger-lever pin. Secure the receiver in the vise, left side up. Take the breech-block assembly in the left hand, lever in normal closed position. Place the extractor alongside the block in its normal closed position. Slide the block part-way into its grooves, meanwhile holding the trigger back, so the sear will be out of the path of the hammer. When half-way in, push the extractor up slightly ahead of the angle of the block until it is home. Slip the taper pin into the lever-pin hole and secure the extractor, but do not push the pin far enough through to interfere with the block. Press the block up while feeling with the pin for the lever hole, and when it is entered, tap the pin clear through the receiver, then turn down the stop screw. The hammer is generally furnished with a fly that is reversible. Turn the fly one way in its slot and the hammer will rest in the half-cock notch when the block is closed. Turn the fly the other way in its slot and the hammer will come to full cock on closing the block. For target shooting this is the more convenient method, but for a hunting rifle the

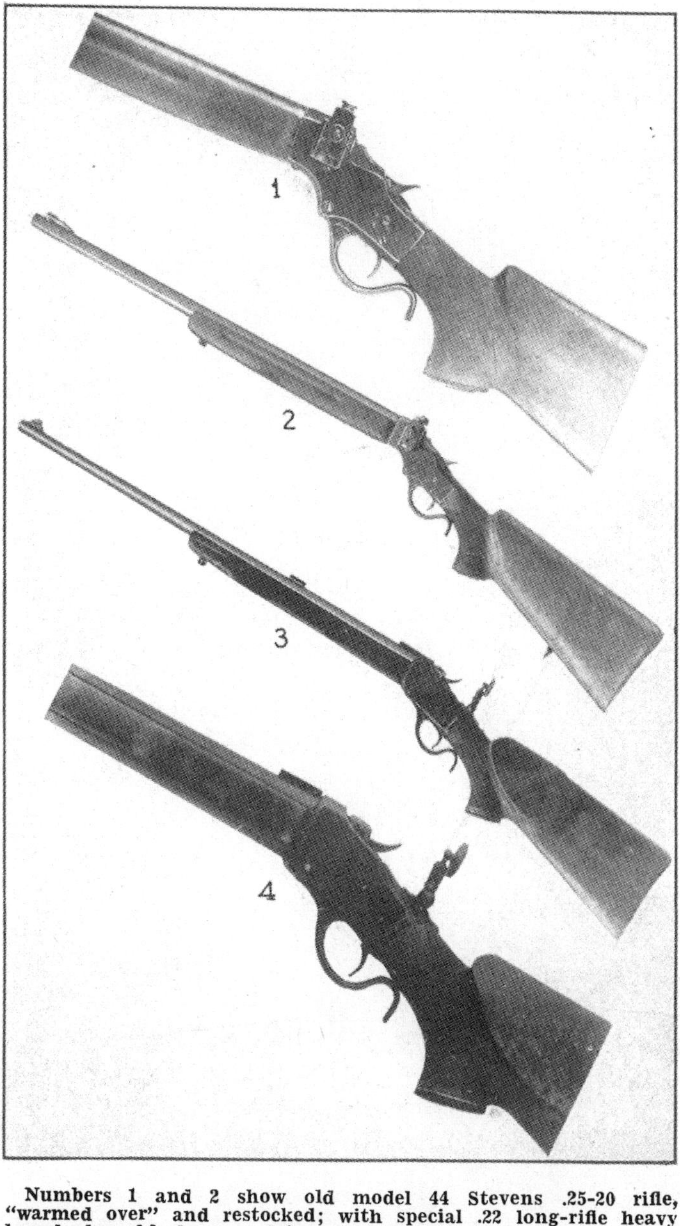

Numbers 1 and 2 show old model 44 Stevens .25-20 rifle, "warmed over" and restocked; with special .22 long-rifle heavy barrel, breechlock and firing-pin altered; fitted with Lyman 56 rear sight and King red-bead front sight mounted in drive-in ramp. 3 and 4, Winchester .22 long-rifle single-shot, with Lyman No. 1 tang sight and gold bead front sight.

other way about is safer, and is to be recommended. The sear is put in as a unit, held by its pin in the frame, and controlled by its spring, which lies along the upper part of the receiver.

A "warmed-over" target rifle. If the young gunsmith has access to a good lathe, he can convert a target rifle into a sporter very easily. Take a Model 52 Winchester rifle, for example. The barrel as it comes is 28 inches long and too heavy for hunting. Saw four inches off the muzzle end—even more; I have seen some rifles of this model with barrels only 20 inches long, and they were very trim. Turn up a brass plug to fit the muzzle perfectly, bore a hole in the plug to fit the headstock spindle, with a shoulder on the plug so it will not enter the barrel too far, make a longer plug to fit the chamber and the tailstock spindle, use a lathedog to prevent the barrel from turning on the centers, then turn the barrel down, a straight taper from the muzzle to a point just forward of the fore-end tip. Smooth the barrel with a fine-cut file, then set it in your padded vise and drawfile it until no tool marks show. Follow with emory cloth, then crocus. Blue it later on, but make a front-sight band first and when the sight has been lined up, blue the whole shooting match at one time.

You can purchase a ramp to fit the barrel, and sweat it on, but if you have a discarded barrel, saw off a two-inch section from the large end and make your own ramp. Ream it out until it will fit the barrel at the muzzle—it must go an inch further back when finished—then with a hacksaw cut pieces off the tube, leaving a half-inch lug on which to mount the sight. Four or five cuts lengthwise will leave the tube much smaller. Put it in the vise and file it to shape; that is, until it is a tube with walls only 1/32-inch thick and with a lug just about high enough for a gold bead sight to match a Redfield or a Lyman receiver sight; or, if you prefer, cut a slot in the lug and fit a blade sight—Springfield fashion. Cutting a dovetail slot in the lug is to be preferred, as this will permit shifting the sight a bit to right or left.

Smooth the lug and taper its top, then matte it by tapping a coarse file, held on it, with a block of wood until the surface is lightly scored. Heat the band, tin it with a soldering copper, then drive it home on the barrel.

The dead weight removed in this way will be about one-half pound only, but the rifle will handle much better for hunting, will look trimmer, and if the stock is trimmed, too, with a thinner grip and a tipped forearm, a carrying strap and swivels, it will make a swell outfit for hunting small game.

Improving a Magazine-catch. The next time a customer asks you to restock a Model 52 Winchester rifle, show him how this may be done through taking five parts out of the magazine assembly and adding one new part. This will do away entirely with the archaic push-button on the side of the forearm, and the new part you put in instead will scarcely show when the stock is finished and its jewelry added. The lower sketch in Fig. 12 shows the regular magazine-holder. There is one screw at each end. Remove the front screw only, set under it the self-spring magazine-catch we are discussing, then turn the screw down again. The new lock (S) is 1¼-inches long, ½-inch wide, made from annealed steel $\frac{1}{32}$-inch thick. The thumb-piece (the top) is cross-hatched with a knife file, blued and hardened. The top extends above the magazine-well only ⅛-inch. With it the magazine is snapped in or removed merely by pressing the spring. While not necessary, the device works a trifle better when the guard is cut away slightly just forward of the magazine well.

Chapter Sixteen

OF VARIOUS MATTERS WHICH INTEREST SHOOTERS.

The young gunsmith must get into the habit of regarding every visitor as a menace to his peace of mind—a carrier of pestilence to every piece of steel he touches. The younger the visitor is, the more he must be watched. Boys cannot resist the temptation to snap the hammers or firing pins of firearms, especially pistols and revolvers—always while pointing them toward someone's mid-section. This is generally harmless, though with rim-fire arms snapping repeatedly may damage the breech. Slip an empty case into the chamber, and let the customer snap the hammer on its soft primer. With bolt-action rifles snapping does no harm. And after the customer has departed, wipe every piece of steel he has handled with an oiled cloth. It takes only a moment to wipe a gun or rifle from end to end, and this will prevent rusting from hands that are moist, as some hands always are. One man can leave finger-marks all over a gun without harming it, while another person's hands are poison.

While they were cleaning rifles after a match, one shooter asked another, "How long does it take to get a cloth nice and oily, for cleaning?"

"Oh," replied the other, "about two years, I should say."

There is something in that. Every man should keep, in a tight drawer or box, a flannel cloth that has been oiled repeatedly. Every time a firearm is handled, it should be wiped all over with one of these cloths. This is the sign manual of the careful man, who takes pride in keeping his guns and rifles beyond danger of rust. Nowadays some one in every family takes mineral oil at bedtime. When a bottle is nearly empty it is discarded. Save these empties and push your flannel cloth into one, letting the small amount of oil left in it soak into your cloth. Nothing is half so good, as this oil does not gum, it is colorless, and it may be wiped over metal and wood in a jiffy, acting as a perfect rust preventive.

It is common practice with some gun owners to oil the mechanism of a gun liberally, then stand it in a cabinet without giving the surplus oil any attention. This practice ruins good guns, as you will see if you will dismount a nicely stocked gun and observe how thoroughly saturated is the wood around and below the lock. While this soaking with oil does not benefit any wood, its effects will not be so injurious if the insides of stocks be thoroughly oiled with linseed. Rifle barrel and receiver mortises should be oiled thoroughly before the parts are assembled, and about once a month all lubricating oil should be wiped out.

And about cleaning gun and rifle bores: Very often one hears well-posted .22 caliber shooters say they never clean their rifle bores, as the ammunition they use is proof against rust. All right, believe that yarn if you like and are willing to pay the price some humid day. Common horse sense, however, will tell you the only way to treat good rifles is to clean them at once after shooting them. All needed for a .22 barrel is pushing a couple of patches with a good solvent through the bore, followed by two dry patches, then a good heavy grease like Rig, B. S. A. or Winchester gun grease.

High-power barrels require thorough cleaning as soon as possible after they have been fired. If this method is followed religiously, there need be no difficulty in keeping rifle bores bright until the next time they are to be used. Saturate a bronze brush with Chloroil and push it through the barrel four or five times. Follow with the same solvent on a tight patch of new cotton flannel, then with three dry patches, end-

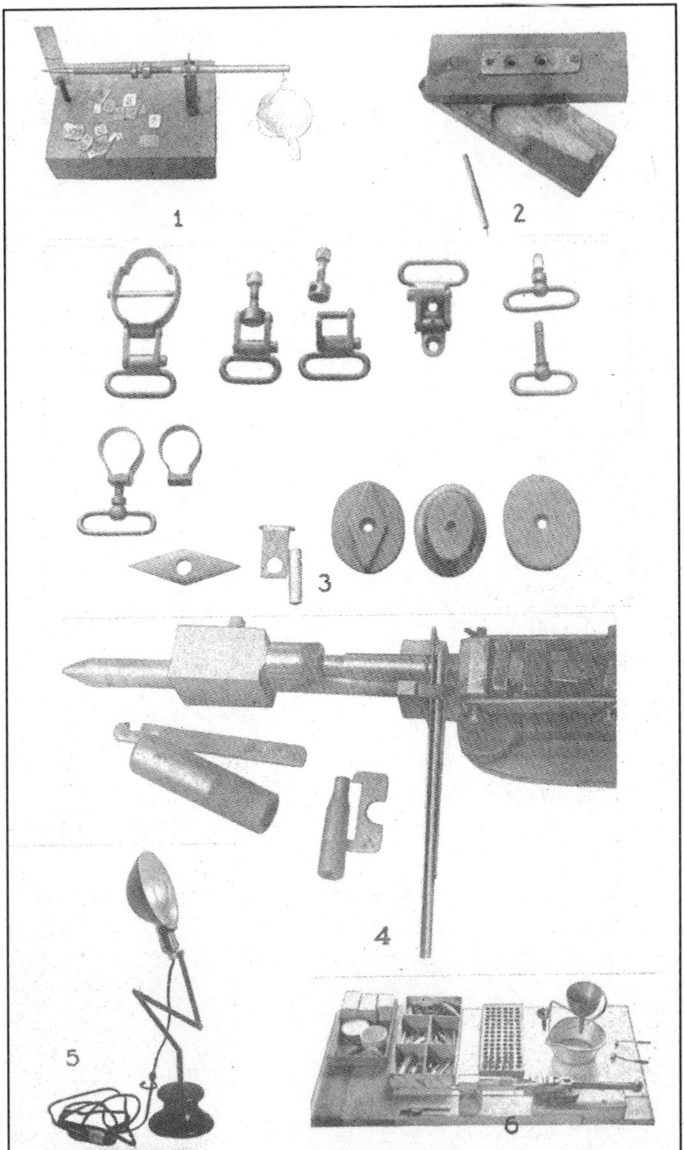

Fig. 26. Gadgets. 1, Cooper type powder-weighing device. 2, decapping block and pin. 3, stock jewelry photographed on a sheet of glass over a black box. 4, primer magazine attached to loading tool. 5, adjustable working lamp fixture. 6, loading board with reloading tool and gravity charger attached.

ing with one of the greases named above. While it is always wise to push a greased patch through the barrel twice each week, one treated as described will seldom if ever actually need further cleaning.

There are three sorts of cylindrical brushes commonly sold for use in rifle bores: mild steel, hard bronze, and natural bristles (many of these are synthetic, of course). For oiling the bore the bristle brush is good, but for cleaning after firing the bronze brush is the best, as with it one can scour, and it will not injure the lands as a steel brush might do. But these brushes should be pushed entirely through the barrel, and not reversed *in the barrel,* as this tends to break down the wires unduly. Whatever is used, be sure the brush be kept in a tube, away from grit, when not in actual use; and before inserting the cleaning rod, wipe it from end to end with a cloth.

Slotted cleaning rods for rifles should be prohibited by law. They cause no end of trouble, and they are a mechanical error. Usually one of these rods is made by flattening a round rod for an inch or more at one end, then cutting a long slot in the rod. Used to pull a patch through the barrel, it is good enough, but when one is pushed, the patch extends back beyond the flat portion, a jam is often the result, and the harder the rod is pushed, the tighter the patch sticks. All sorts of shapes are used to hold the patch against slipping, but when all is said, a plain cylindrical knob is hard to beat. For a .30-calibre rod the knob should be one-quarter-inch or even less; for a .22-calibre rod, about .189-inch. Better still, make the diameter of the knob according to the thickness of the patch used, and try to use the same grade (thickness) of cotton right along.

For a shotgun field cleaner, use a piece of ⅜-inch tubing about ¾-inch long, bore two holes clear through, and use two pieces of cloth for patches. One end of the tube can be bent in slightly, either by spinning in a lathe or by bending in the vise, to hold the knotted end of a length of stout braided cord, like codline. Attach a small weight at the other end, to drop through the barrel, then pull the greased patch through.

For a revolver or pistol, use a length of rod with a loop bent at one end, for a handle, and a knob at the business end. And have a good bristle brush as well, not only for wiping out the barrel, but for getting into corners of the frame and cylinder.

The old-time hickory cleaning rod has passed out of the picture, at least with small-calibre rifles. I saw one not long ago, made by an Adirondack guide. I wonder how many muzzle-loading rifles were abraded with the grit these old wood rods carried into the bores. Polished steel is better.

There is probably no one best oil for firearms mechanisms, but it is safe to use sperm oil, provided it be acid free. Firms like Eimer & Amend (see Chapter XVII) will supply pure sperm oil. It is economical, as four ounces of it should last a very long time. Oil for locks should be free from gumming, but if locks are washed out now and then with thin crude petroleum, then wiped dry and coated lightly with sperm oil, they should function freely for months. Use an old toothbrush for cleaning. Mobiloil E is cheap, and it works very well on the outside of bolts; but if it gums a bit on guns left in dry places, thin it with crude oil, particularly in the winter. Reel oil is good, too, but a bit expensive for shop use. Just now graphite is used a lot, combined with some thin oil, but it is messy stuff. Gunslick is one of these mixtures. Use it sparingly. Too much attention cannot be given the bolts of rifles in cold weather. For hunting it is really better to wipe all parts dry than to use too much oil, and have them "freeze" up when taken out in zero weather. Very often target rifles are brought into the shop with the complaint that the bolts will not function at all. Cleaning usually cures this "ailment."

When black powder was supplanted by Semi-smokeless, Lesmok and similar combinations for loading .22 rim-fire cartridges, in the '90's, target shooters had doubts about what sort of stuff to use for cleaning bores. Dr. Walter G. Hudson then used a formula that is still good for cleaning. It was composed of 6 parts sperm oil, 2 parts each mineral turpentine, astral oil and acetone, and one part amyl acetate. No trouble to prepare, and the odor is not quite so "skunky" as with other cleaners. I used to shoot with "Doc," as we called him, and together and separately we tried to persuade shooters to use blue ointment in barrels suspected of leading. No one likes to ask, in a drugstore, for blue ointment, but this embarrassment may be gotten over with in one session by buying two or three ounces of the stuff—enough to last ten years. In the '80's we shot softer lead bullets than now, and leading was not rare. After cleaning a barrel that is leaded, use a thin patch liberally smeared with the ointment, and leave it in the barrel until your next shoot. If there was a trace of lead in the bore, it will disappear when a clean patch is pushed through the barrel.

In every well-regulated rifle range one will find cleaning racks where shooters place their rifles in grooves while they wipe out the barrels. Outdoor ranges often are similarly equipped. Elsewhere—and even in some gunsmiths' shops, there is no suitable place to support a rifle while it is being cleaned, so some men rest the muzzles of their rifles on the floor or the ground while cleaning. This is very bad practice, for, when a cleaning patch is pushed clear through the barrel, then pulled back, it can be expected to pick up grit or sand enough to scratch the bore and impair its accuracy. To avoid injury, some barrels are crowned, but many of the finest target barrels are cut off flush at the muzzle, and if such a barrel be placed on a gritty floor, it will certainly be exposed to dust and grit, and very little of this will go a long way toward ruining the sharp edges of the lands. It is better practice to hold a finger over the muzzle, or butt the muzzle against a clean upright while performing this "off-hand cleaning," or rather left-handed work. It is so easy to fit up a holder similar to the one mentioned in Chapter III, in the use of which both the rifle and the cleaning rod may be kept free from dust and grit.

We who are accustomed to taking good care of rifle bores in climates that are humid will understand the surprise I had at one time in the Rocky Mountain country, when a friend unrolled from a piece of newspaper a spare barrel for his target rifle, and told me that barrel had not been used for several years. It was in absolutely perfect condition, though the barrel had merely been wiped dry after it had been shot the last time, then stored in a closet. We could not do this near sea level.

Leather Work

Working on guns inevitably leads to some leather work. Nearly all hunters use gun or rifle carrying straps, all rifle shooters use slings, and all these articles must be changed by some one, to suit the owners. Why not go into this, too? No special equipment is needed. You can buy suitable leather, buckles and keepers, or make some of them yourself.

The service rifle sling may be purchased so cheaply that it would not pay to make one like it. It consists of two main parts. The forward end is about three feet long, has a double row of holes in the free end, and a two-prong claw to fit these holes, for length adjustment. In use the free end is passed through the forearm swivel of the rifle, then the claw is hooked on, and you have a loop, which in turn is confined near the center by two keepers of leather. The buttstock end is a simple piece about two feet long, with a bronze ring for attaching to the forward loop, and a claw. It is passed through the butt swivel on the rifle and hooked back on itself. For field service both loops are pulled up tight, so the strap will lie flat under the rifle. For shooting, or for carrying, various length adjustments are made, to suit the individual.

You can make the leather parts from ordinary strap leather, and cut the claws from hard brass 1/16-inch thick, attaching each one with three small copper or aluminum rivets. Make the two keepers from 5/8-inch leather, folding them while wet around the doubled strap, then clamping for awhile, after which put about ten stitches in each one, using orange or yellow waxed linen thread. Swab the strap with Viscol or neatsfoot oil; when this has set, rub with harness soap.

Target shooters use only the forward loop of the regulation strap, but pad this in two places, usually, with sheepskin, wool-side in, to prevent muscle tremors from affecting the aim.

Carrying straps for hunting rifles are sometimes made adjustable for length. A buckle is used at one end, or lacing—to avoid rattling of metal fittings. After many hunting trips in mountainous country I found that a very simple strap about three feet long could be used both for carrying the rifle, and for steadying one's aim, if not too long after it had been adjusted. A quick-detachable swivel is made fast to the front end by sewing, and a plain swivel snap-hook is put on the butt end. Pass the left arm twice through this strap. It is quite efficient. The hardware for this jigger is a plain stud with eye, on the forearm—the same stud one may also use with the target rifle—and a screweye in the buttstock.

If called on to make revolver or knife holsters, make a rather snug paper pattern of the gun (or the knife), it is to be made for, fold a piece of leather, lay the straight edge of the pattern parallel with the fold, then cut with a sharp knife around the open side. Punch generous holes one-quarter-inch from the curved edges, and lace with latigo leather, rawhide or very heavy braided cord. The loop for strap can be put on with aluminum rivets. Prepare the holster when the leather has been wetted then allowed to partially dry, run an ornamental line near each edge, using a small coin, then stamp with almost any implement you may have handy. The ends of straight and taper reamers, end-milling cutters, tubes, nail-ends with grooves sawed in them—there is no end to odd things that may be used to imprint parts of tracings or regular designs on leather. More elaborate tools for this work may be purchased in sets from Southwestern saddlemakers, and some Mexican firms.

Carrying cases for rifles and guns. The ordinary full-length rifle-carrying case has not kept pace with modern trends. It is too narrow for bolt-action rifles, though it is good enough for lever-action rifles. Some of the leather-working firms have recently brought out improved man-size cases, but there is still room for improvement along these lines.

No firearm should be left in a cotton-lined case indoors. Rust will creep into it when the air is humid. Leather is somewhat better, especially soft leather with a woolly surface, and some cases are now made of this material. The well-known zipper has been applied to take the place of the old-time flap and buckle at the large end, and in some cases there is an inner pocket for small articles, and a compartment for a full-length cleaning rod. Why not add a pocket for a rifle scope, and have your case a complete unit for rifle, scope, cleaning rod and screwdriver, even a place for spare iron sights or a few cartridges?

For a good many years I have carried over the right shoulder, in going to and returning from the rifle range, a case made to order along these lines, and it has proved satisfactory. It is simple, with no patches to loosen and no leather edges to fray and get ragged. With the experience gained I would suggest as an ideal case one made from soft leather, with a full length adjustable shoulder strap, a flap and buckle at the bottom, with a width of seven inches for eighteen inches along the lower end, and with a scope pocket on the outside —that is, away from the body when the case is carried over the right shoulder. The open edge of the leather case should be secured with latigo leather lacing, just as is found in holsters for heavy revolvers. The scope pocket should be full and roomy, and to that end it should bulge considerably, like the bellows pocket in a military coat, and the flap cover of the pocket should have a strap that will fit friction tight under a leather loop in place of a buckle.

Since the previous paragraph was written, Allen Bros.,

Buford, Ga., have made a leather case for me along the lines mentioned. The leather is thick but soft, and waterproof. It is roomy enough for any bolt-action rifle, but the scope pocket was made for such scopes as the Malcolm and the Lyman 5A, or nearly 17 inches long. While this pocket could be made longer and higher up on the case, to accommodate the 22-inch high-power scopes like the Fecker, Lyman and Unertl, my suggestion would be that for a scope of this length the outside pocket be omitted and the scope carried in a plain leather sheath case, inside the rifle case. There is abundant space for this at the bottom of the case, with the scope resting under the bolt-handle. A full-length cleaning rod can be kept inside the case nicely. Usually full-length rifle cases of leather are quite expensive, but this Allen case costs very little and is so sturdy that it should outwear a half-dozen duck cases.

Kit boxes, cabinets and arms chests. One thing leads to another. Why not try your hand at making a sample kit box? Make it for a certain purpose, then, if others are made, vary them to suit certain customers. The work is very easy, and the material is abundant.

If a friend's specialty is pistol or revolver shooting, suggest to him a wood kit box. Make it from a solid piece of light wood like white pine or cypress, thick enough to take the revolver, with hinged cover and bottom of thin stuff. Lay the revolver on the plank and trace its outline, cut through on this line with a keyhole saw, smooth the edges nicely, then glue blue, green or red velvet all around, with a cut-out piece of the same goods for the bottom. Bore holes for cartridges or cut out a square segment for boxed cartridges, run a groove at one side for a cleaning rod, and after some staining or varnishing, you will have a very neat kit. For top and bottom use $\frac{3}{16}$-inch plywood, baywood or walnut.

For shooting-kit boxes red cedar is ideal, though it is heavier than you would at first think. The McGraw Manufacturing Company, McGraw, N. Y., makes candy and stationery boxes from this aromatic wood, and possibly they will make knock-down boxes to order, sizes to suit. They made a couple for me, at any rate. The material was supplied with sides and ends cut for locking, so all else needed was to glue all corners, set the bottom in and fit the top, saw out the cover and sandpaper.

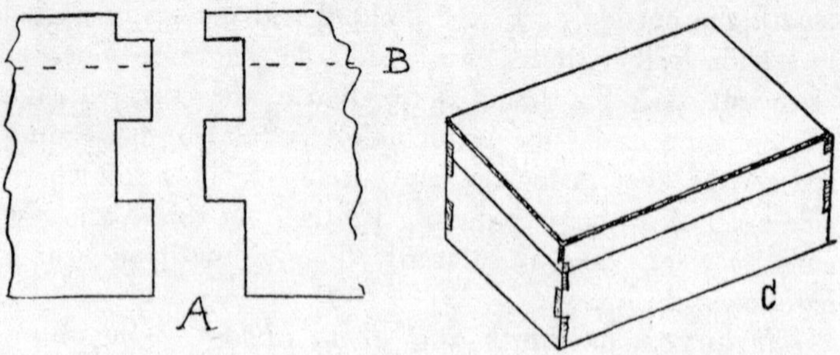

Of course it would not be worth while to try to do this corner-locking by hand except in a rough way, but if you want a kit box in a hurry, try the method shown with this. Cut the ends and sides to finished dimensions, then cut out the edges like A to a tight fit, glue and clamp them over night, using a square to be sure they are true. Cut the bottom piece so it will set in rather than over the bottom edges; it is the stronger method. Glue it in place, clamp it, then fit the top over the edges and glue it. When all members have dried, cut all around the box at B, for the cover. C shows the completed box. Use two or three small brass hinges, and a snap catch—all ten-cent-store stuff.

Pressed steel kit boxes are often used by shooters, but of course they are heavier than wood though waterproof, but if one wants a given size or shape, making it is more satisfactory. This is especially true of boxes in which to carry rifle telescopes. Some very handsome ones are made from three-sixteenths-inch plywood.

The publisher has suggested that I carry this thing about kit boxes to its logical conclusion—arms chests and other containers for shooting irons, but at the time he did not know that all my life I have had a mania for making boxes of all sorts, for camp kits, cameras, revolvers, pistols, and even full-length affairs for rifles. And now that he (Mr. Samworth) is willing, I will spin a yarn or two about this failing of mine (it was inherited by a small daughter, who, one Christmas, threw away all her nice presents and kept the boxes they came in).

My first serious offense in this direction was the making of a locked-corner red cedar box in which was stowed a full cooking kit of aluminum and sheet-steel utensils. The cover had a strut holding it open, for a table. A piece of cedar was attached to the opposite side, for another table. It had removable legs, hinges and a hasp, for locking shut. It was a beautiful thing to behold, and it fitted into our cruising canoe as if made for the purpose, as it certainly was. But one day, in breaking camp in a flooded backwater of the Mississippi River, barefooted because of the slimy mud, I slipped and dropped the box, on a corner, and it was never the same after that. On a rainy day I purchased a wide cypress board with which to make another box, but before I arrived home with the board it curled so much that it took me a week to flatten it out again and soak it with linseed oil.

When I go to our club outdoor rifle range I act as my own jackass, carrying everything needed in a pack except a rifle, so kits must be compact. One of these holds a spotting scope and a folded stand; a rifle scope, a box for thumb-tacks and pasters; spare sights, screws and a driver; cleaning kit, barrel clamp for rest shooting, and other odds and ends. A box of this sort should have partitions, made of thin wood or sheet aluminum. It should be made purposely for certain articles and be no larger than is absolutely necessary.

On a box in which to carry a target revolver more ingenuity may be expended, and if two revolvers are carried, the box may be patterned somewhat like the old-time duelling-pistol cases, with compartments for the two revolvers or pistols, and for cleaning things and cartridges. These may be lined with felt, billiard cloth or velvet—purloined from your wife's sewing basket while she is away from home. Some boxes are covered with leather, others not but sanded and waxed, with brass hinges and hasps. You can buy them ready made, but it is more fun to make one.

The next step is a case in which a shotgun or a pair of guns is to be arranged for; or a gun with two sets of barrels. The body may be made of a solid piece of wood, as already described, cut out to fit the parts, and with a cover of thin wood; cover with leather, if desired. Then it is but a step to a full-length rifle box, though this is clumsy except for transporting by motor car. Practice first on a plain box until size and shape are determined on. If your dealer is good-natured, he may let you pick a box from his shipping room—one made for shipping a rifle as it comes from the manufacturer. For a Springfield rifle or one of the .22-calibre target rifles the length will be about 46 inches, but as these boxes are usually pine, the weight will be unimportant if carried in a car. There is abundant room for one rifle, a scope and a supply of cartridges. Put in thin partitions with cleats to prevent the contents from shifting, and line with felt at points where an unprotected rifle might be rubbed. Three hinges and two snap fasteners, with a leather handle secured with D-rings, will make a very efficient outfit.

If you like the notion, use better wood and make the box a shade deeper, lock the corners, glue all parts, then saw through an inch or so from the top, so the cover will be reinforced. This will give more room for hinges and hasps. And if you make the box from new wood, shape it somewhat like a violin case—smaller at one end. For example, a Model 52 Winchester rifle will go in a case the inside dimensions of which are as follows: Length 46½ inches;

depth, 2½ inches; width at one end, 6½ inches, at the other end 3 inches, leaving room for numerous articles.

In the home a cabinet for one's firearms is the thing. Its size will be determined by the space available, but its form may be very simple. In the stores one can purchase a kitchen cabinet of any handy dimensions for just a bit more than material to make one would cost. A broom cabinet is ideal, as it will be high enough for any rifle or gun, leaving space at one side for inserting shelves for one's shooting kit. And one can have choice of colors or plain hardwood, to be oiled or painted at one's option. If a cabinet of this sort be selected, it should have a shelf about forty inches from the bottom, with round holes in it, so rifles and guns may be put in upright and secured safely. In the gun compartment bore as many two-inch holes as space will permit in this shelf and stand the guns upright. In this way a space a foot square will take three or even four guns. Toward the back put in a couple of tool clips, for cleaning rods, and several brass brads for hanging carrying straps, etc. Put in short shelves at one side, for small articles. And if the outside of this cabinet be painted or waxed, leave the inside as is, so the bare wood may absorb dampness, if any.

When a family moves into a new house, the women folks decide the question of what is to be placed in the various rooms, so the nominal "head of the house" must make shift in some small room wherein he is permitted to keep his treasures. Chances are there may be space for a desk and a chair or two, but no available floor space for the gun cabinet he hopes to put in the room. Make a hanging cabinet five feet long. If it is only two feet wide it will hold two or three guns and one's kit; and as quite a bit of weight will be put in it, make the back and door of thin plywood set in tongued-and-grooved frames—picture-frame style; it will save a lot of weight. And support the jigger with three or four husky screws.

Our grandfathers and military men leaned toward arms

chests—something strong enough to be carted about in springless wagons—made somewhat like a carpenter's tool chest. One may buy a chest or make one, and on it he may expend his ingenuity in fitting it with trays, drawers, partitions ad lib. Make it from fairly thick wood, with cleats around the ends, panels in the cover, and plenty of brass at the corners. Lay out designs to suit your fancy, and practice on them with your checking tools, or work in initials, dates, monograms, etc., with one of the little tools in the Hand-ee set. Run a vine pattern around the end cleats, dig up the family coat of arms, if any, and work it in. You can get a barrel of fun out of this thing, if you carry it far enough; and at the same time have the satisfaction of knowing that there will be no duplicates of your handicraft.

Reloading Tools. The illustration 6, Fig. 26, shows a compact outfit for reloading rifle cartridges, and is mentioned to show how the gunsmith can make up various articles every reloader needs, if he uses ammunition for more than one rifle. The outfit is mounted on a board about 15x30 inches in size, so that it may be used on a bench or table, and stored when not in use, without disturbing any of the equipment.

The reloading tool shown is a Belding & Mull, fastened on a block and set up for the Hornet cartridge, but with extra parts for reloading the .30'06, the .270, the .250 and the .25-20 cartridges. For the .270 parts there are adapters to take any one of the smaller cartridges, so that, for the Hornet, the proper adapters are inserted whenever wanted. This also applies to the bullet-sizing tool (not shown). These adapters you can easily make to order.

The gravity powder charger is one made up from scraps. The reservoir was from a discarded ceiling-light fixture, a brass funnel-shaped cup on the end of which a bored-out .22 High-power case was soldered. At the elbow of the standard an extra piece of wire was soldered, carrying a tiny funnel. A piece of flat spring-wire, soldered at the top of the reservoir, fits into a saw-cut in the cartridge case, to form the cut-off. A bit of brass wire, oval shape, soldered on the spring, acts as a push-button on the cut-off. Unlike some powder loaders, this reservoir will function just as long as there is sufficient powder in it to fill a cup held underneath—the weight of powder in the reservoir having no influence on the charge which is being thrown.

In filling cases, a charge-cup is held under the reservoir outlet tube, the oval wire pushed toward the reservoir, then released, powder flows into the charge cup, then the cup is passed under the wire, to scrape off the surplus powder, which is then dumped into the small funnel at the left when a case is held under it, then set in the loading-block, at the left. As powder flows into the charge-cup precisely alike each time, the only thing necessary, in obtaining uniform charges, is to avoid jarring or tipping the charge-cup after it has been filled.

It is only necessary to make a charge-cup for any given weight powder charge. These are made from small cases with a piece of wire soldered on, for a handle. Instead of using round wire for this, make it from flat stock, so its edge will not catch any powder and vary the quantity slightly. On each handle mark with india ink the exact charge and the kind of powder. Weigh charges until right, cutting off the top of the case until correct.

The Pacific powder scale is one of the best low-cost weighing devices available to reloaders. A very similar one was made by Mark Cooper, who wrote about it in the *American Rifleman,* and a copy of his device was made and used by me (1, Fig. 26). The base is a block of wood two inches thick. The standard is a flat annealed steel, bent double with 60-degree notches cut in the tops, then the piece hardened and polished. The beam is a piece of drillrod eight inches long, threaded half its length, and with a sharp point. A saw cut was made and a piece of hardened steel set in and brazed, its lower edges ground to an edge and buffed. The large end has a wire ring set in a hole, the wire bent to carry the pan, which is a piece of thin aluminum hammered spoon shape. The pointer's position is shown on a narrow strip of white pyraline set in a slotted wood plug alongside. One india-ink mark may be made for the balancing point, or other short marks added to designate the weight of various powder charges. One or two nuts on the threaded portion may be turned to counterbalance the weights placed in the pan.

Borrow from your druggist a set of grain weights, and cut a set from brass, copper and aluminum sheets, marking each one with a scriber. Fifty, 25, 20, 15, 13, 11, 10, 9, and smaller weights down to 1, with 1/2, 1/5 and 1/10-grain weights will complete the unit. Set the pointer to balance a certain weight, then pour powder in the pan.

Bullet-seating Devices. Reloading ammunition, to lots of men, means merely decapping and recapping cases, filling them with powder, then seating factory bullets in them. Expensive and elaborate tools are not needed for these simple steps. The gunsmith can make all the devices needed except a tool to seat primers. This may be one of the old-fashioned shot shell priming tools, with a half-circular bushing fitted to it.

None of the elaborate reloading tools are so handy and rapid as a plain decapping plug. Make one from standard tubing with 1/16-inch hole, and a piece of piano wire a shade smaller and a quarter-inch longer than the tube. The tube should be a slide fit in the case. If cases of two calibers are to be reloaded, turn down half the tube to fit the smaller case, and the decapper can be reversed to fit the case in hand. Bend the wire a trifle, so it will not drop out of the tube of its own weight, and grind the ends round, then forget about it, for it will never wear, buckle or break—piano wire is so hard.

Bore a hole in a piece of flat steel large enough for a primer to pass through it. Countersink the hole with a large drill, so the head of a case will fit into it; and a screw-hole at each end, and fasten the plate atop a small wooden box, to catch dead primers as they are driven out of the cases. Better still, make a regular decapping block like 2, Fig. 26 from two pieces of wood about four inches square; a hole in the upper one, the bottom one with a generous pocket routed out with an augur bit or on a drillpress. Hinge the blocks at one end, and when the pocket becomes filled with dead primers, turn the top around and dump them in your junkbox.

If you have a piece of .22-caliber rifle barrel, cut it off to about five inches and ream one end until the rifle case it is to be made for will enter it easily as far as the shoulder. Bore a hole in the other end and ream it to fit the case half-way. Bore another hole a shade larger and ream it until the case will enter almost to the head.

From a rather thick piece of flat steel make a base with a hole in it just the size of the head of the case. Bore a smaller hole in its center, so the base, in use, will not touch the primer. Turn up a piece of drillrod a shade smaller than the muzzle-end of the steel tube, and bore and ream a hole in the rod to fit your favorite bullet. Thread one-third of the top end, tap a short piece of tubing to fit, then fit a wooden handle to the tubing. As a lock, fit a nut under the handle.

In use, a filled case with a bullet atop is slipped into the tube, the tube set in its base, then the handle is pressed down as far as it will go, and there you are. Cost, one hour's work.

My first loading tool for high-power cases was made from the muzzle end of a .22-caliber barrel. A four-inch piece of steel was fitted to the sight-slot, a bent piece of steel was hinged on the first bar, with a wooden handle on the other end. Over the end of the barrel a spring-hook was fitted into the second bar, to act as a catch to lift loaded cases. The tube was reamed at the top end for a case; the other end threaded for a piece of drillrod, a wingnut fitted to this threaded rod, and the result was a very satisfactory adjustable bullet-seater. Of course the drillrod was bored and reamed to fit the bullet. In use the device was turned bottom up, a bullet and a case inserted, the lever pressed down, then lifted, removing the cartridge.

Cleaning Primer Pockets. This simple method is quite efficient, as it will actually clean the pockets thoroughly, but will not grind away any metal. And for the work one can use either a lathe or a small hand-drill, the drill-stock held in a vise.

Saw off a two-inch length of brass tubing one-quarter-inch in diameter outside; the inside will probably be around one-eighth-inch. Smooth the ends, then fit in the hole as many pieces of one-thirty-second-inch electric light wire as will go in snugly—say ten. Cut these a half-inch longer than the tube, let them extend that far out of the tube at one end, then run a bit of soft solder into the mass, to hold all parts securely. To compensate for wear on the active ends of these wires, as needed heat the tube a bit, push the wires further out of the tube, then let cool.

If you have access to a lathe, seat the tube in its chuck, hold an empty case against the wires and spin for a few seconds. These wires, being a bit hard but yet softer than the brass of the primer pocket, will wipe out all primer and powder residue and leave the primer pocket bright but not abraded at all. Spin the device as fast as possible, but do not put much pressure on the wire brush, else it will be bent and its wires broken down. Lacking a lathe, fasten any small hand-drillstock in a vise and turn its handle while holding the cases against the wire brush. Common wire is too soft, but the single wire that was used before multiple stands of thin wire were put into lamp cables is stiffer, and works nicely, wearing down only after long use.

If the rotation of the lathe-chuck is counter-clockwise, after a few turns the small bundle of wires will be bent slightly in the reverse direction, but this twist, being very slight, will serve to hold all the wires together, so their ends will enter the primer pockets without spreading and turning over. This jigger really cleans primer pockets.

If you have one of the Handee electric hand-tools, the brass tube and its wires may be used in it, provided an extra bit of wire be set in one end, to fit the chuck. A three-thirty-second-inch piece will serve. Solder it in the brass tube and use it in

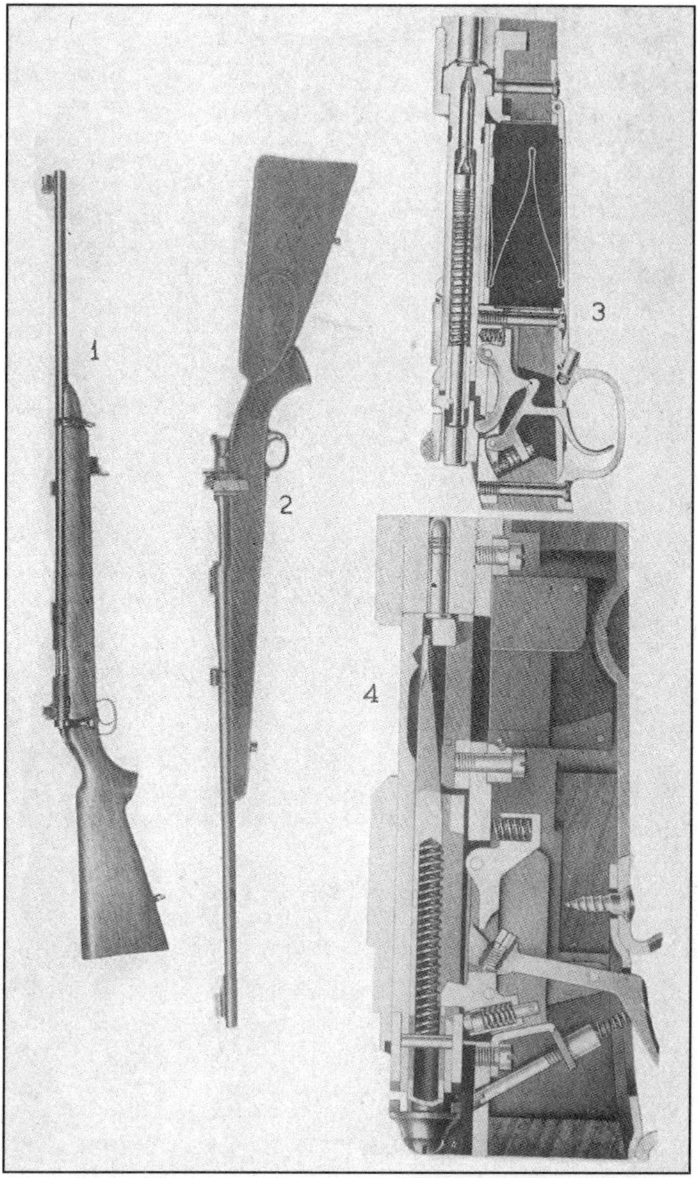

Fig. 27. New Winchester rifles. 1, standard Model 52, and 4, its trigger and sear mechanism. 2, a restocked Model 70 rifle, and 3, its trigger and sear mechanism.

the chuck. Remember that this hand-tool spins at terrific speed, so hold the tool over a block of wood on your bench, to steady it, and go easy with the wire brush, so this will not be crushed out of shape when a rifle case is being cleaned.

Clean out the primer pockets at least once for every four or five times cases are reloaded and fired. It is no trick at all, and cleaning 100 cases is only a matter of a few minutes' attention, now and then.

A Primer Magazine. Feeding primers singly into a Belding & Mull reloading tool is one of the clumsiest things you can think of. Tell your customer so, and get his order for a simple magazine to fit that tool. Make it in this way: Bend a length of flat brass around a $\frac{3}{16}$ x ¼-inch bar, leaving the edges slightly separated, so you can see the primers in this tube. Cut a piece of hard steel to fit the tool in the place of the regular case-head-bar, if you know what I mean —for I have never heard what it is called by the makers. On the right-hand end leave an ear extending up half-an-inch. Bore holes in this ear and in the left edge of the magazine, and rivet. Along the other side of the magazine fit a length of thin spring steel—an old-time corset-steel is just the thing. To this spring attach a short piece, and bend it twice, so it will cross the top of the device, extend down a quarter-inch, and act as a push-button for the spring. Rivet the spring along the right side of the magazine, but first set in its further end a tiny pin, with a hole through that side of the magazine to let it enter and act as a primer stop. Hinge a bit of steel on the loose end of the magazine, to close that end after it has been filled with primers. Bend the other end of the magazine so primers cannot slip through there, then file off the lower edge on a slant until a primer will just slip through.

In use the magazine is set into the reloader, with the magazine hanging down at right angles (4, Fig. 26). When the case is neck-sized and ready to be primed, tip the magazine up, depress the "push-button" spring until a primer drops out into the primer recess in the tool, then the spring is released, sealing the magazine, which is then dropped to place. The lever is turned up, the tool sets the primer—and repeat. A magazine 5½ inches long will take 25 large rifle primers. This is a convenient length, though longer tubes are still handier. Of course the primers must be put in singly, but it is easier to do this at one time, rather than once for each primer.

Gas-Check Bullets and Moulds. In the '90's nearly all riflemen used lead bullets of one sort or another, and the life of those rifles was much longer than is the case now, when jacketed bullets cut the accuracy life of barrels to a few thousand rounds. A generation has grown up, and the youngsters know little about the possibilities of hard lead bullets with gas-check cups fitted to them—and by this I mean real accuracy up to 200 yards.

Seating gas-check cups on bullets is a nuisance. Try this stunt: Put a tight fitting brass ferrule on the end of a small tool handle, then bore a hole a half-inch deep in it, the size a trifle smaller than the bullet to be used. Continue the hole with a quite small drill, try the point of a bullet in it, and if it will stick until you can lift it, fill the hole with bullet lubricant, making it quite slippery. Spread a lot of cups on your bench, push a bullet into the tool handle, seat the base in a cup, then press it home. Twist the bullet out of the hole with the right thumb as you pick up another bullet with the left hand. This work can be done rapidly, once you get the hang of the thing.

The large makers of moulds will not make cherries and mould-blocks for every person who wants a special bullet—except for those who are willing to pay for the cherries, too, and this makes one's pet bullet a very expensive proposition. The inevitable result has been that skilled gunsmiths have taken up this work, and they will make cherries and moulds for almost anyone who will make up a pattern, from brass or steel, for them to follow in fashioning a cherry. Cutting the blocks follows as a mere detail, though of course this can only be done by men who have and can use precision lathes of the best sort.

I have already mentioned the Cramer Bullet-mould Company. Another man who has taken up this work is Vernon Gipson, 1934 Touhy Avenue, Chicago. I have used one of his moulds, made for a special bullet which experience helped me to design, and which is very accurate for target work on all sorts of days. I also have examined special bullets he has designed for the Hornet and other high-power .22-calibre rifles, three different patterns for the .270 calibre, one .250, and several for .30 '06 rifles. His prices are very reasonable indeed, and his workmanship superb. He contemplates making and fitting barrels, too, I believe. This is good news, for while there are several private barrel-makers equipped to do this work well, it seems that they, like artists, are likely to be temperamental, so that getting a good barrel the same year it is ordered is a thing that requires the patience of a modern Job.

Altering Bullet Moulds. If a customer tells you the lead bullets he is shooting do not give satisfaction, ask to examine his mould. If it casts a flat-point bullet, it is easy to ream out the cavity to a round point or a sharp point, a shape that has better wind-bucking qualities but will not be so good for hunting. Try various twist drills in the cavity, and use one that will almost reach the point. Grind the sides of the drill until it is just a shade too large to go clear down to the point, then bore carefully, in a lathe between centers, if you have access to one. Examine the result frequently. If the shape is right, turn down a bit of hardwood to a point similar to the bottom of the cavity, saw a slot in the end of the stick, fit a tiny piece of crocus cloth in the slot, and with oil on the cloth polish the bottom of the cavity perfectly smooth.

Another bullet may have several very narrow lands—to form the grease cannelures in the bullet. This may sometimes be remedied by turning up from drillrod a tiny cutter with teeth cut diagonally across its face—a milling cutter, really. Cut away enough metal for a shank, chuck the cutter in the lathe, set up the tailstock with a drillpad against which the mould-blocks must be held securely, then, as you gradually close the jaws of the mould, you can ream two of the objectionable ridges into one, and the result will be one wide instead of two narrow lands at that point. Of course this requires nice adjustment for the position of the cherry, as you will mar a neighboring ridge if the cutter be allowed any play; but with the mould held solidly against the tail-stock drill-pad and the tail-stock locked, this need not permit any transverse movement of the cherry. To polish the cut, drill a small hole in the base of a bullet, fit a short piece of rod in the hole, coat the bullet with oil and tripoli, fit into cavity, then polish thoroughly.

Venting Bullet Moulds. Old-timers of the lead-bullet days were—most of them—past masters in making good bullets. Their boys are, too, for that matter, though the majority prefer jacketed bullets. But if a customer complains that his mould throws freak bullets now and then, the remedy for this is usually quite simple. Vent the mould for him. In casting bullets both the lead and the dipper must be kept very hot, and this applies to the mould, too, though it must be a bit cooler than the metal, else when lead is poured into the mould it would remain fluid too long to be practical. One tilts the mould on its side, inserts the muzzle of the dipper, tips both upright, then pauses for a moment until certain the cavity is filled. Imagine what happens. The cavity is filled with hot air that must be driven out or imprisoned at the bottom or at one side. If the latter, there will be a wrinkle at that point on the bullet. Remedy matters so the air may rush out while the lead is running in. If the base of the bullet is not perfect—does not fill the cavity full and square—take a needle file with a fine knife point and cut across the top of one mould-block a groove about $\frac{1}{64}$-inch deep, tapering to a mere scratch at the edge of the cavity. Cut this groove clean and keep it clean while casting bullets.

Cast a few bullets, examine them with a magnifying glass and try the caliper on them for roundness and uniform shape all along the bearing surface. If the vent be properly cut, the bases of the bullets will be clean and square—a necessity for accurate shooting. Remember that the ogive or the point of a bullet may be marred a bit without greatly affecting its accuracy—the base never.

If the lands of the bullet be uneven, lower or thinner in one place, before removing the bullet from the mould, examine it with a glass, to determine which half of the mould holds air, then cut a vent into that place; if the result is not just right, cut still another vent in the opposite block, always being sure to get into the exact spot where the air seems to be imprisoned. And do not let anyone tell you that you will ruin a mould in this way. I have examined moulds made by a world-famous riflemaker. One of these has six vents in it, and a favorite mould of mine, which casts perfect bullets now, was not worth shucks when new. It has seven vents. Another one, which turns out beautifully balanced bullets but has a sharp point, has one vent in each block, to offset its early tendency to let air deform that sharp point on one side. However, if vent you must, hold your breath and work with all your skill.

The young rifleman, and all gunsmiths, should join the National Rifle Association. Membership will entitle them to purchase supplies through the Director of Civilian Marksmanship, in Washington, at moderate cost. It will bring to them every month the *Rifleman's Bible,* the *American Rifleman,* with its seventy-two pages of valuable information, stories, reports, and advertisements. It will give them a standing if they wish to visit the Mecca of all shooters—the great National Rifle Matches at Camp Perry, near Toledo, Ohio, and the membership card will show all and sundry that a member is an all-wool and a yard wide person.